# DR. SADLER AND THE URANTIA BOOK
## The Historic Origins of a
## Spiritual Revelation in the 20th Century

**Sioux Oliva**

Printed in the United States of America

First Printing, 2014

Library of Congress Cataloging-in-Publication Data
Oliva, Sioux

Dr. Sadler and The Urantia Book: The Historic Origins of a Spiritual Revelation in the 20th Century
Sioux Oliva—First Edition
Includes bibliographical references and index

ISBN 978-0-692-30610-9

For George

*Though we may believe unreservedly in a certain set of truths, there is always the possibility that some other set of truths might be the case. In the end, we have to act on what we believe; we cannot wait for confirmation from the rest of the universe.*

—Louis Menand, *The Metaphysical Club*

# CONTENTS

# PREFACE

When I was seventeen years old, I came across *The Urantia Book* for the first time. A massive text, it offered a series of papers written in an authoritative style that spoke to my spiritual desire—a longing for connection. For my birthday, my parents bought me a copy. I then became a reader. The teachings from this book became the framework for my religious views. The book describes in marvelous detail the unique and wonderful personalities that call our universe home as well as the physical aspects of the universe itself—a place created to assist us in evolving spiritually through an endless adventure of growth until we attain eternal life. The book introduced Jesus as a celestial being who did not die for our sins but rather came to Earth to teach us how to have a loving relationship with God as well as with each other. It taught that our universe is inhabited by a myriad of celestial beings that work to bring God to us and through some unique spiritual partnering, help us to attain eternal life. *The Urantia Book* presented an overwhelmingly positive philosophy that carried me through my life even through long periods when I wasn't actively studying the text. It answered countless questions about my spiritual growth. It gave me reason to feel secure in my life knowing the universe was here to support me as an enduring spirit. Without question, it was the most important book in my library.

I decided to research the origins of *The Urantia Book* when a friend (also a reader of the book) asked me to research its origin. My friend wanted something that he could hand to his friends and family with a "straight face." There were recent challenges to the veracity of the origin of the book, and readers had a difficult time explaining it to others. I was a good candidate. I am very familiar with the book, have a doctorate in American history, and have professional experience using research methodology.

One of the greatest challenges to writing this book was that no direct records remain: the scribe, William Sadler, had all of his papers burned after his death and no copies of or notes on the original Urantia papers exist. Documents from archival research were therefore used to reconstruct and tell the story. Until now no histories have been written about William or Lena Sadler, although some have written about *The Urantia Book.* Some were authored by believers who sought to support the oral history about the book's origin. Other writers sought to shed doubt on its claims of epochal significance. But no writing has yet been done were by a research historian utilizing primary source material.[1] Weigh the evidence I present in this biography about William Sadler. Was he connected with the cosmic mind circuit while writing *The Urantia Book* or was he a genius? Or are the two connected as one and the same?

---

[1] Mark Kulieke's "Birth of a Revelation" is a brief account of the oral history of the book. Larry Mullins' *A History of the Urantia Papers*, tells the origin story and early history to validate the book as a divine revelation. Ernest Moyer's *The Birth of a Divine Revelation: The Origin of the Urantia Papers* was written to help others understand the celestial activities occurring on the planet and to help people who are seeking God. Martin Gardner in his *Urantia: The Great Cult Mystery* traces the history of Sadler's possible involvement in the writing of the text and refutes the science in the book. He argues that Wilfred Kellogg, Sadler's brother-in-law, was the contact. Gardner suggests that Sadler had a larger hand in writing and editing the Papers than he was willing to admit. Gardner wrote, "In brief, Sadler did not write the UB. He merely edited and wrote portions of it. This would explain both the varying styles of the Papers, as well as the tendency of Sadler, as editor, to inject his own preferences for certain unusual words and phrases" (363).

# INTRODUCTION

In the summer of 1911, a group of celestial beings began to communicate through a sleeping man in Chicago. From then until 1929, William and Lena Sadler, both physicians, had what they estimated as "probably 250 night sessions" during which a "stenographer made voluminous notes" as the celestials spoke through the patient.[1] The celestials explained they were on Earth to study and observe as they traveled from one universe to the other. They were here, they said, to perform various duties, one of which was to bring spiritual enlightenment to the planet through the papers they dictated. This experience began a three-decades-long saga that resulted in a 2,097-page work, *The Urantia Book*.

Drs. William and Lena Sadler were well known in the medical community as pioneers of preventive medicine. They were dedicated to human health in the Seventh-day Adventist sanitariums and the slums of Chicago. As practicing physicians and teachers, they brought to light the deplorable health conditions of the day. They lectured in the medical community, the general community and they wrote more than forty books and hundreds of magazine articles. By day they practiced medicine: William Sadler was a general practitioner, surgeon, and later a psychiatrist; Lena focused on women and children's medicine. By night they recorded celestial beings. These two worlds never overlapped. The Sadlers also never involved their colleagues in these revelatory nights except to once ask a few of their colleagues about the mystery but they kept it secret from others.

This book argues that William S. Sadler was a religious genius, a prophet, and the "contact" for the Urantia papers. When he acted as the scribe for these papers he transcended his normal functioning mind and became connected to the cosmic mind circuit of the universe. This was a great mystery to him. Throughout his life he said that even if he told everything he knew about the celestial contacts, we would not understand because he did not fully understand. As a psychiatrist, he could not fully explain why he was receiving celestial messages and writing them down. In his opus, *Theory and Practice of Psychiatry*, he surmised that he may have been in contact with the cosmic mind he believed endowed human beings with superior spiritual insight. He wasn't really sure. William Sadler never claimed to be the source of this material, in fact he created an origin story that evolved over time so that he could keep his distance and finish the work he believed he was destined to do. Unlike other discoverers of sacred sources, such as Madame Blavatsky, Joseph Smith, Ellen B. White, or George Gurdjieff, Sadler never profited from *The Urantia Book*.

William told the most complete version of the origin story of the Urantia papers to Harold and Martha Sherman on August 20, 1942:

> About thirty-five years ago, when Lena and I were young physicians together, we decided to move, but the place we suggested was not yet available and we were directed to a furnished apartment in the neighborhood which we took for several months until our place was ready. We had been there about two weeks and some of the tenants had apparently learned we were physicians, and one of them—a woman living directly below us—rapped on our door about 11 p.m. as we were in the act of retiring. She said, "Will you please come downstairs with me? Something has happened to my husband. He's gone to sleep. He's breathing very strangely and I can't wake him up."
>
> We slipped on some bathrobes and went down to her apartment where I saw a medium-sized man, approaching middle age, asleep in bed, breathing very fitfully. He would take a couple short breaths and then hold his breath for a time long enough for any normal human to have gotten black in the face, but nothing happened. I took his pulse and was surprised to find it was normal. I then tried to arouse him with every known method, even to sticking pins in him, but failed. His wife seemed to be a somewhat nervous and superstitious type. She was frankly frightened, even though I assured her that he seemed to be in good physical shape despite his peculiar actions.
>
> We sat about and waited for him to return to consciousness, during which time his body gave several violent jumps and starts. Finally after about an hour, he awoke and looked around and saw us. We had propped him up on pillows and he now turned to his wife and asked, pointing at us, "Who are these people?"

She explained we were doctors she had called in when she found she couldn't awaken him, and he said, "What's wrong? What's happened?" I asked him, "How do you feel?" He said, "I feel fine!" I said, "What have you been dreaming about?" He said, "I haven't been dreaming at all!" I said, "You've been jumping about on the bed." He said, "I don't know anything about that. I can't understand it."

I made him promise that he would come to my office the following morning for a complete physical exam. This he did, and I gave him every test but found him to be in excellent physical shape. I got his family history and there were no cases of insanity or epilepsy among any of his antecedents or present relatives. In my investigation of psychic phenomena I had witnessed many so-called trance states, but this phenomenon he experienced seemed to be something different. Most of the trance cases I had contacted were that of emotionally unstable or hysterical women, but here was a hard-boiled businessman, member of the Board of Trade and Stock Exchange who didn't believe in any of this nonsense and who had no recollection of what happened during these strange, unwakeable sleep states. I told him I would like to keep him under observation, to which he readily agreed.

Nothing happened for several weeks and then one night, about the same time, his wife called us and said he was having one of those spells again. We went down and I gave him more tests and tried new ways to rouse him, all without effect. His labored breathing, its sudden breaking off, and then no breathing at all, would have been alarming had not his pulse remained strong and even throughout. The whole thing was baffling. When he awakened he was as before, unconscious of anything having transpired. This sort of experience was repeated at irregular intervals and at different times of night until the fall of that year, when we were able to move to the residence of our choice. This man's lease expired that same fall and he moved into an apartment house in the same block in order to be near us.

One night, when we were called to his new address, and as we sat by the bedside, Lena noticed that he kept moistening his lips as though he was preparing to speak. She said, "Perhaps he wants to talk to us. Maybe if we asked him a question we'd get an answer." She did so, and to our great surprise he did reply but it was not his voice. It was that of what we afterward learned to be a student visitor, on an observation trip here from a far-distant planet. This being apparently conversed with us through this sleeping subject, and expressed ideas and philosophies which struck us an entirely new.

I had been led to believe, through previous study and research, that all such manifestations, however phenomenal, were the work of the subconscious. I, therefore, got this man in my office several days later, since other entities were apparently coming through him, and secured his permission to submit to hypnotism that I might explore his subconscious. It was difficult to get him under, but when I finally did so, I was amazed to find no consciousness whatsoever of the subjects discussed by these purported beings which we had, by this time, started to record.

I now felt that I needed help in solving the causes behind this mysterious phenomenon and I called in other doctors and scientists, friends of mine as well as Houdini and Thurston. They were equally unable to furnish any explanation.

We now, finding that we could communicate by direct voice with different student visitors and other beings, began to look forward to each "contact" as we came to call it, and enjoyed the opportunity of asking questions which always brought the most stimulating and unexpected answers. We took to writing out questions in advance about the universe and to asking them, whenever given the chance. Finally, as a test, I worked out fifty-two questions privately and memorized them in my own mind, deciding to wait to see whether these so-called student visitors might be able to divine what was in my own consciousness.

One night a particularly electrifying personality seemed to be present from a distant planet and had greatly excited us by his comments. As he was about to go, I addressed him, saying, "How can you prove that you are who you say you are?" He said, "I cannot prove it, but you cannot prove that I am not!" He then stunned me by continuing, "However, I have just secured permission to answer forty-six of the fifty-two questions you have been holding in your mind."

Lena, spoke up and said, "Why, Will, you haven't any such questions, have you?" And I had to admit, "Yes, Lena, that is the exact number."

This personality then proceeded to give me the answer to the forty-six as promised. When he had finished, he said, "If you people really knew what you had here, you wouldn't take up our time asking silly, trivial questions like this. You would ask us something really significant and important."

We got home about 1:30 that night but there was no sleep in the Sadler household. We stayed up the rest of the night discussing and formulating questions that we might be prepared for the next contact.[2]

The Sadlers experience launched them into becoming the stewards of the 196 papers of celestial communications. The medium was never revealed. These richly detailed transcriptions were compiled into *The Urantia Book*. Published in 1955, the book describes its purpose as to "expand cosmic consciousness and enhance spiritual perception for the people on Earth."[3] It explains the origins of human beings, as well as their nature, history, and destiny in great detail. It asserts that human beings were created in the image of God, endowed with free will, are indwelt with a fragment of God that leads us through the universe until we reach Paradise, eternal life. The philosophy of *The Urantia Book* is consistent, essentially Christian, and reflects early twentieth-century scientific facts and truths.[4]

When asked about the purpose of *The Urantia Book*, Sadler said,

[It] is an attempt to unify present-day scientific knowledge and religious truth. The main purpose ... is to help the average person to a better understanding of Jesus' religion. This means an emphasis on the religion of Jesus as contrasted to the religion about Jesus.

*The Urantia Book*, while presenting many new concepts, devotes much attention to the exaltation of much that is old—home, education, and social equity.

Remember, it is not the purpose of *The Urantia Book* to start a new church. The book condemns sectarian religions. The book is a gift to all religions including Christianity.[5]

The meetings began in 1923, when the Sadlers launched a weekly lecture and study group of friends and patients at their home, also their office, on Diversey Parkway in Chicago on Sunday afternoons. This group became known as the Forum. Sadler introduced the Forum to the writings of the celestials during one of their early discussions. The people attending the Forum were fascinated by this topic and the celestial papers became the sole focus of the meetings. Over seventeen years, more than three hundred people would ask questions that the celestials would answer. As legend has it, celestial visitors would transmit their revelatory material at night to a group of six people known as the Contact Commission. The commission consisted of the Sadlers, Lena's sister Anna, her husband Wilfred Kellogg, Emma "Christy" Christensen, and later the Sadler's only child, Bill Jr.

These celestial conversations happened outside of the Forum meetings—no Forum members ever observed these events. In the first hour of the meetings, a topical paper would be read (usually by Sadler) that the celestials had previously transmitted through the mind of the human subject. The second hour of the meeting was reserved for Forum members to ask questions, which the celestials would answer in succeeding night sessions, and the answers read to the Forum the following Sunday. These subsequent answers allowed the papers to be revised as the celestials gave increasingly enriched detail to the Forumites (as they referred to themselves). And, with few exceptions, all of the Urantia papers were recorded based on input by the celestials in response to these questions. This process continued until 119 papers were completed. The last seventy-seven papers, totaling seven hundred pages, "The Life and Teachings of Jesus," appeared all at once in 1935. The celestial beings dictated the Jesus papers to the scribe—they were not the result of a Q & A. The Forum can best be described as an active partnership between humans and celestials. Sadler explained that the celestial beings were very real to them. They frequently talked with them during the "contacts."

Sadler wrote that during the early years of contact the celestials "tested" the contact personality, rehearsed the technique of communication and set the stage for the subsequent presentation of the Urantia papers. No two contacts were alike. The humans seldom met the visiting personalities more than once. The celestials appeared to determine, patiently, how best to modify the theologic beliefs and philosophical opinions held by the humans. They achieved this by building a consistent narrative that was logical, reflected current science theories, and progressive religious views. Sadler said that without realizing it, their fundamental religious views and attitudes had been considerably changed by the celestial communications over the seventeen-year period of the Forum.

To understand the remarkable nature of the Sadlers' involvement with the creation of *The Urantia Book*, it is necessary to tell the story with two distinct panoramas. Part I describes the nature of the Sadlers' lives while fully engaged in their medical practice. Part II details their enlightened evenings dedicated to bringing new spiritual revelation to the planet. The first few chapters describe these remarkable people and their early medical practices. These chapters are followed by delving into the history of William Sadler as a writer and how he was led to be the channel for *The Urantia Book*.

Part I commences with Chapter 1, which provides background on William and Lena Sadler's early lives and how their views were formed within the Progressive era in Chicago. This chapter also introduces the people who were part of their extended family and lived with them their entire lives. Chapter 2 describes William Sadler's medical practice and the training he received from his mentor, John Harvey Kellogg, at the Battle Creek Sanitarium in Battle Creek, Michigan. Chapter 3 illuminates Lena Sadler's work as a physician, in which she focused on preventive medicine for women and children. Lena's early death in 1939 ended her participation in the Urantia papers Forum. Chapter 4 outlines the Sadlers' philosophy of preventive medicine that included faith as an element of overall health. The Sadlers began their public campaign with their health lectures on the Chautauqua Circuit. Their topics included their belief in the field of eugenics. Eugenics appeared to hold promise as a way to engineer better humans until the Nazis showed the horrible consequences of this thinking during World War II.

Part II starts with Chapter 5, which tells the story of the Forum in the Sadler home. The Forum members included professionals in all walks of life as well as many of Sadler's patients, each of whom read the papers and asked questions to assist in revising the manuscript. Chapter 6 tells of the nature of the celestial communications during the Forum years. Chapter 7 depicts William Sadler's writing style and highlights a few of his most popular books. Chapter 8 delineates the *The Urantia Book* by its four sections and describes its religious philosophy. Chapter 9 represents the architecture of *The Urantia Book*, how its style is similar to but also far advanced from the writings in William Sadler's books. Lastly, Chapter 10 is an examination of Sadler as the channel and scribe of *The Urantia Book*.

---

[1]   Sadler, *The Mind at Mischief*, 382–83.

[2]   Praamsma and Block, *The Sherman Diaries*, 131–36.

[3]   *The Urantia Book*, 1007.

[4]   Most people have never heard of *The Urantia Book* and no religion is organized around its teachings. However, the book has been widely sold and translated and fraternal organizations, conferences, and study groups for readers have been established. Some 750,000 copies of *The Urantia Book* are in print in English, and another 200,000 in Spanish, Portuguese, Russian, French, German, Dutch, Finnish, Lithuanian, Korean, Italian, Polish, Hungarian, Swedish, Estonian, Romanian, and soon Bulgarian. Urantia Foundation, the original publisher, lost the copyright in 2001, and since then the book has been available as a free download. Records show that it has been downloaded 177,000 times in 116 countries since 2008. The leading countries downloading the book are Russia, the United States, France, Italy, Mexico, and Brazil.

[5]   Sadler, "Consideration of Some Criticisms," 14

# PART I

———◄•►———

# THE SADLERS' LIVES

*There is a Universal Intelligence whose emanations radiate to all who are in harmony with the Divine Mind. Every soul who is "in tune with the infinite" enjoys the possibility of receiving messages and inspirations from the Holy Spirit.*

—Dr. William S. Sadler,
*The Physiology of Faith and Fear;*
*or, The Mind in Health and Disease,* 1912

# 1

## THEIR RULING PURPOSE

*We are all part of God's plans for the future. And these plans are so alive, so adventuresome, so challenging, and so beautiful that it does seem important we learn to appreciate, however dimly, that these plans do affect us. It is the magnitude and the complexity of God's challenge to us that obscures our comprehension of this challenge. It is the vastness of the unfolding adventure that makes it hard to understand. It is the endlessness of the eternal future that staggers our imaginations. And all of this is contained in the symphony of the concept of the master universe in* The Urantia Book.

*God's plans are partially disclosed in the master universe. And if we can comprehend these plans just a little better, we may be intrigued, challenged, and even inspired by the grandeur of the magnificent adventure that is being offered to us. If, perchance, this Study of the Master Universe can bring God's plans just a little closer to our comprehension—closer to our feeling for the living truth of expanding growth, to the thrilling beauty of high adventure, and closer to the rewarding goodness of intelligent love—it will have served its intended purpose.*

—Bill Sadler, *A Study of the Master Universe*

IN THE FOREWORD OF HIS BOOK, *A Study of the Master Universe*, the Sadlers' son, William Junior (Bill), explains that *The Urantia Book*—which asserts celestial authorship—was written like a symphony rather than a textbook: "wonderful themes of concept and movements of unfolding truth appear and reappear as the long story unfolds." He was painfully aware of the limitations of the human mind, he tells us, but still believed that people could begin to understand what the universe had in mind for each of us. This thought—that human beings would be better off if they understood the loving universe they live in—is what fueled the Sadlers' actions to bring *The Urantia Book* to the world.

The ruling question of the Sadlers' lives was to find a path for people to lead a faith-enriched life devoid of fear. The answer to their question was to share the revelatory spiritual knowledge they had gained over three decades of contacts with celestial beings to bring a new era of spiritual consciousness. Disappointed with organized religion, they believed that Earth was waiting for an unencumbered religion of Jesus that would construct a new and appealing philosophy of living. From their celestial contacts, they learned that Jesus was a supernatural being who came to Earth not to start a new religion but to teach us how to have a relationship with God and with each other. This was the religion *of* Jesus, not *about* Jesus. *The Urantia Book* would illustrate an all-powerful love that could bring freedom through faith. The Sadlers believed that faith was a vitalizing attribute of the human mind, which carried tremendous psychic possibilities and extraordinary therapeutic powers.

William Samuel Sadler was born in Spencer, Indiana, on June 24, 1875. At the time, Spencer had a population of about thirteen thousand people. Laid out in 1820, Spencer lies in Owen County, about twenty miles from Bloomington.[1] Sadler's father, Samuel Cavins Sadler, had been born in Indiana in 1855 and taught music for a living before he became a salesman, and was semi-active in the Seventh-day Adventist Church (SDA). His mother, Sarah Izzabell Wilson, had been born in Spencer on July 26, 1856. She would become a doctor before her son did by training in-house with Adventist Shryock in Seattle, Washington. Sarah had accepted the Adventist message with her parents after hearing Elder S. H. Lane, a Michigan native, speak locally when she was twelve years old.[2] The Adventist religion was in fact spread in the mid-nineteenth century by evangelizing from town to town.

The Sadlers' early religious views were grounded in the gift of prophecy, a theme that ran through their entire lives. Prophecy was the root of Seventh-day Adventism when the sect began in the early 1800s under William Miller in Lower Hampton, New York. Miller had had a vision revealing the long-awaited Second Coming of Jesus and that Earth would be engulfed in fire sometime between March 21, 1843, and March 21, 1844, which dates he calculated from biblical readings. Miller spread his vision in public gatherings and through posters, newsletters, and charts. Many thousands of "Millerites" heard, read, and believed his messages. Scholars estimate that as many as a hundred thousand people sold their belongings and moved into the mountains to wait for the Second Coming. Miller's first date came and went with no appearance; he picked another, October 22, no Jesus, and then another, October 23, same outcome. After this, he quit and the Millerites disbanded. Within days, other ex-Millerites began to have visions that convinced them that the dates Miller chose were correct but that the message was not that Jesus was coming back to Earth, rather it was when he would enter the heavenly sanctuary.[3]

Two former Millerites who had these visions were James Springer White (1821–1881) and his wife Ellen Gould White (1827–1915). Ellen's visions were compelling and convinced her listeners that God had chosen her to be his prophetess. The Whites concluded that she had the biblical gift of prophecy as outlined in Revelation 12:17 and 19:10. Subsequently, White became the prophetess of the newly formed Seventh-day Adventist Church. Although White's visions now had an audience, her visions had actually begun when she was seventeen. It was after the Miller episode that her messages were recognized as being divinely inspired. Between 1844 and 1863, she had somewhere between one and two hundred visions, usually in public places or meeting halls. Later in life, her visions occurred at home during the night.[4] An important Christian pioneer, White wrote more than five thousand periodical articles and forty books. Some controversy focuses on the validity of her visions and her reliance on uncited sources in her writings.[5]

William Sadler's parents, Sarah and Samuel, had married in Owen County on September 24, 1874.[6] They had three children, first William and nine years later the twin girls, Catherine and Mary.[7] After Catherine died at age three, William was home schooled because his parents were concerned that he might catch a communicable disease if he attended a public school.[8] Samuel worked on the SDA Sabbath-School Association as a board member in the late 1890s.[9] According to some reports, he sold Bibles door to door rather than continue to teach music. Sometime before 1910, the Sadlers would separate: the census for that year identifies Sarah as widowed and head of the household.[10] She would die in 1946, age eighty-nine, in Seattle.[11]

In 1889, the Sadler family moved to Battle Creek, Michigan. Battle Creek was home to the Battle Creek Sanitarium, the center of SDA activities. The sanitarium, known as the San, was the place where the influential and wealthy came to learn at the hands of the master—John Harvey Kellogg. For fourteen-year-old William Sadler, walking into the San for the first time would be a seminal moment. Because he lived in Battle Creek, young Sadler's talents (intelligence, deductive reasoning, charisma) were recognized and nourished by the two most important people in the Seventh-day Adventist religion—John Harvey Kellogg and Ellen Gould White—who introduced him to a world he would not have known had he remained in small-town Spencer.

Battle Creek's sanitarium was the largest institution of its kind in the world: a bustling tiny "city" dedicated to wellness and housed in an impressive structure that was famous around the world. The main building held between three and four hundred patients at one time. In 1891, more than sixteen hundred patients were treated. The San was a mass enterprise both inside and out: more than four hundred acres were cultivated for fruit and vegetable gardens to feed the patients. As a sanitarium pamphlet pointed out,

> at that time there existed no [other] institution which combined the comforts of the home and the hotel with the medical advantages of the hospital and the added facilities and equipment requisite for the administration of baths of every description, electricity in its different forms, medical gymnastics, and other rational agencies, with careful regulation of diet.

Sadler's most significant mentor was John Harvey Kellogg. For a home-schooled young man from a small Indiana town, the San offered a whole new world of sophisticated thinking. Because it drew the wealthy and influential, the San was full of people who were successful, stimulating, worldly, and interested in the Progressive era's new approach to health and diet. Kellogg early understood the value of having a celebrity clientele. For example, the San hosted William Howard Taft, William Jennings Bryan, John D. Rockefeller Jr., Alfred Du Pont, J. C. Penny, Montgomery Ward, Lowell Thomas, Thomas Edison, Henry Ford, George Bernard Shaw, Admiral Richard E. Byrd, and many others.

Sadler noted later in life that he had never met anyone who accomplished or could accomplish more than Kellogg. A description of Kellogg demonstrates his vigor:

> Kellogg, himself, was living proof of the value of his teachings on diet and health. Although he was small in stature (5 ft. 4 in.; 163 cm) and had had his left lung destroyed by tuberculosis before he was 20, Kellogg was a dynamo of human energy, a personification of the work ethic, who needed only 4 to 5 hours of sleep a night, went cycling or jogging every morning, dictated 25 to 50 letters a day, adopted and reared 42 children, wrote nearly 50 books, edited a major magazine, performed more than 22,000 operations, gave virtually all of his money to charitable organizations, loved human service, generally accomplished the work of ten active people, and lived in good health to age 91. Most who knew him considered

him a many-sided genius. Always a doctor, he had the rare ability of communicating to every patient the impression that their case was his number one concern.[12]

Not only did he have medical skill, Kellogg invented a number of surgical tools to improve safety and decrease pain, and electric blankets to keep his patients as comfortable as possible.[13] His work ethic was intense; Schwartz noted his longest period of continuous dictation was twenty-four hours. Kellogg's recognizing young Sadler's potential gave Sadler the confidence to accomplish much in his life. According to author T. Coraghessan Boyle, Kellogg had built a "bastion of right thinking, vegetarianism, and self-improvement, a citadel of temperance and dress reform and, not coincidentally, the single healthiest spot on the planet."[14] Boyle described the San in his book, *The Road to Wellville:*

> In the thirty-one years of his directorship, Kellogg had transformed the San, as it was affectionately known, from an Adventist boarding house specializing in Graham bread and water cures to the "Temple of Health" it had now become, a place celebrated from coast to coast—and across the great wide weltering Atlantic to London, Paris, Heidelberg, and beyond. Twenty-eight hundred patients annually passed through its portals, and one thousand employees, including [*sic*] twenty full-time physicians and three thousand nurses and bath attendants, saw to their needs. Six stories high, with a gleaming lobby half the size of a football field, with four hundred rooms and treatment facilities for a thousand, with elevators, central heating and cooling, indoor swimming pools, and a whole range of therapeutic diversions and wholesome entertainments, the San was the sine qua non of the cure business—luxury hotel, hospital, and spa all rolled into one.[15]

Besides Kellogg, three other people would help shape Sadler's life as a lecturer, writer, physician, and spiritual leader. Sadler's maternal uncle, General Thomas A. McNaught (1826-1919), was his first mentor in childhood. Sadler cited McNaught as the major influence in his love of storytelling and history. McNaught served in the Mexican War (1846-47) in the 3rd Indiana Volunteer Infantry Regt. His Civil War service began in September, 1861, when he helped to form the 59th Indiana infantry. The 59th elected him their Captain in October of 1861. In August of 1865, he was appointed Brevet Brigadier General.[16] McNaught was wounded (probably in the leg) in one of the assaults on Vicksburg. In an earlier encounter he had a horse shot out from under him. He probably participated in at least fourteen significant battles. Among the most prominent events he participated in were the Vicksburg Campaign, the assault in Missionary Ridge at Chattanooga, the Atlanta Campaign, Sherman's March to the Sea, and the last major battle of the war, Bentonville. The General would regale young Sadler with his Civil War battle stories.[17] As a child, Sadler became interested in history and public speaking after spending time with McNaught. With the stories he heard in mind, he staged battles between toy soldiers in his backyard when he was eight.[18]

Sadler's second mentor when he was a youngster was a family friend, General Lew Wallace, author of *Ben-Hur: A Tale of the Christ* (1880). Wallace lived in Crawfordsville, Indiana, which was about fifty miles from Spencer. Wallace's *Ben-Hur* was the best-selling novel of the nineteenth century and remained at the top of the best-seller list until Margaret Mitchell's *Gone with the Wind* was published in 1936. It has never been out of print. Between 1880 and 1912, *Ben-Hur* sold more than a million copies.[19] Wallace allowed the young Sadler free access to his personal library, which housed Wallace's large collection of history and religion books. Sadler told many people that he read Wallace's history books while visiting him.

Wallace's interest and questioning of religion could have influenced Sadler in giving him an example of how to approach the question of belief and faith. When Wallace was curious, he studied the Bible and wrote *Ben-Hur* as a truth-seeking exercise. Sadler would have been able to see how reading and writing was a way to come to terms with perplexing issues. Wallace reported that writing *Ben-Hur* sorted out his beliefs about God and Christ. He wrote in his autobiography, "When I had finished writing *Ben-Hur*, I said to myself with Balthazar (a character in the novel who was one of the three original wise men), "God only is so great. I had become a believer."[20]

Ellen Gould White was also an important mentor to Sadler in religion. A prolific writer, she was also the prophetess of the SDA church. It is not known exactly when she met Sadler, but the encounter most likely would have been in Battle Creek. The gift of prophecy is one of the twenty-eight fundamentals of the Seventh-day Adventist Church. White's prophecy was the reason William Sadler's family were Adventists. This belief would have been a part of Sadler's life from childhood and would have been strengthened once he was at the San and saw people's lives change for the better. Even as an older man and no longer an Adventist, Sadler indicated in his letters that he had spent a lot of time with the Whites, such as when he and Lena were in San Francisco in 1901. Sadler was aware of the controversy about White's testimonies, having experienced them firsthand. In a famous letter Sadler wrote to White in 1906, he questioned the veracity of her testimonies. White never responded.

Lena Kellogg Sadler also grew up in an unusual world. Her well-known family would bring her both privilege and opportunity that few women in that era realized. Her father, Moses Kellogg, was a half-brother to John Harvey Kellogg and Will Keith Kellogg. John Harvey ran the Battle Creek Sanitarium and Will Keith was the proprietor of the W. K. Kellogg Company (maker of Kellogg's Corn Flakes). Both were excellent models for hard work and service to humanity. They also fully supported Lena in her becoming a physician. Lena was a remarkable woman with many accomplishments: she was a doctor as well as a trained nurse, a mother, a published author, an equal partner with her husband in their medical practice, and the president of several women's medical organizations. She dedicated her life to helping other people both medically and spiritually.

When Lena was born in 1875, her family was just starting to build the institutions in Battle Creek that would make the city famous as a spa destination. Battle Creek became known as Health City because it was the center of Adventist activity. At their institutions, Seventh-day Adventists also endorsed therapies based on what was called the *water cure*. The water cure, or hydrotherapy, involved more than two hundred types of baths to help optimize health.[21]

On September 8, 1890, fifteen-year-old William Sadler entered Battle Creek College. The campus was a leafy seven acres, half covered by buildings and the other half intended for "out-of-door games."[22] His guardian is listed as S. I. Sadler (his mother) of Crawfordsville, Indiana.[23] Students at Battle Creek College were expected to begin each day with religious services in the chapel. The college held Sabbath services and hosted a Sabbath dinner every Saturday, and Wednesday evenings found the students at the Missionary Society, where they were to develop into "active Christian laborers."[24] All of this fed into the highly religious nature of Sadler's young life. His life and religion were being melded into one. Everything one did in life should be devoted to work for the kingdom of heaven on Earth.

Sadler attended Battle Creek College for only one year. Why he left is not known. He returned to the San and, after working for Kellogg as his secretary, became a health-food salesman for the Kellogg brothers' Sanitarium Food Company. This, he told others, is when he began to distinguish himself as a man of ideas. He convinced Kellogg that doing demonstrations in retail stores would help increase the sale of Sanitarium Foods. A sample campaign Sadler tested in Michigan City, Indiana, was so successful that Kellogg had to increase his food manufacturing business. The result was the creation of the Sanitas Food Company managed by W. K. Kellogg. In the Kellogg brothers' agreement, the Sanitarium Food Company retained the production of Granola and the previous lines of breads, biscuits, and cereals. Sanitas Foods would produce the new, flaked cereals and vegetarian meats they had developed in the sanitarium kitchens.[25] This experience was the genesis for W. K. Kellogg's later speech, "What Every Salesman Should Know About His Health."[26] The Sanitas Company was quite successful and spawned numerous competitors in Battle Creek. In 1907, Sanitas became the Kellogg Food Company, most famous for its Corn Flakes brand.[27]

In 1893, when they were both eighteen, William met Lena Celestia Kellogg, who was at the time studying to become a nurse, and they fell in love. On December 3, 1897, they married in Paris, Illinois.[28] After their marriage, they moved to a dormitory in Chicago that housed many students working at the Seventh-day Adventist Medical Mission. This location allowed the couple to do Adventist outreach and social work while living frugally. The 1900 census has them living in Chicago Ward 2, as boarders, with forty-seven other people in the same house.[29] The Sadlers would have two sons: William Kellogg Sadler (Willis) was born on July 5, 1899, and died nine months later on April 26, 1900. He is buried in Battle Creek. William Samuel Sadler Jr. (Bill) was born on December 15, 1907.

Lena's training as a nurse was based on the Nightingale system, a style her uncle, John Harvey Kellogg, would have become familiar with while training to be a physician at Bellevue Hospital in New York. Florence Nightingale (1820–1910), born to an English upper-class wealthy family living in Italy, was a deeply religious woman who believed that God had called her to serve as a nurse. Nightingale laid the groundwork for modern nursing when she served in the Crimean War, where she was dubbed the "Lady with the Lamp" because she made rounds at night to care for injured soldiers. Nightingale opened the first school for nurses in 1860 at St. Thomas' Hospital in London.

The Nightingale system was feminist in that it put women in charge of their own work. Rather than a male hospital administration overseeing the nurses, Nightingale favored an independent, women's nursing organization, which would have its own funds, a separate home for nurses, and a female superintendent. Janet Wilson James noted that the Nightingale model "thus in a sense restored to women, in a secular framework, a measure of the autonomy they had lost in Protestant countries with the decline of the religious nursing orders."[30] The Nightingale system of apprenticeship training was taught around the world in the middle to late nineteenth century. Nurses were trained using hands-on experience in a hospital ward under the eye of a physician or a ward matron. Nurses in training wrote case notes of their work that were reviewed by their supervisor.[31] The Battle Creek School added to this model with Adventist principles adding care that was both holistic and compassionate to spiritual needs. To attend the Battle Creek Training School for Missionary Nurses, women had to be of high moral character, have a good disposition, be in good health, and have a high school diploma.[32]

Being trained at Battle Creek would have given Lena Kellogg a sense of independence that few women outside the Adventist culture would have shared in the late 1890s. Women were accepted and supported in the SDA medical world. William Sadler, because his mother was a doctor, grew up being accustomed to women having strong roles. It was easy for him to support Lena's becoming a physician after her nursing training. Oral history within the Urantia community explains that Lena attended medical school because William encouraged her to do so after the loss of their son Willis at nine months. Sadler told her, "You can have another baby, and perhaps in the meantime, since you have always wanted to do it, you can study medicine."[33] Before becoming a nurse, Lena had been a public school teacher. Once she had become a doctor, the Sadlers were a team both professionally and privately: they performed surgery together, had adjacent offices, taught and wrote together, and supported each other's work.

Lena began her medical practice in the American Medical Missionary College dispensary, which was supported by the Seventh-day Adventists in Chicago. Her work consisted of treating woman and children and providing secondhand clothing to the less fortunate. In 1907, she reported some of her experiences in a letter published in *The Medical Missionary*:

> I have just finished an exceedingly interesting week at the Dispensary. I never enjoyed any work so much in my life as I do this. I find that the people in the Stockyards district are simply suffering for want of clothing, and I trust that all will be done that can be consistently done to provide for the suffering ones in this direction. I send with this letter a brief description of two cases that come to my mind at this moment.
>
> The Dispensary is located in the midst of four square miles of moral desert and temporal destitution. The mere statement that there are Christian workers in that region who need our assistance in carrying on their labors of love should be sufficient to lead us to ask, What can I do? Almost any of us could raise a box or barrel of partly worn clothing and send it prepaid to the Dispensary. Why not do it? Do not send paper rags, or cast-off clothing that cannot be worn on account of its being too ragged or too dirty. We all have clothes that are laid aside for various reasons which we are not depending upon, and which have good service in them. Mend them up in good shape and send them to the A.M.M.C. Dispensary, 888 Thirty-fifth Place, Chicago.[34]

Living in Chicago was a key factor in shaping the young couple's lives and provided incredible stimulation. Even before they moved into the city, they frequently ministered to the poor and received medical training at local SDA institutions. In the early 1900s, Chicago was the second largest city in America and a cultural landmark for progressive thinking. Henry Adams, referring to its prominence in the late nineteenth century, wrote that if one wanted to understand America and her civilization, "Chicago was the first expression of American thought as a unity; [and] one must start [t]here."[35] Chicago hosted the World's Fair in 1893. In 1896, the year after the Sadlers arrived, Chicago hosted the Democratic National Convention and elected William Jennings Bryan to run against William McKinley in the presidential campaign.

Chicago, along with New York, was the center of the advertising business for the nation. As Barzun describes it, "the turn of the century [1899–1900] was a turning point indeed; not an ordinary turning point, but rather a turntable on which a whole crowd of things facing one way revolved till they faced the opposite way."[36] Merchandising was changing with the dramatic rise in commercial advertising. Sadler himself would advertise his medical practice, much to the horror of the American Medical Association, which considered physicians who advertised to have extremely bad taste. The 1890s saw both advertising type and pictures replete with repetitious slogans and excessive claims. McClure's and other magazines grew thicker by as many as a hundred pages as companies made extravagant claims for their products: Post Toasties cereal would cure appendicitis; medical contraptions would cure housemaid's knee (bursitis on the knee). It was endless. The city of Chicago began to modernize as comfort was replaced by convenience. The new appliances demanded that new skills be learned in order to master the new fangled items. Homes began to have central heating and electric toasters, irons, sewing machines, and dishwashers. This, of course, revolutionized women's work in the home. For men who worked outside the home, typewriters became popular, as did telephones and electric elevators. The Sadlers would have been some of the first to see the Chicago Wheel, better known today as a Ferris Wheel, which debuted at the Chicago World Fair in 1893, or to go to a theater and see a motion picture.[37] They could go to a department store, use a coin telephone, and ride an escalator. The Sadlers lived in a city that had street lamps, "street trees," and well-maintained, paved streets. The elevated rail system, the El, had 34.8 miles in 1900 and 70.3 miles in 1914. The world was rapidly modernizing and Chicago was a showcase of new inventions.

The city was also progressive with its architecture. The first modern skyscraper was built in Chicago in 1885 using steel supports instead of cast iron ones. This development was rapidly followed by technically advanced steel structures with glass and terra cotta skins. Architects in Chicago were effectively world leaders in visionary city planning and new styles of architecture. Many famous and innovative Chicago architects changed the course of structure and style. Daniel Burnham gave Chicago and the world a powerful vision for the city. He built some of her first skyscrapers, directed construction of the 1893 World's Columbian Exposition that inspired the "city beautiful movement," and created an urban plan for Chicago. Louis Sullivan started the Chicago School, which emphasized the verticality of these new sky-scraping buildings. Frank Lloyd Wright built many of his Prairie-style homes in Oak Park outside Chicago in the early 1900s. This style was a reaction to mass production and residential living that occurred with the Industrial Revolution: the idea was "better homes would create better people."[38]

Sadler would begin his medical career in Chicago by attempting to live his religion by practically saving souls. His mentors would be reflected in his life in numerous ways. From General McNaught, he learned to love history and tell a good yarn to entertain people. From Lew Wallace, he learned the power of the book as a teaching tool and how writing could bring new spiritual truth to oneself and others. In Ellen Gould White, Sadler observed the power of a prophet and also how the source of her testimonies could turn up errors that could prove troublesome to believers. He would also become a prophet (although he denied it throughout his lifetime), a spiritual writer, a minister, and a teacher of salvation. John Harvey Kellogg was an inspiration for him to practice medicine, to take a scientific approach to problem solving, to teach through the lecturing group called the Forum and to write books on health for a popular audience. Sadler's writing was a blend of both White's and Kellogg's styles in the way he used sources—sometimes he disclosed his sources and sometimes he didn't. Also like John Harvey, he learned to write several books on the same topic. It is important to understand that Sadler did all of this his way.

Another person central to this story is the Sadlers' son Bill, who was the inspiration for his parents to find a way to live a practical, spirit-led, fear-free life. His mental illness as a young man was an impetus for his father to delve deeper into studying psychiatry. William Sadler wrote that the job of the psychiatrist was to help a mentally ill person successfully integrate their personality to a consciousness that is aware of the higher meanings of life. Sadler believed the mentally ill had a chance to develop an "adequate philosophy" of life if a supportive family surrounded them. The Sadlers would observe their severely ill child largely recover from his psychotic state, grasp the incredible complexity of the Urantia papers, and teach and write about them at the highest level. No antipsychotic medications were available in the early twentieth century. Thus they turned to faith in treating disease because it compelled healing.

Bill's later accomplishments were a far cry from his younger life. His troubling story is contained in his military records. Running away from home in March 1924 at age sixteen and a half, he joined the Marines under the assumed name of Winston Stefan Stevens (retaining his WSS initials). He also lied about his year of birth (stating 1904 instead of 1907), where he lived (New Orleans), and what he did (sales). He even found a man, Arthur A. Hawkins, from New Orleans to swear that he was Winston Stefan Stevens's uncle. Hawkins stated that Winston had been born in LaGrange, Illinois, on December 15, 1904, and that both of Winston's parents were dead.[39]

It is not known when Lena and William Sadler discovered the whereabouts of their only child. However, in February 1927, Bill Sadler requested that his name be changed to the correct one, William Samuel Sadler Jr., and that his military records reflect it as well. There are sworn statements in his military records file from his father, William Sadler; his uncle, Wilfred Kellogg; and close family friend, Emma "Christy" Christensen, stating that he was indeed William Samuel Sadler Jr. He was very bright according to a report of the examining board in February 1925—scoring four out of a possible four in aptitude. In February 1928, after four years of service, Bill was honorably discharged. His nonmilitary federal service began in November of 1928, when he went to work as a clerk in the office of the Chief National Bank Examiner, who happened to work with Christy Christensen. In September 1930, he resigned.

On June 23, 1932, Bill again left home without telling his family and reenlisted in the Marines. On June 27, 1932, he was brought unconscious to the U.S. Naval Hospital in Washington, DC. The report, called a medical survey, diagnosed him as in a "constitutional psychopathic state" on July 1, 1932. The medical report spells out his suicide attempt in late June by an overdose of veronal (sleeping pills), his being brought into the hospital in a coma, and his remaining in that state for two days. Sadler told the attending doctor that his son's behavior had been so erratic prior to his leaving home that he had two psychiatrists observing him without his knowledge. As a younger man, Bill had had several episodes of being catatonic and bedridden for days at a time. Because he was not considered suitable for the Marines, he was honorably discharged into his father's care.[40] His discharge papers state that even with a discharge for disability he was given an "excellent" for character. His illness appears to have abated after his return to Chicago and he became more involved with the Urantia papers, playing a vital role in the Forum from the 1930s to the 1950s. Bill married his first wife, Leone Gill, in 1935.[41] They had three children—William III (who died in 1955 at the age of nineteen), Patty, and Charles—but later divorced. His 1958 marriage to Florine Seres lasted until his death on November 22, 1963.[42]

As he regained his mental health, Bill would begin serving in a leadership capacity in the Urantia community in Chicago. In 1933, he was elected assistant cashier of the District National Bank of Chicago, where he remained for the next three years. In 1935, he married and got a job with Standard Oil of Indiana as an investment custodian for its pension fund. In the early 1940s he became a consultant for a firm of consulting engineers. In 1947, he set up his own aptitude testing firm, Sadler and Associates, at 333 North Michigan Avenue.[43] The young Marshall Field IV was reportedly a client.[44]

When asked what Bill was like, John Hales, a Forum member, said that he was "a lot of fun." He described him as gregarious, enjoying a cocktail, telling "off color" stories, and being a "people guy." Another Forum member, Carolyn Kendall, remarked that he could be intimidating at times. She never had a conversation with him, she said, but did observe him for years. When someone in the Forum would repeatedly ask questions Bill apparently felt were dumb, for example, he would cut them off and tell them what he thought. Carolyn, however, also told the story of her bringing her then-fiancé, Tom Kendall, to an Urantia Forum picnic. After talking with William Sadler, Tom was still unsure what to think of the Forum. Carolyn introduced him to Bill, who did an incredible job of explaining the meaning of the papers. Bill's charisma and knowledge convinced Tom to read the Urantia papers and join the Forum. Not only did Tom join the Forum, he later became a trustee of Urantia Foundation.[45]

Bill Sadler became one of the main teachers in the Urantia papers Forum as the papers were being written. After the book was published in October, 1955, he gave a series of lectures at Urantia Book Societies. The tapes of these talks give a nice window into his thorough knowledge of *The Urantia Book* as well as how he taught. Bill served as the first vice president of the Urantia Foundation trustees and was the first president of the Urantia Brotherhood (the first organization of readers devoted to the study and dissemination of the book). In August 1958, after he had retired from the presidency of the Urantia Brotherhood, Bill gave a series of talks in Pasadena for the West Coast Urantia Society. Two stories help illustrate his talks. The first was given on August 23, 1958:

> I'll tell you the only prayer I ever heard in my whole life that was answered verbatim. It's many years ago. And I never crammed religion, much less *The Urantia Book*, down the throats of my kids. But any time they asked questions I told them as much as I thought they should know. And I suppose they were about five and four … oh, let's say four and six and eight. And they had heard about Jesus. And I had never told them a smidgeon about Jesus. And they wanted to know all about Jesus.
>
> "Well," I said, "When you monkeys get ready to go to bed I'll tell you all about him." So I sat down and I took the gospel of Mark. I was afraid of *The Urantia Book*. Number one: It's too long. And

number two: you can't depend on the discretion of children. You know, they're going to talk about this, that and the other thing and "Where did you hear that?" I took Mark as a prompter and in about an hour and a half, in their language, I told them the story of Jesus, taking my cues from Mark and drawing on the [Urantia] papers. And when it was all over, the kids were real quiet. They were little tykes then, and I can remember they still had feet in their pajamas. I can see 'em sittin' around.

It's a real dramatic story, you know, if you've never heard it before. And of course it ends rather horribly. It's tense. It's a terrific tragedy. The boys were quite solemn. And my daughter, Pat, is like her grandmother—she shows her emotions, and she just cried, she sobbed.

That night she knelt down and she prayed the only prayer I've ever heard which I know was answered. And this is what she said, "Dear God, please tell Jesus I think he was just wonderful."[46]

The second, given on August 17, 1958, confirms Bill's anti-institutional religion attitude:

A damn sweet old gal with nearly white hair came to see me. And her heart is troubled. You know, there's not many times in my life when I got as white-hot boiling mad as I did this afternoon.

Here's your problem: this is a sweet little Alpheus twin [in *The Urantia Book* the Alpheus twins are good-natured, simple-minded, apostles] she's no brain. She was brought up in a church where they "sprinkled." And her mother was "sprinkled" along with her. And her mother died.

And she got converted to a church where they "dipped" [baptized]. And that stupid jerk of a pastor had told her [that] her mother can't go to heaven because she hasn't been dipped. What did he think she was, a sheep? I had to get up and leave the table and look out the window. The old gal thought I was praying. I was trying to get my anger down to the place where I wouldn't pop an artery. I said I'm going to talk to this old girl. "Shame on a minister for doing that to a poor soul like you, honest parishioner." I said, "Look, let's paraphrase Isaiah: come now let's reason together."

I said, "Do you have any children?"

"Yes," she has a son.

"Love him?"

"Oh, yes."

"Do you believe God loves him more than you do?"

She thought a minute.

I said, "It's kind of like the difference between moonlight and sunlight. After all, where's your love come from?"

"Yeah," she says, "He must."

"Love you and your mother the same way?"

"Of course."

"You believe God is all-powerful?"

"Yes."

"Do you think really, if God wants your mother in heaven as a daughter, that this minister is big enough to keep God from getting her?"

She grinned. She said, "Of course not."

I said, "Swell, just don't let your pastor know he's that small. He thinks he's bigger than God."

This is the sort of thing that raises the guard in me and represents one of the reasons for the antagonisms toward the churches which I find in many thinking Americans today. This sort of balderdash! That's sectarianism at its worst.[47]

Bill was also a founding member of Urantia Foundation, which published *The Urantia Book,* and the first president of the fraternal organization Urantia Brotherhood. The other members of the Contact Commission were Wilfred and Anna B. Kellogg and Emma "Christy" Christensen. Wilfred and Anna lived with the Sadlers in Chicago. Anna Kellogg was Lena's sister, two years younger, and in 1912 married her distant cousin Wilfred Kellogg in the Sadlers' home in La Grange. Wilfred—born in 1876 in Berkshire, Vermont—worked for the Sadlers his entire married life as a business manager, agent, monitor, and question collector at the reading of the Urantia papers during the Forum evenings. He was also a founding trustee of Urantia Foundation, where he served until his death in 1956. Mark Kulieke, who knew Anna, reported that she was "a comfortable and reassuring person, helping to put people at their ease." Kulieke described Wilfred as a "thoroughly reliable and businesslike individual."[48] Anna and Wilfred had a daughter, Ruth, who was born deaf in 1914 and died from pneumonia in 1944.

The last member of the Contact Commission, and part of the extended Sadler family was Emma Christensen, known as Christy, born on January 29, 1890, in Brown County, South Dakota. Her parents, Nels Christensen and Thora Rosalie Nana Bald, had both been born in Denmark.[49] Life on the South Dakota prairie was bleak, however, and thus Christy decided to leave the isolated community and make something of herself.[50] She went to college, secured a good job, and at a time when women did not hold many leadership positions became the chief bank examiner in Chicago.[51] The story of how Christy came to the Sadlers has its own celestial connection. In July 1922, Christy was hit by a car and ended up in the hospital. One of the Sadlers treated her and a friendship developed as she recovered. At this time, the Urantia papers were starting to come through more and more rapidly. The Sadlers told the celestials they needed a secretary. "Don't worry," the celestials responded, "we'll find [one] for you." As the Sadlers got to know Christy, they described the contact with the celestial beings and said they were in need of a secretary a few evenings a month. Christy agreed to help and moved into the Sadler home in the mid 1930s when Lena was ill with breast cancer. After Lena died in 1939, Christy remained at 533 until her own death in 1982. Asked by a member of the Forum 55 years later why she had done so, Christy explained, "Well, I was curious, but I didn't know what I was getting myself into at the time."[52]

In a draft of his 1960 history, Sadler noted that during the early years their "unseen friends" were testing the sleeping subject to set the stage for the presentation of the Urantia papers. Their primary contact, he wrote, was a type of celestial being called a "midway creature." Sadler went on to explain that during the sessions they were introduced to many new and strange ideas about the "universe of universes" and the eternal destiny of humans. They learned that the cosmos was far flung with trillions of inhabited worlds and that there were scores of celestial personalities. They spent upwards of two decades, he explained, "extending our cosmic horizons, enlarging our theologic concepts, and expanding our over-all philosophy."[53]

The Contact Commission spoke with the celestial beings first through the sleeping subject and then on their own. They were an unlikely group to bring an epochal revelation into reality: a pair of married physicians, their business manager, a sister/nurse, a bank examiner, and a son. All of them led conventional daytime lives. At night, however, they formed a group, spoke with celestial beings, took notes, typed up the papers to review, and brought the papers into book form. Sadler described their responsibilities as follows: "The Commissioners were the custodians of the Urantia manuscript, keeping the carbon copy of the typewritten manuscript in a fireproof vault. They were also charged with full responsibility for supervising all the details connected with the publication of the Book, securing the international copyrights, etc." Sworn to secrecy, "We were enjoined to refrain from discussing the identity of the Contact Personality and, after the publication of the Book, to make no statement at any time as to whether the "subject was still living or was deceased."[54]

Sadler was talented and influential in his craft but he was not a revolutionary physician, psychiatrist, or a writer who changed the academic conversation in his chosen fields. However he did have a brilliant mind that worked far beyond what was usual for him when he was in a superconscious state—what he called the cosmic mind—in which he would have personal contact with the intelligences of the universe. When this phenomenon occurred, he could write far above his normal style. The experience gave him extraordinary access to spiritual realities inconceivable in his conscious mind. Later chapters offer more detail on and into the circumstances that made him a revelatory figure who has remained largely unknown—which was how he preferred it to be.

---

[1] http://www.owen.in.us/owenhist/owenhis2.htm

[2] C.A. Purdon obituary, *North Pacific Union Gleaner*, August 13, 1946.

[3] Kayla Webley, "The Millerites," May 20, 2011, http://content.time.com/time/specials/packages/article/0.28804.2072678_2072683_2072697.00.html

[4] Arthur White, *Ellen G. White: The Early Years*, 123–24.

[5] SDA beliefs include that the Bible is the inspired word of God; that there is one God reflected in the Holy Trinity, which is three unified eternal persons. Through Jesus people gain salvation. They also believe that all people are given gifts from God. These gifts are listed as faith, healing, prophesy, proclamation, teaching, administration, reconciliation, compassion and self-sacrificing service for the betterment of mankind. Prophecy was thought to bring the church comfort, guidance, and correction. This belief goes hand in hand with the fact that the Bible is the standard which all teaching and experience must be tested. The SDA Church also advocates that its members act in harmony with the principles of heaven. These character traits require the members to maintain a high standard of Christian taste and beauty, treat their bodies as temples of the Lord, which means no meat, alcohol, tobacco, or using illegal drugs or narcotics.

[6] Owen County, Indiana, Index to Marriage Record 1850–1920, inclusive vol., W.P.A. Original Record, Book 30, p. 402

[7] The girls were named after their grandmothers: Mary was Samuel's mother, and Catherine, was the name of Sarah's mother and grandmother. See http://trees.ancestryinstitution.com/tree/8232177/family?cfpid=1632086624.

[8] Vonne Meussling, interview with Meredith Sprunger, April 24, 1970.

[9] *Seventh-day Adventist Year Book for 1890*, 24

[10] Thirteenth Census of the United States 1910 (NARA Microfilm publication T624, 1,178 roles), Record Group 29, National Archives, Washington, DC. The census shows Sarah lived in Ward 7 in Seattle with her mother, Catherine, age seventy-six, her daughter Marie, age twenty-five, and an Aron S. Lenewever, age thirty-two, who was probably a boarder.

[11] Interestingly, Samuel lists himself as living in Peoria as a boarder and married for nineteen years in the 1900 census, although his wife was not living under the same roof. He stated he was divorced in the 1910 census.

[12] Shurtleff and Aoyagi, "Dr. John Harvey Kellogg and Battle Creek Foods."

[13] Ibid., 123–27.

[14] Boyle, *The Road to Wellville*, 6.

[15] Ibid.

[16] Email with Scott Forsythe, October 25, 2014. McNaught marched in the Grand Review of the Army in Washington

City in May 1865 with Sherman's Army (spruced up Army of the Potomac marched first with Sherman's command following in the uniforms they wore in the field).

17  Blanchard, *Counties of Clay and Owen*, 880–81.

18  Meussling, "William S. Sadler," 22.

19  In 1893, a study of libraries found that 83 percent of them carried the book and it was the most widely read of all their holdings. By 1900, the book had been printed in thirty-six editions and translated into twenty languages. Ulysses S. Grant read Ben Hur in one thirty-hour sitting. President James Garfield also read it and wrote Wallace, "With this beautiful and reverent book you have lightened the burden of my daily life." Wallace's message that piety brought prosperity served as an appealing message to those who wanted to take part in the Gilded Eras material successes.

20  Lifson, "The Book Shook the World."vol.

21  Ibid., 21–56.

22  *Fifteenth Annual Calendar*, 5.

23  Researching the school records demonstrated that he attended for only one school year since his name is not listed in the roster for Fall 1891, nor any time up to 1893, when he began work for the Sanitas Food Company. His quarterly classes freshman year were algebra, rhetoric, bookkeeping, elementary physics, and Old Testament in the fall along with Bible study and lectures. In the spring quarter he took physiology, botany, Latin, German, New Testament, and civil government as well as the required biblical lectures.

24  *Fifteenth Annual Calendar*, 10.

25  Schwartz, *John Harvey Kellogg*, 209–10.

26  Meussling, "William S. Sadler," 25.

27  Schwartz, *John Harvey Kellogg*, 211

28  Marriage record, County Court Records, Film # 1301880 - 1301882.

29  1900 Census Place: Chicago Ward 2, Cook, Illinois, Enumeration District: 41: Roll T623_245, page 8B.

30  James, "Isabel Hampton," 206

31  McDonald, "Nightingale System of Training."

32  Jones, Herrmann, and James, "Adventist Nursing";– see also McCabe, "Medical History of Michigan."

33  Meussling, "William S. Sadler," 27. The source for this quote is listed as "Sadler's Papers," for which the whereabouts are currently unknown.

34  "An Opportunity to Help the Poor," 30.

35  Adams, *Henry Adams*, 1031.

36  Ibid., 615.

37  The original Ferris Wheel, sometimes also referred to as the Chicago Wheel, was designed and constructed by George Washington Gale Ferris Jr. At a height of 264 feet, it was the largest attraction at the World's Columbian Exposition in Chicago, Illinois, where it opened to the public on June 21, 1893. It was intended to rival the 1,063 foot Eiffel Tower, the centerpiece of the 1889 Paris Exposition.

38  This quote is from the Idealistic Romantic movement and used by Prairie style architects in the American Midwest in the late 1800s and early 1900s. Idealistic Romanticism was part of the Arts and Crafts movement, which sought to free people from the constraints of the Industrial Revolution and harness the power of imagination to escape into a more natural refined aesthetic.

39  William S. Sadler Jr., military personnel records, file in author's collection.

40  "Report of Medical Survey" dated July 1, 1932, in William Samuel Sadler Jr.'s military records from the National Personnel Records Center, St. Louis, MO. Copies in the author's collection.

41  Cook County Marriages, file # 1439839.

42  Ibid., # 2494155.

43  Jim Mills, "Memorial Service for Bill Sadler, Staff Room, Wesley Memorial Hospital, Chicago, Illinois (November 30, 1963): 2.

44  Carolyn Kendall, telephone interview, February 21, 2014.

45  Ibid.

46  William S. Sadler Jr., talk in Pasadena, CA, August 23, 1958, www.ubhistory.org.

47  Ibid.

48  Kulieke, *Birth of a Revelation*, 38–39.

49  The 1900 census shows her living in La Prairie, Spink, South Dakota, with her father, Nels, age forty-nine, and six siblings, the eldest of whom were fraternal twins, Frank and Mary. Christy was eleven years old and third to the youngest.

50  John Ploetz, "Remembering Christy," 2011, in author's collection.

51  On February 9, 1920, Christy married Christ J. Davidson in Clay, South Dakota. There is no record of a divorce, nor did Christy mention this prior marriage to any known Forum members. By 1920, Christy was living in Minneapolis, Minnesota, as a boarder and states herself as single on the census. Her job was assistant chief clerk. Christy resigned from this job in September 1920 to move to California to work in the San Francisco Treasury Office. In a letter from the chief examiner of Minneapolis, he stated that Christy had been "an employee of this office practically from the beginning (8–23–1915) and has most credibly handled the rather trying duties of this position." The Treasury Office in Chicago would employ Christy until she retired as chief clerk in October 1946, at fifty-six years of age. Her retirement was due to disability.

52  Kendall, "We'll Find a Secretary for You," 5

53  Sadler, *A History*, 4.

54  Ibid., 22

# 2

## BRINGING RELIEF TO HUMANITY

*Every one of our sanitariums is established to be a missionary agency for the relief of suffering humanity. We are to minister to the needs not only of the bodies, but of the sin-sick souls, of those who come to our sanitariums, in order that they may receive a knowledge of the truth, and have the faith that works by love and purifies the soul. Our observance of the Sabbath will make its impression upon hearts, and questions will be asked that will need to be answered.*

—Ellen Gould White, *Manuscript Releases*, 169

THE NEXT THREE CHAPTERS ADD CONTEXT and highlight the Sadlers' professional lives. Due to the fact that Sadler instructed that all his papers be destroyed, his story is pieced together from other available documents. Because Lena was president of the American Medical Womens' Association, a collection of her papers is available at Drexel University in their Women in Medicine collection. The Sadlers were in the mainstream working as doctors in their daytime lives. At night, however, they were knowingly on the edge and wisely kept their celestial contacts within a closed group of trusted people. Sadler was aware of what could happen to prophets, and it was clear that if it was known that "midway creatures" were visiting his home at night, a gaggle of reporters would be at his front door. In addition, the "contact" was not interested in fame or fortune from his writings, so there was no need to share the information. They therefore followed the celestials' admonitions to work as a closed group until the book was published. Even then, there would be no publicity because the revelators told them that the book was ahead of its time and would best be spread gradually person to person.

The Sadlers were born in a transformative era. New discoveries in science—from the theory of evolution, to germ theory, to anesthesia, to genetics—changed the way people perceived the natural world. These discoveries also spurred a conversation in the world of religion.

This era meant America would need to create a new culture to help them "cope with the conditions of modern life," brought on by the industrialization and urbanization in the wake of the Civil War. America became transformed into an urban nation in the late nineteenth century. American writer Louis Menand noted, "The Civil War swept away the slave civilization of the South, but it swept away almost the whole intellectual culture of the North along with it."[1] That is, before the war, working on your own farm or in some home-based business meant long hours, but your time was your own. After the war, the Industrial Revolution changed the model. It brought a loss of personal freedom and a loss of economic independence as people moved off the farm and into cities to work in the factories. The average factory workweek consisted of ten-hour days, five days a week, and a half-day on Saturday. Wages were so low that by the early 1900s, three out of five adult male workers did not earn enough money to support their family.[2] These changes forced Americans to think differently now that they were subjected to a new way of life.

Along with losing the "simple" life on the farm, these new urbanites were identified by city dwellers as having lower ethical standards because without financial means they ended up living in slums. The middle-class Progressives—classic liberal reformers in the late 1800s and early 1900s—perceived this decline in "moral and civic purity" in the city and began to focus on social and economic reform. The Progressives sought to regain a higher standard of living within the urban landscape.[3] These changes helped usher in the Progressive era in the United States in the late 1890s. The Progressives were a group of artists, politicians, social scientists, writers, and thinkers who agreed that America needed a spiritual reformation to fulfill God's plan for democracy in the New World.[4]

The impact of the Industrial Revolution was most profound in American cities, where the poor lived in dark, dirty, and inhumane slums. From 1890 to 1900, immigration caused the population of the United States to grow by 20 percent. In urban areas, the change was profound. For example, Chicago had a population of three hundred thousand in 1870. By 1890, the number had exploded to well over one million. At the same time, 40 percent of American rural townships saw their populations shrink between 1880 and 1890.[5] America's immigration boom shifted Chicago's population to being almost half foreign born in 1890.[6] To compound the overcrowding, cities were dirty and poor working people lived in squalor. The changes caused by the Industrial Revolution begged for cultural and political reform to improve society. Practitioners of this "social gospel" directed their moral outrage at poverty, hunger, racism, segregation, and sexism. Cities were crowded, unsafe, and harsh places to live for those who worked in the factories and were forced to live in squalid tenements. Reform was viewed as necessary.

The media helped highlight the plight of the poor urban dwellers. In 1890, Jacob Riis, in his book *How the Other Half Lives*, brought heart-wrenching photographs of the urban poor into people's homes. Another book, *Working People and Their Employers*, published in 1894 by Pastor Washington Gladden, described what he witnessed in 1876 during a workers' strike at a shoe factory in Springfield, Massachusetts. Gladden preached to many factory owners from the pulpit on Sundays. Concerned with what he saw, he took a stand and supported the workers' efforts to unionize against the horrible work conditions he witnessed. This act reflected a shift in American Christianity, from complacency to action in order to improve the way people in cities lived.[7] Gladden wrote in the introduction to *Working People and Their Employers*:

> Now that slavery is out of the way, the questions that concern the welfare of our free laborers are coming forward; and no intelligent man needs to be admonished of their urgency. They are not only questions of economy, they are in a large sense moral questions; nay, they touch the very marrow of that legion of good-will of which Christ was the founder. It is plain that the pulpit must have something to say about them.[8]

This dire situation was communicated to the public via journalists as well. In 1906, Theodore Roosevelt coined the term "muckraker" to describe the type of journalism that exposed social problems: legal, ethical, social, and public policy issues. Newspapers and magazines performed the job that the Internet, television, and radio do for us today. By the early 1900s, magazines such as *Collier's Weekly, Munsey's*, and *McClure's* were already in wide circulation and avidly read by the growing middle class. *Collier's Weekly* became a major proponent for social reform. By 1892, it had a circulation of more than 252,000 and was one of the largest magazines in the United States. Muckrakers shifted the way middle-class Americans perceived government and big business, and they helped marshal support for reform during the Progressive era. Upton Sinclair's article, "Is Chicago Meat Clean?," in *Collier's* magazine in 1905 caused the Pure Food and Drug Act bill to be introduced in the Senate. In 1906 the Senate passed the Federal Meat Passage Act. Sinclair's novel *The Jungle* (1906) caused uproar among the public because of the descriptions of the appalling working conditions in packing plants and the rotten and diseased meat sold for food. When President Theodore Roosevelt read the book, he called for an immediate investigation of the meat industry. Within months, more legislation came from Sinclair's description; the Pure Food and Drug Act was passed in 1906. The book was translated into seventeen languages and became an international best-seller.

An excerpt from *The Jungle* demonstrates the horrible working conditions in Chicago's stockyards area known as Packingtown, the largest meat packing area in the United States. The men and women there were poorly paid to work six days a week, ten hours a day, in dark unheated rooms that were hot in summer and freezing in winter. They worked on floors covered in blood, meat scraps, and foul water. Most of them were immigrants from Poland, Slovakia, and Lithuania who lived in tenements in Packingtown next to the foul-smelling packing houses located near four of the city's dumps.

Other journalists, such as Nellie Bly, Ida Tarbell, and Lincoln Stephens, wrote about corrupt politicians, sweatshop working conditions, and other social injustices. "The middle class awoke to the mockery that the factories and the cities were making of the American dream, and, as had the Populists in the 1890s, turned to reform with enthusiasm."[9]

This era also ushered in new action for churches. The religious wing of the Progressive era was called the Social Gospel. Sadler's life's work was clearly inspired by this call to reform society. He joined in the work of the Social Gospel in the late 1890s. This was no doubt because he lived in Chicago, one of the centers of this cultural shift. Louis Menand wrote, "Chicago seems to have struck the social-scientific mind at the end of the nineteenth century as an animated simulacrum of social life, a sort of living textbook."[10] Historian William Cronon in *Nature's Metropolis* argued that Chicago was the most important city to shape the landscape and economy of America during the second half of the nineteenth century. Chicago was the gateway to the expansion of the west.[11] Jane Addams, who started Hull House, and many other reform-minded individuals called Chicago their home. They shared the Social Gospel's belief that using science, technology, expertise, and education were the best ways to make the United States more socially responsible and more Christ-like in character.

According to historians Ronald C. White and C. Howard Hopkins, the Social Gospel caused people to take action outside the churches to intersect with political, social, and economic life in America, to bring the total message of Christian salvation to urban society in new ways. Social Gospel actions included settlement houses, like Jane Addams' Hull House, who helped poor immigrants improve their lives by offering daycare, health care, and education. Social Gospel practitioners sought to fight injustice, suffering, and poverty in society. In their eyes, living a Christian life should be a "crusade for justice and righteousness in all areas of the common life."[12]

One of the fathers of the Social Gospel was Walter Rauschenbusch, who beginning in 1886, ministered to the tenement dwellers in New York City's Hell's Kitchen. Rauschenbusch's new vision was outlined in his 1907 book, *Christianity and the Social Crisis:* "Instead of a society resting on coercion, exploitation, and inequality," he proposed one that "reflected Jesus' teachings of love, service, and equality."[13] He asked Christians to serve by transforming society to bring dignity and respect to the poor in urban areas. This new theology asserted that the redemption of society though Christian ways would help the individual become part of the kingdom of God. He wrote:

> But it is the human element in the city's life, which must chiefly concern us. The filthy slum, the dark tenement, the unsanitary factory, the long hours of toil, the lack of a living wage, the back-breaking labor, the inability to pay doctors' bills in times of sickness, the poor and insufficient food, the lack of leisure, the swift approach of old age, the dismal future—these weigh down the hearts and lives of multitudes in our cities. Many have forgotten how to smile.[14]

Rauschenbusch's experience was further elaborated in his 1917 book, *Theology for the Social Gospel*, in which he argued that Christians should have a new vision to reform society so that it would become more just and humane. He outlined six social sins as "religious bigotry, the combination of graft and political power, the corruption of justice, the mob spirit (being 'the social group gone mad') and mob action, militarism, and class contempt."[15] A practical approach to service for Christians, the Social Gospel spread across the cultural world in many forms. In addition, religious journals wrote their parishioners about the problem. In 1912, the Presbyterian monthly *The Biblical World* published an editorial titled "The Social Gospel" in which they outlined this social message:

> The industrial struggle looks very dark. We often cry, "Who is sufficient for these things?" But wherever Christian men have tried to find the light they have found it. We dare not to despair. We are laborers together with God, and there is nothing too hard to accomplish with him.[16]

For their expression of the Social Gospel, Seventh-day Adventists established sanitariums as places to heal, teach, and introduce the non-Adventist public to their philosophy. The Adventists were pioneers in proclaiming the healthful effects of clean air, sunshine, exercise, vegetarianism, and pure water. In the late 1860s, sanitariums were created to care for the sick and to assist in disseminating health instruction based upon the visions of Ellen Gould White. White's 1860s visions were full of direction for her people to "act upon the light which God has given in regard to the health-reform."[17] After her vision on December 25, 1865, she wrote,

> I was shown that Sabbath keepers should open a way for those of like precious faith—to be benefitted without their being under the necessity of expending their means at institutions where their faith and religious principles are endangered, and where they can find no sympathy or union in religious matters.[18]

These visions led to the opening of the first health institution in Battle Creek in September 1866. Battle Creek became the epitome of these institutions. The sanitarium proved the most famous, luxurious, and indispensable method to spread this new way of living to a rapidly changing nation. The first sanitarium in Battle Creek was a large home on eight acres of land. The Adventists added a two-story addition and named it the Health Reform Institute. The need to train more people came with the success of the institution—especially after John Harvey Kellogg assumed control in 1872. Initially they had doctors come and teach the staff. Because of the difference in the way non-Adventists approached lifestyle and medicine, the need for their own college was acute. Money was raised to enlarge the Battle Creek Sanitarium in 1877, where medical and health training continued until the American Medical Missionary College opened in 1895.[19]

In 1901, Kellogg sent the Sadlers to San Francisco to open an SDA medical mission. While he was there, Sadler wrote Ellen White's son, W. C. White, as his mind was firming up his life plan:

> I am but a young man, but I have put my shoulder to the wheel. I have settled on my purpose for life, and I am hungering and thirsting for knowledge as how to best do that which God has entrusted to my hands. I know you will pray for me and the work here, and, too, for our brother with whom I am associated in this good work.[20]

The Sadlers began their medical training at Cooper Medical College, now part of Stanford University, in 1901, while they were living in California. After leaving San Francisco in 1904, they returned to Michigan, where they resumed their studies at American Medical Missionary College (AMMC). Kellogg had begun AMMC in

1895 after the wealthy father of one of his patients made him promise on the young girl's deathbed—because of the care she had received from the nurses at Battle Creek Sanitarium—to maintain at least one nurse to work among the poor in Chicago. Kellogg visited the nurses to observe their work. He liked what he saw and began adding more women to the group. Initially the women worked in a basement room with laundry facilities and a bathroom. Soon a Sunday noon meeting that Kellogg conducted began along with dinner for a penny. Kellogg wrote, "Many thousands were fed and not a few were through these means led to abandon their evil habits, and through the Lord's great mercy some of these remain steadfast to this day."[21]

On July 3, 1895, AMMC was incorporated under the laws of Illinois. Financially supported by Battle Creek Sanitarium and wealthy benefactors, it opened for instruction with a class of forty on September 30, 1895.[22] Most of the classwork was conducted in Battle Creek and seminars on dissection and other medical clinics were conducted in Chicago. The students were taught the practical knowledge of disease and methods of treatment at Battle Creek Sanitarium, which was across the street from the school. Tuition remission was available for students who worked summers at the sanitarium, meaning that a motivated young man or woman could work their way through school at no cost to themselves. Students spent a portion of each year in Chicago also doing mission work.

The tuition was $100, or free with board, room, and laundry, for students who worked twenty-six hours a week in the sanitarium and to those "who agreed to devote their lives to missionary work either at home or abroad in a variety of work." This included working in time in the clinical lab, working as a lab assistant for the teachers, assisting in the treatment rooms at the sanitarium, being a doctor's assistant, and doing dishwashing and nursing relief on the Sabbath.[23] The school year was spent doing six hundred hours of didactic work, 675 hours of laboratory work, and about thirty-five hours a week of Bible study. Students spent six weeks in Chicago for each of the first two years. This included five to six hours a day studying anatomy and doing dissection with twelve students on each cadaver. The second two years they spent more time in the city doing clinical work. They slept, ate, and attended classes all in the same building. Shryock noted, "a thick board partition was all that separated our sleeping rooms from the dissecting room."[24]

The school took charge of the students' daily schedules from 5:30 am to having them retire at 10:00 pm. This schedule prepared them for a life of working during the day and studying and writing at night. A normal day's schedule at AMMC followed these lines:[25]

| | |
|---|---|
| Rising hours | 5:30 am |
| Breakfast | 6:00 am |

| Worship | 6:40 am |
| Class work | 7:00 to 10:00 am |
| Practical work | 10:00 to 12:30 pm |
| Missionary study | 12:30 to 1:30 pm |
| Dinner | 1:30 pm |
| Laboratory work | 2:30 to 6:30 pm |
| Exercise | 6:30 to 7:10 pm |
| Silent hour (two sections) | 7:10 to 7:30 pm |
| Study | 7:30 to 10:00 pm |
| Retiring hour | 10:00 pm |

AMMC, besides being an excellent school and free to those who worked for SDA, was also notable for two reasons. First was the number of women who attended the medical school. An ad for AMMC in the Medical Missionary in 1906 stated that "Women are received on equal terms with men."[26] This was remarkable during a time when women could not vote, could not attend most colleges, and had no rights to control their own property. The first graduating class of AMMC numbered fifteen men and nine women. Many graduates were couples who went on to practice medicine together at various Adventist institutions. The Sadlers were one of these couples, along with the Paulsons and Van Dorns. The second reason was the level of rigor in the AMMC program. When the first class received diplomas in 1899, AMMC was not yet accredited by the Illinois State Board. To remedy the problem, the State Board created a special exam and tested the first class and all twenty-four students passed easily.[27]

> The Sadlers graduated from AMMC on an occasion that spanned several days, from June 16 through 18, 1906. On the first day, a baccalaureate sermon was delivered by Professor B. J. Wilkinson of the Washington Training College. Later, a choir sang hymns. On the second day, the celebrations continued. William Sadler delivered the prayers, hymns were sung, and speeches delivered. On June 18, the class officially graduated. The graduation speech was given by Mr. V. L. Fisher and described as:
>
> > From the first to the last … one earnest simple appeal to the principles taught by Jesus and his apostles. The purely scientific aspects of the profession were only alluded to in loyalty and confidence in the course over which they had been led by the land of providence. It was a modest and earnest recognition of the value

and importance of that which had now been committed to them as a class, and an expression of a sincere purpose to be faithful to their high calling as medical missionaries.[28]

After graduating, both Sadlers took the Illinois State Medical Exam and passed. Sadler stated that he was one of four to receive a top grade on the test.[29] In December 1906, John Harvey Kellogg gave them one hundred shares of stock in the Kellogg Corporation to help their new medical practice. The Sadlers opened a joint practice first named the Chicago Institute of Physiologic Therapeutics, renamed in 1910 the Chicago Physiologic Institute and in the 1920s the Chicago Institute of Research and Diagnosis. They had two offices, one at their home in LaGrange, Illinois, and one in the stockyard district of Chicago. Sadler described some of this work in 1907:

> Those who have worked in Chicago in years past would be delighted to come now and see the beautiful facilities that have been provided since the beginning of our work down in Custom House Place. Now we have a splendid three-story building in the Stockyards district, nicely equipped. We have men's and women's treatment rooms in the basement, and we can do practically anything for the sick that can be done anywhere. Two of the Sanitarium nurses are there at work. The work is fascinating. The thing I am desirous to see is an all-around work done for these people. That which led me to study medicine and keeps me in touch with this work at the present time is the hope of seeing a still greater development in our work where body, soul, and spirit shall be ministered to.[30]

Their medical practice was essentially a mini-sanitarium and offered treatments using hydrotherapy, light baths, vibrating machines, heat treatments, and electro-shock therapy.

When he was eighty-five, Sadler shared his feelings with his friend Dr. Meredith Sprunger, a *Urantia Book* reader and minister, about his early years with his office:

> I fooled around and wasted a lot of time for years in the practice of medicine and lost thousands of dollars flirting with the idea of having a sanitarium or institution of some sort. You see, I had been brought up, since I was fourteen years old, in a sanitarium. The practice of medicine, as I knew it, was institutionalized, and as I say, it took me twenty years to get it through my head that I was to

be another kind of doctor, and I wasn't going to have a sanitarium. It would have been a blessing if someone could have sat down with me early during this period and pounded it into my head that I should give up the institutional notion. But it is hard to overcome the results of early training and associations. I don't know how many more inspirations along this line you will have in getting adjusted to the new setup of the Urantia movement. It is really something new in the world as regards religious propaganda, and it is going to be hard for any minister to step out of the pastorate, as you and David Schlundt are doing, and wholly give up the idea of the institutional church.[31]

While working in San Francisco in 1903, Sadler shared his experience as a medical missionary. After treating a woman who was cross, irritable, and being so full of worry that she was making "everyone miserable," she shared that her visits to the dispensary, were making her steps "lighter on my way home, and the sunshine comes home with me, and all in the house feel it." Sadler wrote:

> Then I seized the opportunity to tell her about the sunshine of God's love, and that it was not the doctor nor I that helped her and did her so much good, but it was Christ within us, the hope of glory, that He blessed the treatments, and also was blessing her …. May God help us to be a real comfort to this soul, and to the many others we meet from day to day.[32]

The Sadlers also did something controversial and almost unheard-of in their profession which got them in trouble with the American Medical Association. They advertised: "The Reliance Baths, The Diagnostic Facilities of the Modern Hospital and the Therapeutic Advantages of the Up-to-Date Sanitarium Right in the Heart of Chicago." A deluxe forty-eight page booklet featured their office's medical departments and areas of treatment, including photographs of the following treatments: nervous disorders, respiratory disorders, general surgery, general dentistry, complete examinations, and ear, nose, and throat. Listed in the therapeutic departments were massotherapy, electrotherapy, hydrotherapy, and manual Swedish therapy. This advertising was radical, looked upon as unseemly, and led American Medical Association (AMA) to launch an investigation.

The AMA, as part of its professionalizing program, opened a department of investigation in 1906 to examine complaints about health fraud, quackery, "patent" medicine, and alternative medicine. In 1915, the association received the first of several inquiries about the validity of the Sadlers' practice. The complaints, about ten, were mostly from other doctors who questioned their promotional methods—advertising at Chautauqua events, write-ups in popular magazines, such as *Everybody's* in September 1915 and the *Chicago Examiner* on July 7, 1918. Initially, the AMA was concerned, but after a visit to the Sadlers' facility, an interview with Sadler, and a fifteen-year wait, they closed the investigation. The last letter, dated March 3, 1930, in the AMA file on the Sadlers stated, "The institution about which you inquire is, as far as we are able to learn, a reputable one." The letter went on to confirm that the members were in good standing, but that their methods of advertising and promotion were of "questionable taste."[33] Although advertising by doctors, dentists, and lawyers is commonplace today, the Sadlers were well ahead of their time. In addition, the Sadlers sent letters to other doctors with a listing of their services. This practice provoked some of the letters that were written to the AMA.[34]

On October 16, 1907, Sadler wrote a letter to W. C. White to bring him up to date about his career. He was still attending Sunday evening meetings on the South Side, which he said were on "the same even trend." Teaching was taking over more of his time. He wrote,

> There seems some prospect that within the next year I shall probably be appointed to take charge of the new chair of hydrotherapy in the Post Graduate Medical School of Chicago. This will give me an opportunity to reach about half of all the physicians who come to this city to do post-graduate work. It seems almost too much to expect that such an opportunity should fall to us but the indications look favorable at the present time, and of course I shall do my duty to follow up.[35]

In addition, Sadler was teaching hygiene at the Dunkard's School of Chicago. Dunkard's was a Bible training school with a course of study that lasted two years. Ministers were taught fifty hours a year by Sadler, who saw "an opportunity to inoculate the whole Dunkard people as these workers scatter in the summer all over the country."[36] At the same time, he was preparing his manuscript on health and healing, writing his Chautauqua lectures for the following summer and his lyceum courses for the next winter, practicing medicine privately, and "devoting my energies to following up various openings which are presenting themselves for educational work and for presenting our health principles to the people."[37]

A busy and multidisciplined man throughout his life, William Sadler lectured, taught, and practiced surgery and psychiatry at various medical institutions in Chicago throughout the first half of the twentieth century. From 1907 into the 1920s, he was a professor of hydro and physiologic therapeutics at the Medical School of Chicago, later taught surgery there, was chief surgeon at Bethany Sanitarium and Hospital, and between 1914 and 1930 was a senior attending surgeon at Columbus Hospital in Chicago. Sadler's longest running educational endeavor was lecturing on pastoral psychiatry at McCormick Theological Seminary in Chicago, which he did from 1930 until 1956.[38]

In all respects the Sadlers were a team in both domestic and professional life. They went to medical school, lectured, wrote, performed surgery side by side, and ran their medical office together. In *The Life Boat* in 1903, Sadler shared his wife's support:

> Mrs. Sadler was an enthusiastic supporter of the enterprise and earnestly took hold to help me in every way possible. We had many counsels, and seasons of prayer, over the work, and were rewarded by seeing the hand of God working in many ways toward the accomplishment of our purpose.[39]

In a 1909 letter, Lena called herself "his right hand man":

> The year of 1909 has been full of money spending, not only our own, but money we could hire, and I believe that Doctor Sadler is going to do a wonderful amount of good among the Chicago practitioners, in bringing before them physiologic methods, and has been the case for the last nine years, I am his right hand man. I believe the Doctor is becoming more and more a domestic animal than the previous year. Since the baby came, he actually takes time to sit down and talk and laugh and enjoy life in general.[40]

Sadler would be called a "pioneer of preventive medicine by means of lectures and articles." Not surprisingly, he became involved with medical institutions that were actively educating the public.[41] One was the Gorgas Institute of Tropical Medicine, named for William Crawford Gorgas, surgeon general of the U.S. Army, who had eradicated yellow fever from the tropics, which enabled the building of the Panama Canal. In 1921, the Gorgas Institute began a public health and education program headed by Calvin Coolidge which dedicated itself to bringing "better health and longer life" to American citizens. They sponsored a national publicity campaign of "interesting health talks by physicians of national reputation and prominent laymen, interested in health improvement." More than fifteen hundred physicians joined this health campaign, hoping to increase the life span from fifty-eight to seventy years. It would take between twenty-five and forty years to see the goal realized, they asserted.[42] Sadler gave three radio talks as part of the campaign in 1928 and 1929. The first, given on March 3, 1928, was titled "Heart of Middle Life" and was part of the heart and circulatory series. For hygiene, he spoke on "How to Increase Vital Resistance" on May 5, 1928. The last talk was "Food in Hot Days" and given on July 7, 1929. Sadler also served on the Illinois Governing Committee for the Gorgas Memorial Institute for the city of Chicago.[43]

During the 1930s and 1940s, Sadler worked at two other medical institutions: the North Side Rest Home, where he was the attending psychiatrist and later the consulting psychiatrist, and later as a consulting psychiatrist for the W. K. Kellogg Foundation in Battle Creek, where he served as a trustee from 1937 to 1939. The W. K. Kellogg Foundation was established in 1930 to protect, nurture, and support opportunities for children. During the 1930s, the foundation brought public health care to children in rural Michigan. In 1931, it opened a school for children with disabilities to be taught alongside children without disabilities. This method was called mainstreaming and is still used today.[44]

Sadler lived through the period when the social sciences were professionalizing, from the late nineteenth through the early twentieth century. American intellectuals sought to eliminate the quackery and charlatanism of amateur scholarship and to confer authority on those who possessed it. Both Sadlers became members of the American College of Surgeons (ACS) in 1922. Started by Franklin Martin in May 1913 to further the education of those practicing in the field of surgery, ACS was open to surgeons five to eight years after graduating from specialized training in surgery.[45] ACS held yearly clinical congress meetings, at which leading surgeons from Chicago lectured and presented operating techniques. William and Lena Sadler lectured as a team at the nineteenth annual session on October 17, 1929, representing Columbus Hospital, where they both worked. They discussed blood transfusions, Hodgkins disease, hysterectomy, radium application to the cervix, hemorrhoidectomies, open plastic method, a thyroid case, discussion of x-ray, injection treatment of varicose veins, salpingectomy with adhesions (removal of Fallopian tubes), and tonsillectomies.[46] Eight years later, on October 27, 1937, Sadler, again representing Columbus Hospital, lectured on psychiatry in surgery at the ACS Clinical Congress.[47]

Medical schools for the first time were training doctors using a theory, based on the role of natural science in medicine, medical training, and practice. Courses included experimental physiology, physiological chemistry, germ theory of disease, and pharmacologically based chemical therapeutics, which would eventually lead doctors to displace other types of healers. Through AMA efforts, American society became aware that going to professional trained and licensed doctors was the best way to receive health care.[48]

A letter from 1937 provides a good example of Sadler's standing in the field of medicine. Haven Emerson, a professor at Columbia University in the College of Physicians and Surgeons, wrote to Stuart Pritchard, the medical director of the W. K. Kellogg Foundation, on March 29, 1937.

> I made inquiries concerning Dr. William Sadler of Chicago and have the personal statement of Professor Adolf Meyer that Dr. Sadler would be a suitable person for carrying on an educational campaign among our general practitioners and introducing modern sound principles of psychiatry and mental hygiene into the work of the County Health Departments and medical practice locally.
>
> Dr. Meyer further states that Dr. Sadler has never had any formal adequate training in psychiatry. He is what might be called a "one-man institute" of psychiatry but in his writing and his outlook he is entirely sound.[49]

The Sadlers found themselves living in Chicago, a stimulating city that was helping to drive new thinking in science, philosophy, and religion. William Sadler had a full schedule during the day practicing medicine and psychiatry in his office, lecturing at various clubs, teaching medicine and pastoral psychiatry a few days a week, and writing books and articles for publication. At night, he spent time with his "unseen friends" who, with his help, delivered thousands of pages that blended known science, philosophy, and religion to enlighten humankind.

1  Ellen White, *Manuscript Releases*, x.

2  McNeese, *Progressive Movement*, 32–33.

3  Hofstadter, *Age of Reform*, 5.

4  Cruden, *Ministers of Reform*, ix.

5  Bateman, "Social Gospel."

6  Rob Paral, "Chicago's Immigrants Break Old Patterns," Migration Policy Institute, September 1, 2003, http://www.migrationinformation.org/Feature/display.cfm?ID=160.

7  Bateman, "Social Gospel."

8  Gladden, *Working People*, 3.

9  White and Hopkins, *Social Gospel*, 179.

10  Menand, *Metaphysical Club*, 319.

11  Cronon, *Nature's Metropolis*, xv–xviii.

12  White and Hopkins, *Social Gospel*, xvii.

[13] Rauschenbusch, *Christianity and the Social Crisis*, xi.

[14] White and Hopkins, *Social Gospel*, 53.

[15] Ibid., xvi.

[16] "The Social Gospel," *Biblical World*, vol.151.

[17] Loughborough, *Second Great Advent Movement*, 22.

[18] Ibid.

[19] Shryock, "Summary of AMMC," 3.

[20] Letter, William S. Sadler to W. C. White, SDA Archives, Special Collections, Loma Linda, CA (July 18, 1902).

[21] Kellogg, "American Medical Missionary College," 54–56.

[22] Shryock, "Summary of AMMC," 4. Shryock was in the first graduating class of AMMC in 1899. He moved to Seattle in 1901, where he opened a branch of the Battle Creek Sanitarium with William Sadler's mother, Sarah Sadler.

[23] Ibid., 5.

[24] Ibid.

[25] Ibid., 19.

[26] Sadler, *Medical Missionary* (August 7, 1906), 55.

[27] Ibid., 8.

[28] "Annual Commencement Exercises," vol.1906, 4. AMMC continued for sixteen years until the 1910–1911 school year. It was then amalgamated with the University of Illinois Medical School.

[29] Manning, *Source Authors of the Urantia Book*, 325.

[30] Sadler, Medical Missionary, (January 30, 1907), 38

[31] Letter, Sadler to Meredith Sprunger (February 24, 1960), copy in author's collection.

[32] Sadler, "San Francisco Church Dispensary,"vol. 12.

[33] Letters, brochures, and other documents, Box 119, American Medical Association Health Fraud and Alternative Medicine Collection, AMA Archives, Chicago, IL.

[34] Ibid. Another way they sought new patients was by holding open houses. The Sadlers invited Chicago doctors to see their facilities at these events. One reception was held on Wednesday, December 9, 1908. The invitation requested the "honor of your presence" to "inspect" the Chicago Institute of Physiologic Therapeutics from 9 am to 9 pm. The Institute was located in the Reliance Building, 32 State Street, Suite 223, Chicago.

[35] Letter, Sadler to Elder W. C. White (October 16, 1907): 1, E. G. White Estate Archives, Branch Office, WDF 247.

[36] Ibid., 2.

[37] Ibid.

[38] Manning, *Source Authors of the Urantia Book*, 315.

[39] Sadler, "Story of the Life Boat," vol.335.

[40] Letter, Lena Kellogg Sadler to Mr. and Mrs. C. G. Marcus, January 6, 1909, E. G. White Estate Archives, Branch Office, WDF 247.

[41] Nobel, "Lena K. Sadler," 219.

[42] Gorgas Memorial Institute, News Release, April 1, 1925, Public Health and Education Programs 1921–1990, Health Education Programs and Publicity, Box 32, Folder 25, History of Medicine, National Library of Medicine, Bethesda, MD.

[43] Sadler took three trips to Europe. The first was in September 1911, when he applied for a passport. He sailed on the Donaldson Line Steamers, *S.S. Cassandra* on September 23, 1911, and stayed about three months, returning on December 15, 1911. In April 1919, he applied for a passport renewal in order to "lecture and for instruction on health and hygiene to the American Expeditionary Forces in France" under the YMCA's direction. His last trip was in 1928, returning to the United States on September 22 on the *America* into New York.

[44] http://www.wkkf.org/who-we-are/our-history.aspx.

[45] *American College of Surgeons Directory* (1922): 4–9.

[46] "Daily Bulletin," Clinical College of Surgeons, Nineteenth Annual Session, Chicago, (October 17, 1929): 2.

[47] Ibid., Twenty-Seventh Annual Session, October 27, 1937,2.

[48] For works on the nascent professionalization of the social sciences see Haskell, *Emergence of Professional Social Science*, 89; Abbott, *Department and Discipline*; Furner, *Advocacy and Objectivity;* Menand, *Metaphysical Club;* Wiebe, *Search for Order*.

[49] W. K. Kellogg Foundation, Sadler Letters, #26394.

# 3

――――◄◆►――――

# ONE SOUL WHO SPOKE KINDLY

*Dr. Lena K. Sadler of Chicago has been especially interested in teaching the American public the facts regarding preventive medicine in connection with her public health work. She has given twenty-five years to this important subject .... Among the first physicians to espouse the great cause of teaching laymen the facts regarding health and disease, she has delivered this message from the lecture platform and by means of the printed word and through the radio thousands of times. She considers this the most important contribution she can make to her generation.*

—*Medical Women's Journal,* May 1933

L ENA SADLER WORKED THROUGH ONE OF the nation's most devastating periods with regard to epidemics. Her first exposure to these epidemics would have been in the medical missions in Chicago that served the poor community, an experience that put her in a position to try and alleviate the public health issues of her time. Consequently she created a plan to use women's clubs to raise awareness in her fight to improve public health. Women's clubs came into being in the late 1860s to uplift the moral tone of America through voluntary work with groups such as the YWCA, temperance and antivice crusades, and women's suffrage movements. Scholars have argued that women's clubs gave middle-class women a place to develop leadership capacity and to build group consciousness for reform during the Progressive era.[1]

The Spanish flu pandemic of 1918 was the deadliest epidemic in recorded history, infecting between twenty to forty percent of the world's population, killing 675,000 in the United States alone.[2] Worldwide, it killed between fifty to a hundred million people—more than died in World War I—approximately three to six percent of the world's population. Unlike other flus, which mainly killed children and older people, this epidemic also killed the young and healthy because it overamped the immune system: the more robust the immune system the sicker one became.[3] In Chicago, the Spanish flu killed 8,500 people in eight weeks.[4] In September 1918, Chicago newspapers reported that in the first week of the epidemic, 28,598 people fell ill in Chicago and 176 died. The following week another 6,000 were sick and 600 died. By the third week, 11,239 people were ill and 1,400 died. On October 17, Black Thursday, 381 people died in one day.[5] In one month, October 1918, more than 10,000 people lost their lives in Chicago.[6]

The Health Department, in an effort to control the spread of the Spanish flu issued the following press release on October 24, 1918:

> Special Daily Press Service, Department of Health
> Chicago, October 24, 1918
>
> **Influenza Don'ts**
> Don't live in the dark.
> Don't shut the sunshine out of your home.
> Don't exclude the fresh air.
> Don't fail to keep clean.
> Don't go into crowded places.
> Don't associate with people who sneeze and cough in
>       your presence.
> Don't use common towels.
> Don't fail to practice what you preach.
> Don't overtax your physical powers.
> Cut out evening entertainments.
> Be in bed by ten o'clock.
> Don't fail to sleep with every window in your bedroom open.
> Don't fail to call your doctor for yourself or any other member
>       of your family at the first sign of illness.
> Better be safe than sorry.
> Don't allow your home to become damp, chilly, or uncomfortable.
> Don't fail, if possible, to walk to your work in the morning
>       and to your home at night.
> The open air exercise will be of decided benefit.

Posters with this information were hung at the entrances of theaters, on elevated train platforms (and in the cars themselves), and other various places around the city. The Department of Health produced lantern slides to be shown in every moving picture theater in Chicago. These slides warned the public about the danger of sneezing and asked those with colds to leave the theater. It was an unprecedented health emergency.

Urbanization was a big contributor to these devastating epidemics. The industrialization of America brought millions of people into the cities, which led to an increase in the urban poor living too close together, which in turn made the spread of flu much easier. Chicago's population increased from 109,000 in 1860 to 1.7 million by 1900. The new residents found themselves crammed into overcrowded and filthy tenements with no plumbing and infested by vermin, approximately three hundred people per acre. These were communities where disease easily spread. Even so, Chicago was considered the healthiest city of its size in the world in 1894, but the challenges for the Health Department continued.[7] Since no one knew how to stop it, what a virus was, or that the flu was caused by a virus, the city was powerless to stop its spread as was evidenced by the Spanish flu epidemic. Another problem in treating these epidemics was the immigrants' fear of doctors. This attitude developed as new immigrants heard, or more often knew someone, who had been deported due to being ill with an infectious disease.

Lena Sadler wrote an article, "The Relation of Women's Clubs to Organized Medicine and the Public Health Movement," published in the *Illinois Medical Journal* in 1926.[8] In it, she explained that "club women" are best suited to work with medical women in public health matters because they are well educated, willing to work, progressive in mindset, and committed regardless of their political leanings to social uplift of their community. In Lena Sadler's assessment, they were the most important contact to help bring the "gospel of health" to the lay people of every district, county, and hamlet of Illinois. To prove her point, she gave three examples of how they improved the health of Chicago: they raised $88,951.19 for infant welfare stations (infant welfare stations were storefronts that provided a much-needed source for infants and medical services to children in need),[9] created a plan so that preschool children could get medical attention, and purchased milk for less than a penny per cup for poor children and gave nutrition classes for mothers to improve children's diets.

As for what should come next, Lena Sadler argued that education is needed in the areas of communicable diseases and venereal infections so that women can support legislation to improve the situation; they should be enlightened on proper care of feet and what shoes are best for their bodies to prevent pelvic displacement as well as what a woman should expect from her doctor so that she can "tell the difference between a quack and a well-trained professional."[10] This list continued with a request to educate club women on the importance of prenatal care; cautioned against using untrained midwives; the prevention of tuberculosis (important since they raised thousands of dollars a year to help support this cause); the causes and preventions of heart disease, diphtheria, and scarlet fever; and eugenics. On the latter, Lena, who was a proponent, wrote, "they should be taught to interest themselves in the creation of laws which will find potential criminals; and in legislation which will not only protect, but stop the reproduction of the potentially defective stock of this state."[11]

In her conclusion, Lena explained that by educating club women they could make a big difference in the lives of others—especially for children. She noted that in 1928 one-third of all deaths in the United States were children under six years old. Ten times as many deaths occurred during the half-decade of preschool life as in the full decade of school life. Eighty percent of deaths from diphtheria were children younger than five. Malnutrition and rickets were prevalent in preschool children to the point that 30 percent of all the crippled are found in preschool. If medical women reached out and educated club women, they could better reach the goals of discouraging what is unsocial and unsanitary and to promote what is best for the greatest number of people.[12]

To educate her medical sisters, Lena published an article, "Important: Here's Where We Must Give Our Service," in the *Bulletin Medical Women's Club* of Chicago in September 1926. Lena was the acting state chairman of public health and child welfare that year. In the *Bulletin* article, she suggested seven projects to club members nationwide that would improve conditions of sanitation, health, and prevention of disease across the United States. Her list included the following items:

> *Promotion of a plan for saving mothers and babies in one's county* urged members to educate their community on the importance of prenatal care, such as teaching young mothers how to breastfeed.

> *Promotion of plan for preschool child examinations* noted that thirty thousand history forms had been sent out at the request of club women for children to be examined by a doctor and dentist. The bonus for those reporting a record number of children examined was a $500 prize.

> *Promotion of medical inspection of school children* noted that thousands of children who enter school each year have correctable defects, called for a public health nurse to visit the school, examine the children, and refer them to a family physician to get the care and treatment they needed.

*Promotion of dental inspection of school children* called for a uniform dental chart to be filled out by the dentist and that the child should return for yearly exams.

*No diphtheria* advocated for vaccinations and education: "Let us, as club women, adopt the slogan, No diphtheria in Illinois in 1930."

*Health audits* noted that four hundred thousand people between the ages of thirty-five and fifty die each year from symptomless diseases such as blood pressure and irritated kidneys, that ninety thousand lives each year were cut short by cancer, and that colleagues should familiarize themselves with early signs and symptoms.

*Digest of health laws* urged medical women to work with law enforcement departments to ensure community obedience of sanitation laws and explained that speakers were available free of charge between September and May on numerous health subjects.[13]

In 1900, women doctors in the United States numbered some 7,387.[14] Women's medical societies arose to help them strengthen their professional roles. Lena was one of the founding members of the Medical Women's National Association, later the American Medical Women's Association (AMWA), organized in Chicago on November 18, 1915, at a meeting of the Chicago Women's Club. Membership in AMWA was contingent on a woman's being eligible for the AMA membership. AMWA meetings were always held concurrent with the AMA meetings to allow women physicians to attend those meetings as well as their own. Because women physicians were excluded from some social gatherings at the AMA (they could attend events sponsored by the AMA Women's Auxiliary but found that demeaning), AMWA provided them with their own place to gather. This was important because some of the men who were uncomfortable with women in a "male" profession did not treat women physicians well at AMA meetings. AMWA arose to function in three main areas: as a social group to stress companionship among a unique group of women; as a network for the dissemination of scientific and professional information; and as a means to become involved in social reform activities.[15]

Lena was active in public health during the 1920s and 1930s in the following capacities:

- 1924–1927, state chairman of public health and child hygiene of the Illinois Federation of Women's Clubs (first of two terms)
- 1925–1926, secretary of the American Medical Women's Association

- 1928–1930, president of the Chicago Council of Medical Women
- 1930–1931, vice president of the American Medical Women's Association
- 1931–1933, state chairman of public health and child hygiene of the Illinois Federation of Women's Clubs (second term)
- 1934–1935, president of the American Medical Women's Association

In 1928, when Lena was state chairman of public health and child hygiene for the Illinois Federation of Women's Clubs, she wrote a report of the club's efforts. Her role was to give advice and guidance concerning all questions relating to public health and child welfare activities. Included in the report was a summary of the purpose of public health programs she presented:

- To direct the interests of club women in building a health program suitable to their community needs.
- To work for a closer relationship between club women, parent teacher associations, and the organized professions of medicine and dentistry.
- To interest club women in the study of health legislation and to urge cooperation with the legislation and law enforcement departments of the federation.
- To give professional advice and guidance concerning all questions relating to public health and child welfare activities.[16]

The report stated that Chicago was fortunate to have educational programs from the Chicago Medical Society, Illinois State Medical Society, State Department of Public Health, as well as a very active local board of health. It noted that medical women were active in venereal clinics, birth control and prenatal clinics, and infant welfare clinics. Some of the programs they supported included prenatal care, pre-school examinations, medical inspections of school children, health education in the schools, sight saving, dental hygiene, mental hygiene, and health audits. They also studied and responded to health-care legislation, and worked to promote the diphtheria immunization program in schools.[17]

A description of the diphtheria immunization program in Chicago was described in the "Public Health Report of the Medical Dental and Allied Science Women's Association." The report explained that students who could not afford to go to a doctor were given the diphtheria toxoid at school. Bulletins with information on how to prevent diphtheria were sent to every parent (with a child under eight), physician, teacher, and pastor in the city. Billboards were placed on streetcars, trains, and taxicabs; in addition radio talks on immunization were broadcast. Special folders were printed in all languages and sent to Cardinal Mundelein so he could distribute them to parochial schools. As added insurance when a child reached six months, a nurse would visit the home and urge immunization. It was discovered that even with all this work, one of every three mothers failed to take her child to get the vaccine because money was short, she was indifferent, or she could not find the time to do so. The Board of Health decided to outfit two buses with all needed materials and after eight months immunized 16,496 children who would not otherwise have been immunized.[18] The results of this program were promising. Lena Sadler reported that from January to March 1933, eighty-three cases of diphtheria were reported and four deaths. During the same period in 1929, 384 cases were reported and sixteen deaths. The report noted that deaths outside the city had been rising between 1930 and 1932, but that in the city of Chicago they had been sharply decreasing.[19]

The need for further planning was discussed in Lena's June 1929 report to the Medical Women's National Association, which went out to all members nationwide. It outlined ways that medical women could work with women's clubs "doing constructive public health work" and enumerated the projects she was working on at this time:

- securing a bigger budget for dental hygiene in public schools in Chicago;

- becoming a member of the executive committee of the Illinois Society for the Protection of Medical Research to more effectively fight an antivivisection bill pending in the state;

- becoming a member of an advisory council to a group organized to work for the prevention of hay fever by exterminating rag weed in Chicago;

- arranging a series of health broadcasts by women physicians of Chicago on radio stations; and

- guiding the lay interest in public health by addressing women's clubs and speaking before Farm Bureaus.[20]

In February 1932, Lena Sadler read her paper, "The Preliminary Survey of Emotional Analysis," at a meeting of the Chicago Council of Medical Women. The paper was later published in the September 1932 issue of *The Medical Women's Journal*. It addressed the use of a test for emotional health by investigating the neuroses and emotions of a patient. To check on the patient's psychiatric state, she advised, the doctor or nurse should sit the patient down, "near enough to the desk so that for good relaxation the elbows may rest upon it," and tell the patient that he or she would be asked many personal and intimate questions that could be answered yes or no. If the patient wanted to give a more lengthy answer, that opportunity would be provided later during the interview.[21] First came the neurologic family history of the parents, grandparents, sisters, and brothers. This was followed by the patient's nervous history. Colleagues were encouraged to follow this childhood history with notes on the present nervous condition to trace when the troubles began. Psychologic tendencies were noted to show whether the patient had adopted a "philosophy of life," that is, when they "shaped their life interests around a master motive of a spiritual or personality idea." The paper's discussion of social life noted that many people were leading isolated lives, without hobbies, as well as an unsatisfactory religious life, netted them nothing of true value.

The religious explanation in the article is interesting because it occurred late in the process when the Urantia papers were being written. Much of what Lena Sadler wrote reflects the book's teachings. Second, it was unusual for an article in a professional medical journal to carry information about specific religious beliefs:

> In getting information regarding the religious life we are chiefly concerned with but two points: If they believe in a Supreme Being, and if they believe in a Hereafter, we believe that their religious emotion has a normal outlet. They may or may not be church members. We find a large number of individuals believing in a Supreme Being and in a Hereafter, but they have found the puerile religious tenets of their progenitors and contemporaries confusing and disappointing. Few of them have learned the art to worship in contradistinction to *egocentric* praying: they appear to have adopted religion as a code for living instead of using it as life's shock-absorber and as a solace for embitterments and affliction.[22]

AMWA members also were involved in supporting legislation. At the June 1933 annual meeting, the AMWA Legislative Committee asked members to reaffirm their stand on several public questions, such as approving the Cable Act, which provided that a child born to an American woman abroad would automatically be an American citizen; approving the Child Labor Amendment; approving the World Court; approving the Birth Control Act; and supporting the bill to allow citizens of the District of Columbia to vote.[23]

Many women's organizations, including AMWA, gave their support to the plans for a woman appointed to the Federal Communications Commission through the Women's National Radio Committee.[24] Lena Sadler wrote a letter in response to Mrs. Harold Mulligan, chairman of the Women's National Radio Committee, who asked for AMWA's official support in October 1934.[25] Mulligan stated in her letter that radio "was a man's setup at present, and since radio touches so intimately the lives of most women, and its advertised products are purchased so largely by women, it seems only just that a woman should represent the woman's viewpoint on the Commission."[26] She also pointed out at a later meeting that one problem was that the women needed to coordinate to change the quality of programming on the radio. Young people were influenced by what they heard and Mulligan was concerned that advertisers were "dictating" what people heard on the radio, which meant that "lesser" programs were heard.[27] These women were arguing for what they preferred for "American standard of culture," which in their eyes was classical music performed by elite musicians. The associate editor of *Woman's Home Companion*, Mrs. Anna Steese Richardson, stated that the committee had a wonderful opportunity to "protect the country through radio." If something were not done soon, she said, then radio would end up like the motion picture industry, where no effort was made to improve taste, habits, or methods of entertainment. Congress voted in July 1935, but no woman had been appointed. The effort was not successful until Harry Truman appointed the first woman to the Federal Communications Commission (FCC), Frieda Hennock, in 1948—fourteen years after AMWA began to support the campaign.[28]

Another arena that Lena Sadler used to educate the masses about preventive medicine was the Chicago Century of Progress Exposition in 1933. The fair was originally designed to celebrate Chicago's previous hundred years but came to symbolize Chicago's and America's future in the midst of the Great Depression. Organizers hoped it would help restore popular faith in the nation's economic and political system and to demonstrate that business, scientific, and intellectual leaders could lead the country out of the Depression. The fair created within Chicago a modern dream world to encourage visitors to share in highly controlled fantasies of what living in a modern world was like. As Robert Rydell noted, "The century of progress expositions were theaters of power."[29] They boosted people's vision at a time when the country was near collapse.

Chicago's expo, like other fairs of the era, helped bring scientists into the forefront as the legitimate leaders in how to perceive the world. American scientists after World War I sought to popularize science so that they could rework American culture with "scientific values." Scientists were the intellectual underwriters of the fairs because they helped design and implement the themes of a "century of progress."[30] Rufus Dawes, an oil baron and head of the Chicago fair corporation, said that the fair would be a close alliance between men of science and men of capital."[31] This was a different attitude compared with the previous Victorian-era exposition of 1893; the scientists featured there were anthropologists who showcased the current thinking about evolution and eugenics. At the 1933 fair, the scientists were mostly "hard" scientists who had research supported by corporate laboratories of university-based research programs. This further supported the idea that corporations could be trusted to plan America's future.[32]

Lena Sadler wanted to showcase the gains in women's medicine at the fair. This was due to the fact that women were not supported in the 1933 fair as they had been in the 1893 exposition. In 1933, there were no plans for a Women's Building to demonstrate the contributions women had made to America's progress. Lena and her colleagues were exceptional because they mounted a series of exhibits themselves to demonstrate the progress of women in medicine and the gains in public health. Lena Sadler was part of the team of the Medical and Dental Women's Association of the Century of Progress. On March 16, 1932, they met at the Newberry Hotel for dinner to discuss what kind of exhibit to sponsor at the fair. Agreeing that no one organization could adequately represent all women doctors and dentists, they decided to combine their efforts. Their first step was a vote to support the National Council of Women in its campaign to get a million signatures on a petition to ensure an exhibit on women's work at the exposition.

The new organization would be open to all licensed women physicians and dentists of the Chicago Metropolitan area as well as other interested groups. Later, it decided to invite all women doctors and dentists to become active, nonresident members of the association to help promote the interests of women physicians and dentists during the Century of Progress. It sent out a notice in March 1932, "An Invitation to Every Licensed Woman Physician and Dentist in the United States," with this request.[33]

In addition to their exhibit in the Hall of Science, the women of the Medical, Dental & Allied Women's Association created a headquarters booth on the fairgrounds to welcome visitors. The booth had a large window overlooking Lake Michigan, the stairways, and the gardens. It was roughly fifteen feet square, with chairs and a large table displaying exhibition books with photographs and the histories that illustrated professional women's activities. These included women's hospitals, medical societies, foreign women's professional societies, and women's Greek letter societies. The booth was adjacent to two movie theaters where the women could showcase their activities with "moving pictures."[34]

The official handbook from the Hall of Science at the fair described the Chicago Medical Society and Women's Auxiliary exhibit as follows:

> By the use of large wall charts the progress of Medicine in Chicago is divided into four definite periods. The first chart enumerates the uncontrolled epidemics in Chicago in the period 1833–1858. During this period malaria, influenza, typhoid fever, cholera, smallpox, diphtheria, and tuberculosis, ran wild throughout the Chicago region,

causing the death rate to mount. The Chicago Medical Society was organized in 1850.

The second chart presents the efforts made in sanitation during the period 1859–1881. In this period the first State Board of Health was organized, the first milk ordinance regulating sale was passed and the first investigation of stream pollution was attempted. During this period the mortality rate was decreased.

During the third period of this century of progress in medicine, some of the most remarkable achievements were made in the attempt to control the spread of disease, 1881–1906. We find during this period that Koch discovered the causative agent of tuberculosis; Klebs discovered the germ which causes diphtheria; and Crede used silver nitrate in the eyes of babies to prevent blindness. Chicago Sanitary District was organized, and the Chicago Board of Health issued its first diphtheria antitoxin and made its first medical inspection of schools.

The fourth chart includes the period between 1906–1926, and it is during this period that preventive medicine was most strongly advocated. Each case of tuberculosis had to be reported and the milk pasteurization ordinance was passed. In the fight against tuberculosis the Municipal Tuberculosis Sanitarium was opened for patents. During this period typhoid immunization, chlorination of the city water supply, diphtheria immunization of young children, and hospitalization of typhoid carriers were some of the major steps in preventive medicine.

There is also a large map of Chicago indicating the location of its hospitals, medical schools and medical libraries.[35]

An undated newspaper highlighted the Chicago Women's Club medical day at the fair, "Women Physicians, Dentists and Allied Associates Are Centers of Interest at Fair." It described a luncheon given by the group and noted that "Lena Sadler, who had charge of the program" was assisted by Julia C. Strawn.[36] The exposition ran in Chicago from May 27 through November 1, 1933, and reopened from May 26 through October 31, 1934. Attendance was more than forty-eight million people. On Monday, June 12, 1933, Lena Sadler spoke at the luncheon meeting on the roof garden solarium on "The Century of Progress Exhibition." She later in the same day gave a lecture titled "Doctor and Wife, also a Woman."[37]

On February 15, 1934, Lena Sadler assumed the presidency of the AMWA. She was the first person nominated. The letter written by the colleagues who put her name forward reasoned that she had been a loyal member for years and was deserving of the honor being conferred upon her. Politically, they thought it was a good idea to have a president from the Central Regional Division (which had 213 members) because in the past only three of their members had served as presidents.[38] Public education continued throughout 1934, a different woman doctor speaking every week over the summer at Navy Pier to audiences of between four and eight hundred.[39]

Lena Sadler's health took a turn for the worse in 1932, when she was diagnosed with breast cancer, which led to a mastectomy. In December 1938, she became ill again. In a letter to W. K. Kellogg, William Sadler wrote that Lena had been to the Mayo Clinic to have her arm diagnosed. This led to a disagreement between the Chicago and the Rochester doctors. The Mayo Clinic physicians thought it was cancer and that nothing could be done. The Chicago doctors thought it was scar tissue. William Sadler wrote that all doctors agreed that Lena should be treated by a D. B. Phemister in Chicago. He also related some trouble that he and Lena were having with the press:

> I want to explain to you confidentially why this matter has been put off until after Christmas. About two weeks ago some nosey newspaper reporter (I think they call them "sob sisters") in some way found out about Lena's trouble, and got the idea that this arm had been affected by radium, that she was a "martyr to science," and prepared a sensational article where she tried to sell to newspapers in Chicago, and we were all "needle and pins" here for about ten days, working with editors and trying to keep this thing out of print, and apparently we succeeded. Lena was afraid to go near Billings Hospital, see Dr. Phemister, or do anything during this period.[40]

This letter was followed by another on December 27, explaining that Lena had had surgery at ten o'clock that morning. Her arm had been amputated just below the shoulder joint. He continued:

> It seems Lena and I are destined to have very successful operations as far as the operation itself is concerned, but we are also destined to have no end of complications following our successful operations. Take me: two simple and successful operations for glaucoma and then two cataract operations to follow. And there is still an operation for adhesions elevating my pupil to be gone through with my left eye, but this only means three or four days in the hospital. Lena has

an operation for carcinoma of the breast with x-ray following, and it is successful. She is alive and in good health six years afterwards, and then all this inexplicable fibrosis has to come on, compelling her to lose her left arm.[41]

As she was recovering from surgery, Lena suffered from phantom pains in her arm. In a letter to her uncle, W. K. Kellogg, she wrote:

> I am rid of all the pain which I have had for four years but there remains something that I have heard of but, of course never experienced, "phantom pains"; I can actually feel the outlines of my arm in every particular and there are some most unpleasant sensations. The last two days I have devoted nearly every waking moment to doing things that one-armed people can do and it has helped a lot. I am going to rise above this just like our tribe does; we meet things and go through with them. We do not let anything get us down.[42]

Unfortunately, the phantom pains continued throughout the winter and spring. Her attitude was always upbeat in her letters, she still found joy in her life:

> We have had a few delightful days on the "Deck" this Spring. Oh, what a blessing that Deck is to this grandmother and her grandchildren. It's the biggest thing that has happened to me. How I like it!!!
>
> My surgeon insisted I drive the car, so the family got me a very light small Nash with gear shift on the wheel. I've driven a lot the last 2 weeks—it's good therapy for "the phantom" arm.
>
> I did my first social thing last Wednesday when I accompanied Will to the faculty luncheon at the Theological College. Also we attended the p.m. reception. And so it goes.[43]

There were no further letters until August 8, 1939, when William Sadler sent a telegram to W. K. Kellogg, "Lena's funeral three o'clock Thursday Fourth Presbyterian Church." Lena died at 64 years of age. Her friend Elizabeth Kittredge wrote, "Sadler's death seems a tragedy, but the greater tragedy is her extreme suffering the last months of her life."[44] Her memoriam in *Women in Medicine* was published in October 1939. The article stated that she "had been engaged in the practice of medicine in Chicago with her husband since 1906—together they practiced their profession—not as usually the case, individually—but as partners, each having the benefit of the other's advice and counsel." [45] It continued:

Hundreds of thousands bless Dr. Lena Sadler for her personal message of health which she began to deliver over the United States from
the popular lecture platform thirty years ago and has continued in
books, magazines, and metropolitan newspapers. She has repeatedly broadcast by radio her story of health conservation and disease
prevention. In the last years, she drew very close to countless women
who attended the lectures of Dr. William Sadler, as she helped them
solve their personal problems of adjustment.

And she lived so abundantly and productively, found time for
successful home-making and motherhood and for the cultivation of
warm and enduring friendships. She had a talent for loyal friendship
and her dependability, vivid personality, sympathetic and affectionate
understanding, and spontaneous enthusiasm endeared her to many
within and without her profession.

In the large attendance of the beautiful and dignified funeral
service at the Fourth Presbyterian Church were the President and
many members of the Chicago Medical Society, Chicago Council
of Medical Women, the Medical Women's Club of Chicago, and
personal friends by whom Dr. Sadler was loved, and very many to
whom she had restored faith in themselves and joy in living.[46]

Her obituary in *Women in Medicine* in August 1939, written by her close friend
Mary McKinnin-Harper, illustrates her personality:

... A recent intimate visit with Dr. Sadler is a sacred and ineffaceable
memory. Her keen and continued interest in AMWA [American
Medical Women's Association] and her affection for women doctors
is most evident. With her usual fortitude, she sat in her chair with
her manuscript for the next Sadler book, planning for the continu-
ance of her work. A few days later, after several hours work on her
manuscript, she retired as usual and passed away in her sleep.[47]

Lena began her service as a nurse and became a doctor who was a pioneer in
women's medicine, preventive medicine and public health. First she worked in the
dispensaries assisting the poor in Chicago providing them with clothing and medical
care. She practiced medicine in full partnership with her husband. As an advocate for
better public health she lectured, fought for legislation, and worked with women's
clubs to spread the word. Her service was life-long: secretary, vice-president, and
president of the American Medical Women's Association and state chairman of Public

Health and Child Hygiene for the Illinois Federation of Women's Clubs. Additionally Dr. Lena served as the treasurer of the Medical, Dental and Allied Science Women's Association for the "Century of Progress" (1933 Word's Fair in Chicago), was associate director of the Chicago Institute of Research and Diagnosis (an organization of physicians and surgeons engaged in active practice); a gynecologist at Columbus Hospital and Women and Children's Hospital; and was a special instructor at the Presbyterian College of Christian Education.[48] She also served as president of the Chicago Council of Medical Women. Last, she was instrumental in organizing the exhibits showcasing the gains of women in medicine at the Chicago Century of Progress Exposition in 1933. These exhibits were seen by millions of people. By any measure, Lena was an extremely accomplished woman. There appears to be no hint from her daytime projects that shed any light on her extraordinary nights.

---

[1]   Justin, "Men, Women, and Women Physicians," 7.–

[2]   http:www.flu.gov/pandemic/history/index.html.

[3]   Taubenberger and Morens, "1918 Influenza Pandemic."

[4]   Alice Maggio, "Chicago and the Influenza Epidemic of 1918. "Ask A Librarian" Gapers-Block, Chicago, Illinois web blog, www.gapersblock.com/airbags/archives/chicago_and_the_influenza_epidemic_of_1918. It was called the Spanish flu because the Allies and the Axis powers did not admit to having the disease.

[5]   Ibid.

[6]   http://www.encyclopedia.chicagohistory.org/pages/432.html.

[7]   *Report from the Department of Health, City of Chicago* (1894): 1

[8]   Lena Sadler, "The Relation of Women's Clubs."

[9]   In 1911, eleven such stations were opened by the Infant Welfare Society of Chicago. The women then organized into the Hinsdale Chapter of the Infant Welfare Society Auxiliary working in partnership with Clifford Grulee, an Infant Welfare Society physician ("A Memorable 'Chapter' in Auxiliary History," Infant Welfare Society of Chicago, http://www.infantwelfaresociety.org/twochaptersmerge.html).

[10]   Ibid., 54.

[11]   Ibid.

[12]   Ibid. AMWA #291.

[13]   Lena Sadler, "Important."

[14]   Justin, "Men, Women, and Women Physicians," 19.

[15]   Ibid., 24.

[16]   "Public Health Report," President's Papers, (1932–1933, pt. 3–5), AMWA #12.

[17]   "Public Health Report," President's Papers, (1932–1933, pt. 3–5) American Medical Women's Association at Drexel University Archives, Philadelphia, PA. (#12 in author's collection). What was diphtheria? Diphtheria symptoms are a sore throat, loss of appetite, fever, and most distinctively, a thick grey substance called a pseudomembrane that forms over the nasal tissues, tonsils, larynx, and or pharynx. This pseudomembrane forms from the waste products and proteins from the bacteria that cause the illness. It sticks to the tissues making it difficult to breathe. There were 206,000 cases of Diphtheria in the United States in 1921, which killed 15,520 people. The death rates were about 20 percent of those under five years old and over forty and 5 to 10 percent of those between five and forty. A chart from Franklin Royer shows the decline in deaths in Chicago after vaccines (antitoxins) were given in 1905: At the end of 1921 and the beginning of 1922, there was a diphtheria epidemic in Chicago. Schools were closed. There were 19,901 cases of the disease in Illinois that year with 1,258 deaths—626 fatalities in Chicago.

[18]  Ibid. #109.

[19]  Ibid.

[20]  Lena Sadler, "Report of the Chairman."

[21]  Lena Sadler, "The Preliminary Survey."#

[22]  Ibid., 222.

[23]  Minutes of the Annual Meeting of the Medical Women's National Association, June 12, 1933, 10 am. President's Papers 1932–1933 (pt.4), AMWA #38.

[24]  At a meeting of the Women's National Radio Committee, September 25, 1934, the following women's organizations were present: American Organization of University Women, American Legion Auxiliary, Association of Junior League of America, Child Study Association of America, General Federation of Women's Clubs, International Sunshine Society, Jewish Welfare Board, National Council of Women, National Council of Jewish Women, National Federation of Business and Professional Women's Clubs, National Society of the D.A.R., National W.C.T.U., Service Star Legion, Southern Women's Educational Alliance, N.Y. State Federation of Women's Clubs, and the editor of *Woman's Home Companion.* President's Papers 1933–1934 (pt.6), AMWA #150.

[25]  Letter, Lena Sadler to Mrs. Harold V. Mulligan, October 24, 1934, President's Papers 1933–1934 (pt.6), AMWA #148.

[26]  Letter, Mrs. Harold V. Mulligan to Lena Sadler, October 20, 1934, President's Papers 1933–1934 (pt. 6), AMWA #149–156.

[27]  Ibid.

[28]  Weisenberger, "Women of the FCC."

[29]  Rydell, *World of Fairs,* 11.

[30]  Ibid., 93.

[31]  Ibid., 94.

[32]  Ibid., 215–16.

[33]  AMWA President's Papers, 1932–1933, AMWA #3.

[34]  Letter, Bertha VanHoosen to Esther Lovejoy, April 23, 1933, President's Papers, 1933–1934, AMWA #80.

[35]  "Official Handbook, Of Exhibits in the Division of Basic Sciences: A Century of Progress, Chicago, 1934, Hall of Science" (1934), 150. AMWA #391.

[36]  Malcolm McDowell, "Women Physicians, Dentists and Allied Associates Are Centers of Interest at Fair." Undated newspaper article, Century of Progress ephemera folders. AMWA #395.

[37]  Pamphlet in "AMWA Meetings, 1931–1933." AMWA #225.

[38]  Letter, Olga Stasney, Mabel McAkin, Lena L. Kevin, Helen G. Demis, Dora J. Underwood, and Harriet J. Lawrence, President's Papers, 1933–1934 (pt.6), #AMWA #118–19.

[39]  Letter, from Bertha VanHoosen to Esther Lovejoy, September 23, 1932, President's Papers, 1933–1934 (pt. 1), AMWA #81.

[40]  Letter, William S. Sadler to Will K. Kellogg, December 19, 1938. Sadler letter #26109.

[41]  Letter, William S. Sadler to Will K. Kellogg, December 27, 1938. Sadler letter #26107.

[42]  Letter, Lena K. Sadler to Will K. Kellogg, January 1, 1939. Sadler letter #26104.

[43]  Letter, Lena K. Sadler to Will K. Kellogg, May 2, 1939. Sadler letter #26092.

[44]  Letter, Elizabeth Kittredge to Bess, August 17, 1939, Folder 5, Correspondence, AMWA #338

[45]  McKibbin-Harper, "In Memoriam."

[46]  Ibid.

[47]  Obituary of Lena Sadler in "Women in Medicine," August 17, 1939, AMWA #438.

[48]  Lena Sadler, "Medical Women of Today," 117.

# 4

————◄●►————

# THEIR PHILOSOPHY

*The doctors do not entertain their audiences with mere word pictures, but give practical illustrations. To accommodate them in their program yesterday, women fainted, boys sustained temporary fractures of the limbs, suffered sun strokes, and even went to the bottom of the Dupage river. The hour of emergencies was one of intense interest for the demonstrations were so life-like that the audience fairly gasped and then awakened to the fact that it was only make believe.*

—*Joliet Evening Herald*

THE SADLERS' FOCUS ON PREVENTIVE MEDICINE, their "Gospel of Health," flowered with the Chautauqua lecture circuit. The Chautauqua, as it was known, was a tent show that traveled across America in the summer months. The lectures given were intended to entertain, improve the mind, bring culture, and enlighten the ears and thoughts of the hearer.[1] The Chautauqua programs provided information about current trends in the United States and the world in the safe environment of the attendee's own community. As Vonne Meussling described them, "millions of people found inspiration and emotional succor, intellectual stimulus, and moral reinforcement when they sat in the audiences of Chautauquas everywhere."[2] Generally, the largest Chautauqua shows served fifteen hundred to two thousand people per show sitting in flat folding chairs in a sweltering tent.[3] The season ran from June to August, until children returned to school in September.[4] The events lasted between two and seven days. Prices varied by location and depended on transportation and the quality of program. In general, by 1919, the prices were $1 to $3 a ticket.

In Sadler's mind, Chautauqua seemed like an ideal method to bring his practical truths to the masses. His desire to serve was recognized in *The Lyceum News* in September 1912. Sadler wanted, they wrote in an article, "to do good, not to get money, for it is evident that specialists and surgeons of this sort lose money every day they leave their work."[5] In 1912, when Sadler spoke to the International Lyceum Association Convention in Winona Lake, Indiana, *The Lyceum News* reported that

> Sadler, it may be said, in taking to the platform, where he won signal success as a lecturer, did so that he might the better work out a vision that came to him as a young man just out of college, that is, to educate the people to medical truths worthy of scientific propaganda.[6]

By the summer of 1920, the Chautauqua lecture series had reached thirty-five million people, one-third of the U.S. population. The lectures were presented in more than ten thousand communities across the country. Sadler thus spoke to many thousands of people in his twenty-one-year career as a Chautauqua lecturer.[7] These lectures addressed the science of living, good eating habits, and living a moral life, and included demonstrations and "stereopticon" lectures.[8] He wrote that it was better to prevent a thousand people from getting sick than to cure ten who were already sick. That his greatest mission was to "educate the masses in practical hygiene."[9]

In their 1915 pamphlet "The Sadlers and Miss Willmer: Ninth Annual Announcement," they outlined their performance history as well as their popular health lecture schedule and biographies. Sadler wrote that, in 1906, they had approached the Chautauqua managers located in Chicago with their plans for a Chautauqua health campaign. Everyone turned them down, remarking that the project was "infeasible and impossible." In 1907 the Sadlers managed to get one booking in Appleton, Wisconsin, for a ten-day period of furnishing morning programs and filling in a few afternoon spots when needed. The Sadlers were paid $110 and were to cover their own transportation costs. It was in Appleton that the Sadlers met Sarah Mildred Willmer, who would become part of their troop, and travel with the family for five years until she married Edward van Bond in 1912.[10]

In 1908, Sadler mentioned that he took Lena along "as a helper" for the hour-long morning sessions. The lecture program expanded in 1909, Lena handling the morning sessions and Sadler delivering his health talks in the afternoon. Lena's sister Anna Kellogg joined the Sadlers on the road that year to assist Lena with the morning lectures. The health lectures were practically oriented in that they were billed as being free of impractical fads and teachings of extremists. For the rural and middle-class people served by the Chautauqua circuits, the Sadler lectures were a safe place to hear about a multitude of health topics from a Christian standpoint.[11]

Sadler is listed on a flyer as lecturing on "Faith and Fear," "Long Heads and Round Heads," "Work and Play," and "Americanitis." Wilfred Kellogg assumed a managerial role and booked the Chautauqua and Lyceum events and made all travel arrangements. By 1916, Lena wrote to W. K. Kellogg that "Will[iam] is lecturing in the city to some church, club, or lodge from one to three times a week." This pattern of speaking at local venues and at some outside Chicago continued for decades.

The Chautauqua program expanded when Sadler introduced stereopticon talks in the evening during the 1910 season. The stereopticon was also known as a magic lantern and was a type of slide projector. The device was a precursor to a film projector and used photographs projected onto a screen to tell stories.[12] The stereopticon was a slide projector with two lenses. Stereopticons were a popular form of entertainment before moving pictures arrived on the scene. The topics of Sadler's stereopticon lectures included child life in the slums, modern miracles, and crime and criminals. The slide projector proved a visually arresting method to teach the Social Gospel to those who attended his speeches. John Harvey Kellogg had used a magic lantern at the San to illustrate his lectures in the 1880s and 1890s, which is probably where Sadler first saw it used.[13] Sadler also used his stereopticon to assist in his health lectures and to show images from the slums in Chicago and New York.

The Sadler slum lectures allowed the rural attendees of the Chautauqua lectures "see" the slums in America's rapidly growing cities. Sadler called the slum dwellers "submerged classes" and presented them as "one of the great problems of this generation." Sadler noted that he and Lena were personally acquainted with this "class of people" through their service work and that his "stories of poverty and squalor were presented without the odor of vice and crime." He sought in these lectures to explain that "the story of the children of the slums is a narrative appalling as well as amusing and entertaining." To bring the story home to his rural viewers, he traced the "terrible trail" of "vice and disease" of the slums from the inner city to the boulevards to the country village and country home. He promoted his lectures as a way to argue for intelligent action to deal with the problem of poverty.[14]

By 1911, the Sadlers had fully realized their company and were booked for the entire season. Sarah Willmer became a permanent part of the shows, alternating with the Sadlers in the afternoon sessions, which were expanded to four hours. The Sadlers used the promotional line that they "were a whole Chautauqua in themselves—except the music." Early on his letters reveal that Sadler focused on public health education rather than practicing medicine. On June 12, 1907, Sadler wrote to W. K. Kellogg explaining that he and Lena had worked hard over the previous year trying to break into one of three large lyceum bureaus in Chicago. He told W. K. that they had spent several hundred dollars in advertising in preparation. This letter was one of a series Sadler wrote to Kellogg to seek more time to pay off his loan so that he could purchase more equipment for the July Chautauqua lectures.[15] In a letter to W. C. White in October 1907, he wrote that though he had become a doctor in private practice, he wasn't actually practicing much medicine. He had other doctors assume his sanitarium duties at Hinsdale and the Dispensary so that he could concentrate on "bringing our health principles to the people." "I am working very hard on my various lectures on health and Bible subjects which I am preparing for chautauquas [*sic*] next summer and for the lyceum courses a year from this winter."[16]

Sadler's program was medically based but included strong moral threads throughout the presentations. His most popular lecture was a eugenics-based presentation titled "The Weak and the Strong, or the Tragedy of Civilization," which was described as "a striking presentation of the fundamental causes and the basic remedies necessary to abolish those social strains which unfailingly gravitate toward pauperism, criminality, drunkenness, prostitution, and various forms of mental and nervous instability. A purposeful lecture on eugenics divested of fanciful theories, impractical plans, and sentimental nonsense."[17] Other lecture titles became books: "Americanitis," "Worry and Nervousness, or the Science of Self-Mastery," "The Physiology of Faith and Fear, or the Mind in Health and Disease," and the "Science of Living, or the Art of Keeping Well."[18]

Lena's participation in the Chautauqua lecture circuit helped round out the program with her emphasis on women, children, and the family. Billed as a "physician, mother and lecturer," she was described as "an enthusiastic speaker—possessing an earnest style and direct delivery which enables her to go at once to the very hearts of her hearers."[19] People who attended the Chautauqua lectures would have seen a rare thing: a female physician. Even more rare was that she was married to a fellow physician who was her full partner in their medical practice. For women and girls this could have been either inspirational or threatening. At the very least, seeing a female physician face to face would prove that it was indeed possible.

The demonstration lectures Lena gave ranged from the cause and cure of colds; to how to treat common pains such as headaches; to food facts, an integral part of her Seventh-day Adventist upbringing; to constipation cures; to a discussion on alcohol that focused on "scientific study has shown that the drink habit is largely the result of other exciting causes and predisposing influences." A pamphlet also noted that Lena would present the temperance problem from scientific, sociological, moral, and health perspectives. Her other talks centered on child culture, which was a "lecture teeming with the very latest ideas on child culture"; dressing and feeding the baby; symmetrical child training, which was described as discussing "scientific stair-climbing, physiological sweeping, and how to get physical development out of household duties instead of disease and deformity;" healthful dressing to assist women in understanding what clothes one should wear using twenty-five special charts; and a lecture on childhood purity to help young mothers in dealing with early childhood development, sexual education, and the diseases of social transgression.

The third member of the Chautauqua group was Anna Kellogg. Her lectures were intended to teach mothers how to model their homes on a sanitarium. Mothers were instructed on how to use hot and cold water as home remedies for simple disorders. The informational pamphlet explains that these classes were different from domestic science because they would have followed SDA in emphasizing diet, cleanliness, water cures, and temperance, which differed from the domestic science of the day. Anna's program focused on treating illness, teaching exercise, and educating audiences on how to turn their home into a sanitarium by teaching "modern methods" of preventing household disease and techniques of promoting family health.

The fourth member of their troop, Sarah Willmer, was billed as a reader because she presented "literary masterpieces with a dramatic flair" to entertain her audiences. In keeping with the religious overtones of the Chautauqua Circuit she sought to "to exalt their ideals, to elevate their standards, to improve their tastes, and to increase their love for an appreciation of the good and pure in people."[20] The year 1912 saw the group grow by one when Bill Sadler, age four and a half, began to appear in the demonstration lectures with his mother and aunt as well as in the "Accidents and Emergencies, or What to do Until the Doctor Comes."[21]

Sadler sold his books at his Chautauqua appearances with the understanding that the regular bookseller's profits plus the author's royalties should be turned into the treasury of the local Chautauqua. The Sadlers' promotional material stated that the books were available postpaid and free of charge to the secretaries of committees booking the Sadlers if they requested them. Sadler noted that every Chautauqua but one had handled the books to receive the profits free of charge. Additionally, his publisher at the time, A. C. McClurg in Chicago, published a volume or two of his Chautauqua lectures every year.

The Chautauqua Circuit reached its high point in its fiftieth anniversary year, 1924, and declined rapidly after that date. An estimated twelve thousand towns saw Chautauquas that year and that thirty million Americans attended—nearly a third of the country's population. The decline in attendance is attributed to the rise in automobile ownership, improved roads, and proliferation of radios, which made music, dramas, and lectures available to everyone in their own homes.[22]

What was Sadler like in person? This is a challenging question to answer. There are no videos or recordings of him, little physical record exists, no official biographies, and just a few personal accounts. The best information we have is contained in the five-volume *Sherman Diaries*, a firsthand, up-close account of Dr. Sadler leading the Forum for five years from 1942 to 1947, as witnessed by Harold and Martha Sherman. In addition, G. Vonne Meussling, a doctoral student, wrote her dissertation on William Sadler as an orator in 1970. To discover what his students thought about Sadler, Meussling sent questionnaires to students at McCormick Theological Seminary—ministers in training—to "learn their interpretation of the dynamics of his delivery." She received responses from eighty-eight of the students in the Pastoral Psychiatry class he taught from 1951-1954. These interviews took place sixteen to nineteen years after the students had been in his class. They remembered him.

George Bennett, took a course with Sadler, then 79 years old, in the fall of 1954. He wrote:

> Sadler appeared quite elderly, rotund, with thick white hair (almost silver) thick, gold-rimmed glasses, a heavy-jowled face, almost always wearing a gray suit, starched white shirt, and slightly behind-the-times tie. He walked toward the lectern with short, quick strides, spoke in a strong yet soft voice, started from his manuscript but quickly drifted from it to give almost two hours of lively anecdotes, almost all funny, and only on one or two occasions touching on anything "off-color." He moved about freely, never consulted his manuscript after starting the lecture, gave the appearance of maintaining constant eye contact, and usually dismissed the class a moment or two before the final bell rang. His gestures must have been appropriate since I do not recall them, but I do recall a lot of movement. His speed of delivery and general effect was something like a funny Walter Cronkite might be .... He said he had a "senile" tendency to repeat himself and asked that we interrupt him when this happened.[23]

Another student, John Dilley, recalled Sadler's presentation style: "At times, he impressed me as a jolly little old man whom you would like your children to know. Other times, he would come across as a shrewd business tycoon."[24] Dilly continued, "He always had stories to share ... he would have referred to them as 'case histories.' These stories would just flow from him, one after the other. Very seldom did he refer to notes, and very seldom did he refer to other authors or sources other than himself."[25] Dilly also noted that Sadler had "tremendous audience contact, and was concerned that everyone was following him."

Reverend John W. Omerod, described Sadler as being a forceful speaker in the classroom who made his students feel as if he was speaking directly to them because of his constant eye contact. Omerod said that Sadler was so attuned to the class that he could sense when someone missed a point he that he would re-explain it effectively until he could see that the student understood him.

Sadler never referred to notes. Ronald T. Allin recalled that his tone of voice and quality were not what was significant, he "was so effective at communicating, that I was simply unaware of tone quality and characteristics of his speaking voice. This may be the highest complement one can pay a speaker. His delivery was at times slow and thoughtful and at others rapid and animated." When asked about his voice Robert E. Raymond said it was "clear and penetrating," while Morgan S. Roberts said his voice was "high-pitched but had good inflections."[26]

Charles Dierenfield described Sadler as having a quiet personality while at the same time being highly dynamic. He remembered Sadler "like a 16 cylinder [engine] idling; we knew there was a lot in there if he ever wanted to apply it and so it gave a vitality and quality to his lectures and relationships." Dierenfield reflected that Sadler, "knew exactly what he was doing; that he knew who he was, and was perfectly satisfied with himself." All 88 students concurred that Sadler had these four characteristics:

1. A keen sense of humor

2. Lots of enthusiasm for his subject matter and his teaching

3. Brought his lectures alive by illustrating them with beautiful and relevant stories

4. Total self-confidence[27]

When asked for negative criticism his students responded that while he was warm and intimate while lecturing, he was distant with them in personal conversations. His student George F. Bennett said that when Sadler was asked a question, he would respond briefly and appropriately, but "with sufficient distance to ward attempt to establish a dependency or encourage fantasies of a 'special relationship.'" Sadler's daughter-in-law, Leone, stated that Sadler was dynamic, demonstrative, and extrovert on the platform, but otherwise was an introvert and did not care for trivial talk. Leone also told this story about his sense of humor; "Dr. Sadler when speaking in Detroit was traveling on a street car to his lecture engagement. The man riding next to him asked him where he was going. When hearing the name of the hall, the passenger said, 'Oh, so are you going to hear Sadler speak—what do you think of him?' Sadler retorted, 'Why I wouldn't walk across the street to hear him speak.' When Sadler was introduced on the platform that night, the fellow passenger who was then in the audience laughed throughout most of the lecture."[28]

Another area of focus for the Sadlers in the Gospel of Health was eugenics. Eugenics was believed to be an answer to many pressing problems in the early twentieth century. A cousin of Charles Darwin, Sir Frances Galton, had coined the term eugenics, meaning "good in birth" or "noble in heredity," in 1883. That year he wrote *Inquiries into Human Faculty and Its Development*, in which the term eugenics was first used. He described it as "the study of the agencies under social control that may improve or impair the racial qualities of future generations, either physically or mentally."[29] Darwin's theory of evolution played a role in eugenics, as Galton explained: "it would be quite practical to produce a highly gifted race of men by judicious marriages during several consecutive generations."[30] This would allow the "improving human stock" by giving "the more suitable races or strains of blood a better chance of prevailing speedily over the less suitable."[31] Eugenics was supported by many prominent figures, including Theodore Roosevelt, Margaret Sanger, Alexander Graham Bell, Marie Stopes, Woodrow Wilson, Emile Zola, George Bernard Shaw, F. Scott Fitzgerald, John Maynard Keynes, John Harvey Kellogg, Linus Pauling, and Sidney Webb, Oliver Wendell Holmes, and Winston Churchill.

The Sadlers were not leaders in the eugenics movement in that they did not formulate new ideas. They did, however, disseminate the ideology by speaking at eugenics conferences, writing positively about sterilization, and advocating ridding the world of those who were unfit. Sadler wrote that

> If we should thus conscript our degenerates—sanely classify and properly employ, incarcerate, or sterilize them—within a very few decades most of our charities, which are dealing largely with problems resulting from feeblemindedness, would go out of business; most of our jails and brothels would be empty; our courts would languish for want of cases; and fully two-thirds of philanthropic and reformatory work having to do with poverty, vice, intemperance, delinquency, and crime would presently stop for want of the feebleminded grist which today keeps these mills of charity grinding.[32]

We now know that eugenics was based on incomplete science and was frequently partnered with prejudice and misunderstanding. It certainly was not the answer. Laura Hillenbrand described it this way:

> In the 1930s, America was infatuated with the pseudoscience of eugenics and its promise of strengthening the human race by culling

the "unfit" from the genetic pool. Along with the "feebleminded," insane, and criminal, those so classified included women who had sex out of wedlock (considered a mental illness), orphans, the disabled, the poor, the homeless, epileptics, masturbators, the blind and the deaf, alcoholics, and girls whose genitals exceeded certain measurements. Some eugenicists advocated euthanasia, and in mental hospitals, this was quietly carried out on scores of people through "lethal neglect" or outright murder. At one Illinois mental hospital, new patients were dosed with milk from cows infected with tuberculosis, in the belief that only the undesirable would perish. As many as four in ten of these patients died. A more popular tool of eugenics was forced sterilization, employed on a raft of lost souls who, through misbehavior or misfortune, fell into the hands of state governments.[33]

Ruth Clifford Engs notes in *The Eugenics Movement: An Encyclopedia* that in American history the rights of society versus the rights of the individual have gone in and out of fashion. The hereditarian and eugenics movements reflected this thinking in the early twentieth century by asserting that the good of society was more important than the rights of the individual. The theory argued that curtailing reproduction of the unfit would benefit humanity by reducing disease, and the cost of charity and public welfare programs for those who financially drained the system. The legislation passed under the eugenics movement—mandatory sterilization of the mentally ill and disabled, criminals, prostitutes, and the poor, immigration restriction, marriage license requirements—was considered a humanitarian effort for the good of society.[34]

In the early twentieth century, Sadler's interest began to shift from treatment to the prevention of illness, which he called the mind cure. No doubt fueled by his son's illness, he wanted to learn more about the mind-body connection of illness. When Sadler began his psychiatric studies, eugenics would have remained visible. Ian Robert Dowbiggin in his book *Keeping America Sane: Psychiatry and Eugenics in the United States and Canada 1880–1940* states his research found virtually no psychiatrist who did not at one time or another express a favorable opinion toward eugenics during the Progressive era.[35] Eugenics remained a strong trend in America until the Nazis demonstrated the appalling social ramifications of malignant application.

The eugenics movement became an underlying theme in much of the health-reform movements in the early twentieth century's Progressive era. Prohibition, sexual purity, birth control, antiprostitution, pure food and drug, and anti disease campaigns all had eugenic elements to them.[36] Positive eugenics focused on promoting optimal mating and reproduction of those who were considered to have desirable or superior traits. Negative eugenics, which both William and Lena Sadler advocated, was concerned with the prevention of those with inferior or less desirable traits from having children. The Sadlers advocated sterilization of the unfit. The Nazis practiced macro eugenics, that is, targeted an entire population or group of people they deemed less than ideal. Micro eugenics concerned policies that affected families or kinship groups. These policies were aimed at women and raised special ethical issues from the minute they were introduced.[37]

The Sadlers were most likely introduced to eugenics by Lena's half-uncle John Harvey Kellogg. In fact, the idea of race betterment was everywhere around the Sadlers: in medical school, on the Chautauqua Circuit, in the newspapers they read, and in the medical meetings they attended. Many top universities trained their students in this "science." In fact, more than four hundred colleges and universities taught eugenics theory by the 1920s.[38] Harvard, Columbia, Cornell, Brown, Wisconsin, Northwestern, and Berkeley offered classes in eugenics or offered the study of eugenics as part of a standard genetics course. Eugenics practitioners tended to be "middle to upper middle class, white, Anglo-Saxon, and educated."[39]

Both Sadlers were members of the American Eugenics Society. The society formed in 1922 after the Second International Conference on Eugenics was held in New York in 1921. Alexander Graham Bell was the honorary chair of the 1921 Congress. J. P. Morgan, Leon F. Whitney (son of cotton gin inventor Eli), and Margaret Sanger were among the early members. John Harvey Kellogg was on the financial board. The goals of the society were population control, genetics, and medical eugenics. It advocated eugenic sterilization, segregation, and marriage-restriction laws for the mentally ill and disabled. Some of the society's activities included proposing immigration restriction laws, promoting a higher birth rate among the middle class, and advocating birth control for the poor and unfit.[40] William Sadler is listed as a member until 1956.[41]

Albert Edward Wiggam was a leading publicist for eugenics and lectured on the Chautauqua Circuit. He blended science with "statesmanship, morality, and religion" and said that eugenics was "simply the projection of the Golden Rule down the stream of protoplasm."[42] In 1930, while lecturing at the American Museum of Natural History, he said, "Civilization is making the world safe for stupidity." In Wiggam's Chautauqua Circuit speech, he stated that eugenics was "the final program for the complete Christianization of mankind." He stated in his 1923 best-seller, *The New Decalogue* of Science that

> God is still doing the same thing. However, in our day, instead of
> using tables of stone, burning bushes, prophecies and dreams to

reveal His will, He has given men the microscope, the spectroscope, the telescope, the chemist's test tube and the statistician's curve in order to enable men to make their own revelations. These instruments of divine revelation have not only added an enormous range of new commandments—an entirely new Decalogue—to man's moral codes, but they have supplied him with the techniques for putting the old ones into effect.[43]

William Sadler presented a paper at the Second Annual Conference of Eugenics held at the American Museum of Natural History in New York, from September 22 to 28, 1921. Attendants numbered 393 and came from the United States, Britain, Australia, Belgium, Denmark, and France.[44] Sadler's paper, "Endocrines, Defective Germ-Plasm, and Hereditary Defectiveness," explained that his goal was to "call the attention of the biologists and geneticists here assembled to the great dearth of practical knowledge in the realms of medicine regarding the role of hormones—those secretions of the so-called ductless glands or endocrine system." Sadler also explained that he wanted to secure a consensus on endocrines. To accomplish this task, he listed a thousand people whose opinions he wanted to know regarding the hormone system and heredity. He prepared ten questions and sent them out to zoologists, biologists, geneticists, eugenicists, neurologists, psychiatrists, as well as "educators, and others having large contact with feebleminded, defective and delinquent classes." He found the answers proved his hypothesis, that hormone disturbances could frequently determine heredity factors.[45]

Eugenics was such a strong part of middle-class American culture that the Supreme Court ruled on the lawfulness of sterilization in *Buck v. Bell* on May 2, 1927. The case supported the involuntary sterilization of people until the 1970s. It concerned Carrie Buck, a white teenager who had a child after her rape by a relative of her adoptive parents. To protect those involved from the stigma of having a child out of wedlock, to spare the relative who raped her, and to save her adoptive parents from embarrassment, Buck and her child were institutionalized by her parents in the Virginia State Colony for Epileptics and Feeble-Minded in 1924. She was eighteen years old.

The doctors at the institution diagnosed her, in their words, as epileptic and feebleminded. Years later, she and her child were diagnosed as normal. Because Buck's mother had been considered feebleminded, Harry Laughlin and Arthur Estabrook at the Eugenics Record Office prepared a test case using Buck and asking that she be sterilized. Her guardian, R. G. Shelton, filed suit against the institution to prevent the surgery. After the Virginia Supreme Court upheld the circuit court's decision for sterilization, the case went to the U.S. Supreme Court. The Supreme Court upheld the statute instituting compulsory sterilization of the unfit, including the mentally retarded, "for the protection and health of the state."[46] This decision was largely seen as an endorsement of negative eugenics, that is, the attempt to improve the human race by eliminating "defectives" from the gene pool as was written by Justice Oliver Wendell Holmes Jr. His argument was based on his belief that the interest of the states in having a "pure" gene pool outweighed the interest of individuals in their bodily integrity. Holmes concluded his argument by infamously declaring, "Three generations of imbeciles are enough"[47] in another example of the argument that society's rights superseded the individual's during this era.

Lena Sadler was one of the featured speakers at the Third International Congress of Eugenics, "A Decade of Progress in Eugenics," held at the American Museum of Natural History in New York from August 21 to August 23, 1932. The conference's goal was to "mark the advance made in the field of eugenics, both as a pure and as an applied science." Lena's paper—"Is the Abnormal to Become Normal?"—argued that society should treat "defectives," but demand in return that they give something back: they should be sterilized. She made the following statement at the meeting:

> Here we are coddling, feeding, training, and protecting this viper of degeneracy in our midst, all the while laying the flattering unction to our souls that we are a philanthropic, charitable, and thoroughly Christianized people. We presume to protect the weak and lavish charity with a free hand upon these defectives, all the while seemingly ignorant and unmindful of the fact that ultimately this monster will grow to such hideous proportions that it will strike us down, that the future descendants of the army of the unfit will increase to such numbers that they will overwhelm the posterity of superior humans and eventually wipe out the civilization we bequeath our descendants; and all this will certainly come to pass if we do not heed the handwriting on the wall and do something effectively to stay the march of racial degeneracy, for it is said that even now three-fourths of the next generation are being produced by the inferior one-fourth of this one.

She went on to argue other mainstream eugenic themes. She advocated a federal sterilization law, which she predicted would eventually eliminate most crime, insanity, feeblemindedness, moronism [sic], abnormal sex, and many other types of "degeneracy."[48]

These are harsh words by today's standards, especially for the mother of a son who was mentally ill. It is a good example of the Sadlers, like *The Urantia Book*, being both of their time and transcending time. On one hand, she reflected the thinking of her era with discordant language against the unfit. On the other, she worked tirelessly throughout her life to uplift people both spiritually and physically. By the mid-1930s, forty-one states had laws prohibiting marriage of the mentally ill and feebleminded; seventeen prohibited marriage between epileptics; and four prohibited the marriage of confirmed alcoholics.[49] It is estimated that about six hundred thousand people had been sterilized by the 1960s because of eugenics laws. Many of these laws remain on the books in several states but are unenforced.[50]

William Sadler produced *The Truth About Heredity: A Concise Explanation of Heredity Written for the Layman, Long Heads and Round Heads; or What's the Matter with Germany,* and *Race Decadence.* In the preface of *Race Decadence,* in 1922, Sadler wrote:

> Important as is the health of the individual—personal hygiene, still more important is the health and vigor of the nation—race hygiene ....
>
> It is our purpose carefully to examine the causes and influences which are at work among civilized peoples, which contribute more or less to a possible deterioration of the "stock" of the white races; and also to present an outline of those plans and propaganda which, in the opinion of the author, may tend to combat these deteriorating influences, and otherwise counter-work those conditions which we believe to interfere somewhat with normal human progress; and in subsequent treatises to present a more definite program which we believe will contribute immensely to the immediate improvement of the mental and moral fiber of the white races in general, and the American people in particular.[51]

In 1936, William Sadler published his opus *Theory and Practice of Psychiatry,* by far the longest of his books at 1,231 pages. In its glossary, he defines eugenics as "the science which is concerned with improvement of the human stock through study of heredity."[52] In chapter 8, titled "Hereditary Trends," Sadler discusses how heredity is the base of all neurotic patterns and psychotic types of behavior. He said that these behaviors "in reality . . . have their origin in the nursery."[53] Sadler argued that even though the proof is far from satisfactory, we should recognize that in a majority of cases where a truly feebleminded man mates with a feebleminded woman, practically all the children are feebleminded.[54] One solution eugenics called for was the sterilization of those suffering from defective heredity that manifested itself by feeblemindedness, criminality, or imbecility. Sadler assured his readers that sterilization would not interfere with the "biologic feelings and impulses of the individual" and that they could marry and live out natural lives, but that "at the same time society could breathe more freely, knowing that no feebleminded offspring would result from such marriages between these defectives."[55]

Sadler asserted that a national sterilization law enforced throughout the United States would result in eliminating a large amount of crime, insanity, feeblemindedness, moronism, abnormal sexuality, and degeneracy within a hundred years. This would help eradicate a "troublesome factor in civilized society."[56] He ended the chapter with "The Eugenic Challenge":

> American conditions call for thoughtful consideration—for serious study; the problems of the hour challenge our immediate consideration. Our national life needs to be studied in the light of the rise and fall of other nations. We are but a young people, and now is the time in our adolescence as it were, carefully to take stock, earnestly to inquire into and recognize our fundamental defects, and then with patriotic courage and stalwart stamina to consecrate our hands to the task, and dedicate our minds to the cause, of turning back the swelling tide of moral decadence and mental defectiveness before this dire threat of degeneracy shall have time to assume more serious proportions, and before the racial deterioration which now looms in the not far distant future shall have, to further degree, undermined the stability and intellectual greatness of America and Americans.
>
> The call now to the citizenship of our country is for the reading, thinking half to become students of the great problems of race betterment; to formulate their ideas, revise their opinions, reach sound conclusions, and then, in turn, to become teachers of the other, the unthinking and the careless, half which are driving on heedlessly toward racial decadence and possible national ruin.[57]

Sadler's theory of eugenics propounded in the book was criticized in a United Kingdom periodical, the *Journal of Mental Science*:

> Does anyone really believe that a sterilization law enforced throughout the United States would result in less than one hundred years in "eliminating a large amount of crime, insanity, feeblemindedness, moronism, and abnormal sexuality, as well as many other forms of

defectiveness and degeneracy? Thus within a century, our asylums, prisons and state hospitals would be partially emptied"? And, "If we should thus conscript our degenerates—sanely classify and properly employ, incarcerate, or sterilize them—within a few decades most of our charities, which are dealing with problems resulting from feeblemindedness, would go out of business, since most of our jails and brothels would be empty"?

The reviewer questioned whether such a philosophy belonged in a psychiatric text.[58]

One of the main challenges for William and Lena Sadler, given their belief in eugenics, was the mental illness in their own family, of both their son Bill, and Lena's cousin Wilfred Kellogg, who was being treated by a psychiatrist in the early 1900s. Lena Sadler presented her paper at the eugenics conference the month after her son's suicide attempt. It is hard to imagine that this episode would not have created some soul searching on her part. Her paper reads as angry. Was this due to her internal conflict regarding her son and eugenics theories or was she trapped by societal stigma for not wanting to admit that she had a mentally ill child? William Sadler advocated sterilization for those who were psychotic in *Theory and Practice of Psychiatry*. The Sadlers clearly made an exception with their son as they did with Lena's sister, Anna, in marrying her cousin Wilfred Kellogg. Theory clearly did not meet with reality, at least here.

---

[1] The forerunner to the Chautauqua was the "sawdust trail" of the evangelists who set up gospel tents along the western frontier in the 1840s. It was named this because the evangelist Billy Sunday noticed while preaching in Bellingham, Washington, that lumbermen would sprinkle sawdust on the snowy trails so they could find their way home. He spiritualized this idea and called it "hitting the sawdust trail" which meant coming home to Christ. When an attendee was being converted or repenting, they would walk the center aisle covered in sawdust, shake his hand, and be "home." The trend of tent-based teaching like Chautauqua began as a Methodist-inspired summer camp in upper on the banks of Lake Chautauqua in New York State in 1874. It began under the Methodist Bishop, John Vincent, when he purchased a little-used church campground to train Sunday school teachers. The camp expanded its offerings from religious instruction into cultural edification, upgraded its facilities with an assembly hall, more out buildings to attract the general public. Attendees would travel to the Lake Chautauqua and for a small ticket price could see celebrities, politicians, and entertainers for the summer season. John Tapia argued that Chautauqua transformed the platform arts (arts performed on a stage in front of an audience) and paved the way for the acceptance of radio, sound movies, and television. It capitalized on the desires of Americans for self-enrichment and betterment. Chautauqua combined both entertainment and education with a blend of Christianity, family life, ethical values, and responsible leadership into its programing In 1904, Keith Vawter, owner of the Redpath Lyceum Bureau, decided to take the show on the road in the form of a "tent Chautauqua." He believed that by grouping talent together, preselling tickets to towns along railroad lines, he would save travel costs, allowing him to book nationally known speakers to expand and reach of these events. Teva J. Sheer noted that Chautauquas gave rural people their first exposure to nationally known professional musicians, magicians, lecturers, politicians, plays, dancers, bands, dramatic readings, and even a few animal acts. The lectures covered a wide range of topics: literature, history, travel, religion, and politics and helped to introduce audiences to new ideas about democracy, society, and citizenship. Originally Chautauqua traveled only to states west of the Mississippi, but expanded nationwide as the demand increased. Within a short time, more than Chautauqua assemblies were under way. By 1919, there were some five thousand traveling companies across America. The Chautauqua circuit was a lecture program that presented the Social Gospel to millions of Americans living in rural areas between 1907

and 1932. Chautauqua speakers, consisting of both well-known and the not-so-well known speakers, traveled to towns and lectured—outdoors or in tents—on popular topics. Chautauqua bookers found that the shows worked best in towns under thirty thousand, who had what Vawter called a "strong community spirit" that could be used to make the event a success. This included having the foremost citizen of the town (preacher, lawyer, merchant or manufacturer) to be in charge of the local committee organizing the entertainment.

[2]    Von Meussling, "William S. Sadler," 87.

[3]    "Keith Vawter, Inventor," 39

[4]    Kelly, "What 20,000,000 People Like to Hear," vol.105.

[5]    "Message of Health for the Masses," 33.

[6]    "*Lyceum News,* 8–10.

[7]    Meussling, "William S. Sadler," 69–74.

[8]    "Dr. Sadler's Company," Chautauqua Managers Association, pamphlet (Chicago: Lyceumite Press, 1910).

[9]    "The Sadlers and Miss Willmer," ninth annual announcement 1915, 22. In author's collection.

[10]    Ibid.

[11]    During 1910, Sadler wrote a series of letters to Harry Harrison, head of the Redpath Lyceum Bureau. In October, he asked whether Harrison could get him two or three lectures between then and Christmas to determine whether he would be a "hit" on the lyceum circuit. He sent Harrison a couple of his books with a Chautauqua circular along with the request that Sarah Willmer also be booked. Harrison replied that he could book Sadler in two churches at any time with no pay. Sadler agreed. His lyceum work kept him in front of audiences during the fall, winter, and spring when the Chautauqua Circuit was not operating. Ultimately, Sadler was represented by Thomas Brady, a lecture, entertainment, and musical agent in New York City. A circular states that Brady was "the personal representative and arranged the speaking engagements of a number of prominent men in the United States Senate and the House of Representatives."

[12]    For more on stereopticons see Robinson, From Peep Show to Palace; and Klee, *Before Hollywood.*

[13]    Powell, *The Original Has This Signature,* 65

[14]    "The Saders and Miss Willmer," 10.

[15]    Letter, Sadler to Kellogg, June 12, 1907, W. K. Kellogg Foundation Archives, Battle Creek, Michigan (# 26070).

[16]    Letter Sadler to White, October 16, 1907, Loma Linda University Archives, W.C. White Collection.

[17]    Ibid., 4.

[18]    The biography of Sadler in their pamphlet notes that he was the head of the department of therapeutics in the post graduate medical school of Chicago, where hundreds of doctors attended his clinics. He was also the medical director of the Chicago Institute of Physiologic Therapeutics. The latter was devoted to the "treatment of disease by all known drugless methods." As was typical of Seventh-day Adventist medical treatments, water was an essential factor in that "every form of bath" was offered as was "every physical energy from X-ray to Radium." Sadler required a prescription from a "reputable physician" before he would agree to treat a patient on the road. He was always careful to respect other doctor's patients.

[19]    Ibid., 9.

[20]    Ibid., 16.

[21]    Ibid.

[22]    Stott, *Waxahachie,*113

[23]    Meussling, 48.

[24]    Ibid. 53.

[25]    Ibid.

[26]    Meussling, 47-57

[27]    Ibid.

[28]    Ibid

[29]    Galton, *Inquiries into Human Faculty,* 17.

[30]    Galton, *Hereditary Genius,* 1.

31  Kevles, *In the Name of Eugenics*, ix.

32  Sadler, *Theory and Practice of Psychiatry*, 158

33  Hillenbrand, *Unbroken*.

34  Engs, *Eugenics Movement*, xv.

35  Ibid., x.

36  Engs, *Eugenics Movement*, xiv.

37  O'Toole, *Miller-Keane Encyclopedia*, #.

38  Stephen Jones, "Zoology 61," http://wsm.wsu.edu/s/index.php?id=627.

39  Ibid., 64. Eugenics was an underlying concept in John Harvey Kellogg's books on health reform, his talks and approach to educating his patients at Battle Creek. To further his support of eugenics, Kellogg organized the Race Betterment Society (RBF) in Battle Creek in 1906, in partnership with Charles Davenport and Irving Fisher. Kellogg was a proponent of eugenics in spite of the fact he adopted several non-white children. Kellogg's idea of eugenics was broad: he suggested that the use of alcohol, tobacco, tea, coffee, improper dress, and unhealthy foods led to feeblemindedness, crime, insanity, and pauperism. Long after others had discarded the doctrine of acquired characteristics, Kellogg continued to argue that they would improve future generations. Until his death, Kellogg asserted that positive changes in behavior would uplift future generations. He also believed that segregation was necessary, because he believed that immigrants and nonwhites would damage the gene pool.

40  Engs, *Eugenics Movement*, 7. For further , see Bigelow, "A Brief History"; Haller, Eugenics; Kevles, In the Name of Eugenics; Mehler, "History of the American Eugenics Society–."

41  O'Keefe, *American Eugenics Society–*, 328.

42  Ibid., 59.

43  Wiggam, *New Decalogue*, 17–18.

44  Engs, *Eugenics Movement*, 202.

45  William Sadler, "Endocrines, Defective Germ-Plasm, and Hereditary Defectiveness," 341–50.

46  274 U.S. 200, at 270

47  Ibid.

48  Lena Sadler, "Is the Abnormal to Become Normal?" 198.

49  Dowbiggin, *Keeping America Sane*,– 76

50  Engs, *Eugenics Movement*, 56.

51  William Sadler, *Race Decadence*, v.

52  William Sadler, *Theory and Practice*, 1173.

53  Ibid., 149.

54  Ibid., 149–53.

55  Ibid., 157.

56  Ibid.

57  Ibid., 158

58  Carmichael, book review. 225–27.

# PART II

◆●◆

# THE URANTIA BOOK

*All of us avid readers read* The Urantia Book *in the 1960s. We were fascinated by it and everyone had a copy. Jerry and I read it with a sense of mystery and excitement, since it addressed many subtle questions about the nature of the universe and human experience. We have always wondered about its origin and purpose.*

—Carolyn Garcia,
former wife of Jerry Garcia
of the Grateful Dead, October 2014

# 5

◄●►

# THE FORUM

*Our superhuman friends thus spent upward of two decades in extending our cosmic horizons, enlarging our theologic concepts, and expanding our over-all philosophy.*

—William S. Sadler

IN 1922, THE SADLERS MOVED INTO their new home at 533 Diversey Parkway in Chicago, Christy entered their life, and the Urantia papers Forum was soon to begin.[1] The Sadlers spent their days practicing medicine, writing books, and lecturing. In the evenings, they served as stewards to celestial communications.

The Forum was in essence a laboratory. A paper was read, questions were asked, and a follow-up draft would be read the following Sunday. The Sadlers found the process validating. Had the Forum not sparked any interest, it would have ended. The belief they were doing something important for humankind kept them focused for decades.

It began in January 1923, when Sadler was traveling in Kansas to deliver a talk on Gestalt therapy. He wrote his son, then sixteen years old:

> Say, let's start a Sunday evening Forum at our house. I'll answer and direct discussion on Philosophy, Religion, Ethics and Race Betterment. We would keep open house and invite our friends and patients to come when they felt like it. We don't go to church any place and we ought to set aside that much for our own improvement. Talk it over with your mother.[2]

73

Sadler believed that doctors should maintain contact with their patients. He thought a meeting of "informal discussion and social exchange" would be a good way to accomplish that need.[3] In a 1960 history, Sadler wrote, "This group came to consist of professional men and women—doctors, lawyers, dentists, ministers—together with individuals from all walks of life—farmers, housewives, secretaries, and common laborers."[4]

By the time Sadler arrived home on Sunday, February 11, Lena had invited thirty people. The session would be held from three to five o'clock. The Sadlers proved a powerful draw: they were both well-known physicians who spoke professionally and were well read. For the first two years, Forum meetings were open to all. Forum members brought friends and family to hear talks about primary emotions and instincts, genetics, chromosomes, character, Darwin, heredity, Mendelism, and eugenics.

Another reason the Sadlers may have entertained the idea of a Forum was to help Bill. His mental illness was affecting his success at school and he was increasingly isolated. As it turned out, he ran away from home a year later, in March 1924, to enlist in the Marines, which he did under an assumed name. He was away for the first four years of the Forum.

The meeting that changed everything occurred on a Sunday, November 23, 1924, when the discussion was on false mediums and related phenomena.[5] The talk focused on the differences between trance mediums and alleged spirit visitations. Sadler had experience investigating fraud in spiritualism, the belief that the dead could communicate with the living. Oral history of this meeting notes that a guest asked Sadler if it were possible for alleged spirit beings to actually transmit messages to human beings. Sadler answered that in his experience all cases of psychic phenomena but one he had investigated turned out to be fraudulent. This apparently was the opening he had been waiting for. He then described the sleeping subject case he had been investigating since 1911. Lena did not attend this meeting. On her return, she was shocked to hear that he had spoken of the case. The next week, she brought notes that she had taken during night-time sessions with the subject and read them to the group. The attendees found it fascinating and asked numerous questions.[6]

The Contact Commissioners (group communicating with the celestial beings) heard many strange concepts from the celestials during the contacts. In his 1960 history, Sadler noted seventy-five concepts that were "new and original as presented in *The Urantia Book*, not to mention more than one hundred additional narratives which represent enlargement, amplification, and clarification of existing knowledge." He wrote that their "superhuman friends" had told them that the universe is far flung with millions of inhabited planets, explained the story of the evolution of humankind and the cosmos, that the central universe was called Havona, that there were seven superuniverses, defined the Supreme Being, told them all about the numerous orders of angels, and about the "Thought Adjuster" which is the fragment of God that lives in our mind.

Overall, the development of the Urantia papers fell into four phases over the thirty years:

- *Phase 1: 1911–1923.* The pre-papers period, sleeping subject introduced the Sadlers to the celestial beings who were communicating through him. Forum begins 1923.

- *Phase 2: 1924–1929.* An announcement by celestial beings starts the flow of the first series of the Urantia papers to the Contact Commissioners in response to questions from Forum members. Celestial communication was through written and spoken contact. Sadler stated that some of the papers were just appearing in his home. It is uncertain whether sleeping subject was involved in this series.

- *Phase 3: 1930–1935.* Expanding of text. Jesus papers arrive complete in 1935 (Jesus papers were not the result of Q & A).

- *Phase 4: 1936–1942.* Forum final review of papers for publication.[7]

On September 27, 1924, the group officially attending the Sunday meetings became known as the Forum. They continued the established question-and-answer format beginning on Sunday, October 7, 1924, at three o'clock in the afternoon. In the first hour, a paper would be read. Then refreshments would be served. A second hour of questions-and-answers followed. This process helped refine and expand the papers. This Q & A period continued for seventeen years, ending on May 31, 1942. Over that period, the Forum had 486 members, each of whom signed an oath of secrecy.[8] Approximately thirty to fifty attended the Forum each week. Forum membership was self-selecting because those who stayed believed that celestial beings were communicating with the Contact Commission.

Forum members dressed as for church. They called each other by their first names with one exception. Sadler was known as Doctor, though his close friends called him Doc or Poppy. Sadler was not one to engage in small talk unless the Chicago Cubs were mentioned. A life-long fan, he knew all the players, their positions and team statistics, and was always ready to share his knowledge.[9]

On December 14, 1924, Sadler told the Forum members that he had received a message ten months earlier from an unseen being named Machiventa Melchizedek, on February 11. Melchizedek had announced through the sleeping subject that they would "be receiving a wonderful new revelation." Carolyn Kendall, a Forum member, noted in her history that a Melchizedek being was accompanied by the leader of the secondary midwayers named a-b-c. This was the first time that the Contact Commissioners learned of the purpose of the celestial contacts of the previous decades—preparation to bring this revelation to Earth. She notes that the midway creatures had been planning the Urantia revelation for almost five hundred years.[10]

In The *Mind at Mischief,* the best-selling of all of Sadler's books, Sadler wrote about the origin story of *The Urantia Book* in the appendix:

> In discussions of fraudulent mediums or self-deceived psychics, the reader of this book has several times encountered the statement that there were certain exceptions to the general indictments there made, and was referred to this appendix. It now becomes my duty to explain what I had in mind when those footnotes were inserted.
>
> In the interests of scientific accuracy on the one hand, and of strict fairness on the other, it becomes necessary to explain that there are one or two exceptions to the general statement that all cases of psychic phenomena which have come under my observation have turned out to be those of auto-psychism. It is true that practically all the physical phenomena have proved to be fraudulent, while the psychic phenomena are almost invariably explainable by the laws of psychic projection, transference, reality shifting, etc. But many years ago I did meet one trance medium, a woman now deceased, whose visions, revelations, etc., were not tainted with spiritualism. As far as my knowledge extends, at no time did she claim to be under the influence of spirit guides or controls, or to communicate messages from the spirits of departed human beings. Her work was largely of a religious nature and consisted of elevated sayings and religious admonitions. I never had the privilege of making a thoroughgoing psychic analysis of this case, and am not in a position to express myself as to the extent to which her revelations originated in the subconscious realms of her own mind. I make mention of the case merely to record the fact that I have met one instance of psychic phenomena apparently of the trance order that was not in any way associated with spiritualism.
>
> The other exception has to do with a rather peculiar case of psychic phenomena, one which I find myself unable to classify, and which I would like very much to narrate more fully; I cannot do so here, however, because of a promise which I feel under obligation

to keep sacredly. In other words, I have promised not to publish this case during the lifetime of the individual. I hope sometime to secure a modification of that promise and be able to report this case more fully because of its interesting features. I was brought in contact with it, in the summer of 1911, and I have had it under my observation more or less ever since, having been present at probably 250 of the night sessions, many of which have been attended by a stenographer who made voluminous notes.

A thorough study of this case has convinced me that it is not one of ordinary trance. While the sleep seems to be quite of a natural order, it is very profound, and so far we have never been able to awaken the subject when in this state; but the body is never rigid, and the heart action is never modified, tho [*sic*] respiration is sometimes markedly interfered with. This man is utterly unconscious, wholly oblivious to what takes place, and unless told about it subsequently, never knows that he has been used as a sort of clearing house for the coming and going of alleged extra-planetary personalities. In fact, he is more or less indifferent to the whole proceeding, and shows a surprising lack of interest in these affairs as they occur from time to time.

In no way are these night visitations like the séances associated with spiritualism. At no time during the period of eighteen years' observation has there been a communication from any source that claimed to be the spirit of a deceased human being. The communications which have been written, or which we have had the opportunity to hear spoken, are made by a vast order of alleged beings who claim to come from other planets to visit this world, to stop here as student visitors for study and observation when they are en route from one universe to another or from one planet to another. These communications further arise in alleged spiritual beings who purport to have been assigned to this planet for duties of various sorts.

Eighteen years of study and careful investigation have failed to reveal the psychic origin of these messages. I find myself at the present time just where I was when I started. Psychoanalysis, hypnotism, intensive comparison, fail to show that the written or spoken messages of this individual have origin in his own mind. Much of the material secured through this subject is quite contrary to his habits of thought, to the way in which he has been taught, and to his entire philosophy. In fact, of much that we have secured, we have failed to find anything of its nature in existence. Its philosophic content is quite new, and we are unable to find where very much of it has ever found human expression.

Much as I would like to report details of this case, I am not in a position to do so at present. I can only say that I have found in these years of observation that all the information imparted through this source has proved to be consistent within itself. While there is considerable difference in the quality of the communications, this seems to be reasonably explained by a difference in state of development and order of the personalities making the communications. Its philosophy is consistent. It is essentially Christian and is, on the whole, entirely harmonious with the known scientific facts and truths of this age. In fact, the case is so unusual and extraordinary that it establishes itself immediately, as far as my experience goes, in a class by itself, one which has thus far resisted all my efforts to prove it to be of auto-psychic origin. Our investigations are being continued and, as I have intimated, I hope some time in the near future to secure permission for the more complete reporting of the phenomena connected with this interesting case.[11]

The Contact Commission members served as the stewards of the typewritten manuscript and kept a carbon copy of the transcript in a fireproof vault. The commissioners assumed full responsibility for supervising all publication details, securing the copyrights, and proofreading the galleys. They never disclosed the methodology of how the book was written. These were people who talked about the celestial communications but never revealed the identity of the sleeping subject. Several of them, it appears, received celestial messages from the various beings involved. In his 1960 history, Sadler wrote that the main reason the celestials did not want the identity of the contact known was that they did not want any human to be associated with *The Urantia Book*. They hoped that the revelation would stand on its own declarations and teachings. The celestials were determined that future generations would have the book free of any human connections—they did not want a Saint Peter, Saint Paul, Calvin or a Wesley. Bill Sadler said that the man himself did not want to be known and that the book did not carry the imprint of the printer who brought the book into being. Urantia Foundation is listed as the printer.

The celestial beings and the Contact Commission made an agreement that the humans would always be present together when oral dictation was occurring through the unconscious subject. When the sleeping subject was receiving messages and writing them down, none of the commissioners would be present. The contact person was also involved later when they received written mandates and communications. Bill Sadler told Forum member Carolyn Kendall that the verbal communications occurred by what he called "direct voice." One or more Contact Commissioners heard voices in numerous different places such as Chicago; Pine Lodge, Indiana; and Culver City, California.[12]

In January 1925, the celestials directed the Contact Commissioners to ask the Forum members to write down questions that would benefit mankind. Sadler told Kendall that they decided to start with questions about the origin of the cosmos, deity, creation, and other topics far beyond present-day knowledge. The following Sunday, Forum members brought their questions, which the commissioners narrowed down to about 180. Sadler told her that eight Urantia papers appeared in answer to those questions: "The Universal Father" (two papers), "The Eternal Son," "Universe Arrangement," "The Conjoint Actor," "The Central and Divine Universe," "The Universe of Universes," and "The Seven Superuniverses."

The next nineteen papers covered the personalities from Paradise to the superuniverse level; fifteen papers covered the physical evolution of the universe, administration and personalities of the local universe, the Lucifer rebellion and cosmology; the next nine papers detailed the Edenic regime, its downfall, racial evolution, and two papers on the Melchizedeks; the next three were the bestowals of Christ Michael, the Thought Adjusters, and the Seraphic guardians. The total number of papers in the first series was fifty-six, plus the Foreword. Later in 1925, the celestials asked the commissioners to make the Forum a closed group. Forum members were required to sign a pledge of secrecy and not to discuss any of the information they gleaned at the meetings to anyone outside the group. Thirty membership tickets were issued to the first Forum members.[13]

Until 1931, the celestials approved every prospective Forum member. After that date, the Contact Commissioners took over that role. Helen Thurman Carlson, who said she was the last person approved by the celestials, thought that the revelatory beings had been warning the commissioners about potentially unreliable applicants to the Forum.[14]

Sadler described the process in his 1960 history draft:

> We would read a paper on Sunday afternoon and the following Sunday, the new questions would be presented. Again these would be sorted, classified, etc. …. Fifty-seven papers were received by this method between 1925–1929 …. This program covered several

years and ultimately resulted in the presentation of the 196 papers as now found in *The Urantia Book* .... From first to last, when papers appeared, the questions disappeared. This was the procedure followed for the many years of the reception of the Urantia papers. No questions, no papers.[15]

During phase 3, the Urantia papers were expanded. The first three papers in the original fifty-six became ten. A new religion papers series was added. One Forum member, Lee Miller Jones, spent "hours and hours typing questions to submit to the revelatory commission [celestial beings] so that they could give us new information that would be meaningful to humans."[16] By 1934, the first three parts of the book were complete. The Forum members assumed the entire book was complete. A year later, they received a surprise: Part IV, "The Life and Teachings of Jesus," a series of seventy-six papers, was delivered.

Sadler explained how Part IV appeared in his 1960 history:

> The delay of one year in the reception of the Jesus papers—Part IV of *The Urantia Book*—may be explained as follows: The midwayers were a bit apprehensive about becoming involved in the suit pending in the universe courts—Gabriel v. Lucifer—and they hesitated to complete their project until they were assured that they had full authority to retell the story of Jesus' life on Earth.
>
> After some months' waiting there came a mandate from Uversa directing the United Midwayers of Urantia to proceed with their project of revealing the story of the life and teachings of Michael [Jesus] when incarnated on Urantia, and not only assuring them that they were not in "contempt" of the Uversa courts but instead granting them a mandate to do this service and admonishing any and all persons connected therewith to refrain from interfering with, or in any way hindering, the execution of such an undertaking.
>
> And this is the explanation of why the Jesus papers appeared one year after the other papers had been completed.

Sadler reported that the celestials provided him with a simultaneous narrative of the court proceedings for the trial of *Gabriel v. Lucifer*. For Part IV, "The Life and Teachings of Jesus," the midwayers were mandated by their superiors to draw on the highest human concepts as well as their memories in compiling this series of seventy-seven papers. Another of their sources were notes made by the apostle Andrew (of Jesus' apostles). Part IV appeared in total on one day in 1935. Sadler said, "The biggest surprise was the Jesus papers. We never expected to get a whole new story of Jesus' life. This was a big shock."[17]

Phase 4 of the Urantia papers occurred between 1936 and 1941. Sadler noted in his history that during this final review the celestials asked the Forum members to go through the papers and ask questions about the "clarification of concepts" and "removal of ambiguities." This took several years. During this time, few revisions or amplifications were made to the text. In 1939, the Commission decided to organize a class to study the Urantia papers. They told the Forumites about their plan and those who wished to could join the group. About seventy people raised their hands and the Seventy, as they came to be known, were born. The Seventy took over the Wednesday evening study group that had been meeting at the Sadlers' for two or three years. The group began on April 3, 1939, and carried on until the summer of 1956. During these years, the Seventy class enrolled 107 students. The Seventy was the precursor to the "School of the Urantia Brotherhood" in September 1956.[18]

Sadler and the other Contact Commissioners used the Seventy to assist them in creating this series of workbooks intended to train teachers and leaders across the country. The workbooks would make the study of and the concepts in *The Urantia Book* more uniform. The Sadlers directed members of the Seventy to study the Urantia papers and then write their own papers on different topics to be teaching tools for the future Brotherhood School. At the same time, both Sadlers gave lectures to this group to help them understand the more difficult concepts in *The Urantia Book*. This process developed eight workbooks to aid readers.

Sadler closed the Forum to new members between January 1935 and January 1939 while they reviewed the second series and the Jesus papers. This is also the time when Lena was diagnosed with breast cancer. The celestials asked the Forum members to make a final review of the entire set of papers between 1936 and 1941. The Forum lasted until May 31, 1942.[19] The Forum did not meet in the summer months except for an annual picnic.

At the picnic on June 6, 1942, the Forum was officially released from its duties of asking questions and the celestial messages continued. On June 19, 1943, during the annual summer picnic, Sadler read a message reportedly from secondary midway creatures. Marian Rowley, a member of the Forum, took notes in shorthand. It was discovered later that the source of these messages was Emery Reves's book *A Democratic Manifesto*, published in 1942. There is evidence of awareness of source materials by those in the Forum during those years. A person who worked at Urantia Foundation when Christy was alive gave the author a set of papers, among which is a typed sheet titled "Communication Received in 1945." These words were struck out and replaced, in Marian Rowley's handwriting, with "Excerpts from Emery Reeves

'Democratic Manifesto.'" This document was found in 1982 in Christy's desk as she lay in the hospital dying.

The most important documents for a historian are those written at the time of the events they describe. We have two sets of primary source documents in the form of diaries from people who attended the Forum. Clarence Bowman kept the earliest diary. Harold and Martha Sherman also kept a detailed diary of their attendance. Bowman attended the Forum in the early days, beginning in 1924. Bowman's diaries were quite tiny in size, about three by four inches, and he wrote only a few sentences about the topics and a few messages he heard read.[20]

Bowman's first Forum meeting was on November 23, 1924. He noted it in his diary: "In aft[ternoon] went to Sadlers forum and heard some of his disclosures of fake mediums. He also told us of the phenomena of supposedly extra mundane?? Origin." His second attendance is the first record we have demonstrating that messages from celestial beings were being read to the group: "In aft[ternoon] went out to Dr. Sadler's forum. Wonderful revelations from Machavalia (Machiventa) and ABC were read by the Dr." This pattern continued in early 1925, as Bowman noted on January 11: "In aft[ternoon] went to Dr. Sadler's forum. He read some of the accounts of supervisors of Series 666 (606?) and of sovereign visitors of the universe of nebulon (Nebadon)" and a week later on January 18, "In aft[ternoon] went to Dr. Sadler's. He gave us the answers of 181 questions answered by ABC. Miss Williams and I stayed a while later and heard Mr. and Mrs. Sadler discuss this further," and then on January 25, "Went to Dr. Sadler's forum in aft[ternoon]—he read us some more messages from some of the extra-planetary beings."[21]

The second set of diaries is from Martha and Harold Sherman. They note what paper was read on what date, the changes they noticed in the papers, their thoughts about the material, and their relationships with other Forum members. These Forum diaries total more than twelve hundred pages.[22] The Shermans learned about the Urantia papers from an early Forumite, Harry Loose, a former Chicago policeman and detective. In 1921, while Loose was speaking on the Chautauqua Circuit on crime and criminology, Sherman interviewed him. After the meeting, the two men began to correspond with one another. Through this correspondence, Loose became Sherman's spiritual mentor. Sherman learned from Loose that he and Loose had known each other over many lifetimes and "belonged to a special order of beings who incarnated on Earth periodically to perform important missions."[23] Sherman also learned from Loose that each of us was indwelt with a fragment of God that served as a spiritual guide. Sherman named his fragment Ara. He wrote down the inspirations he received from Ara into a little black book that his daughter Marcia discovered in the family home after his death.[24]

In 1941, Sherman and Loose met again in person. During this meeting, Loose told Sherman about the Urantia papers. Sherman became so interested in them that he and Martha moved from Hollywood to the Cambridge Apartment Hotel, across the street from the Sadlers on Diversey Parkway in Chicago, so that they could participate in the Forum. The Shermans began to attend the Forum regularly in May 1942. They spent the next few months walking across the street to the Sadlers' home to read the entirety of the papers. At the annual Forum picnic in June 1942, Bill Sadler read a message from the Angels of Progress, who were in charge of the Urantia papers. The Shermans wrote that:

> the message released the Forum from its duties of asking questions and direct responsibilities concerning the papers; it was stated emphatically that everyone was now on their own and that it would remain to be seen whether they would prove equal to the "test." It emphasized unity and predicted there would be many human ideas on how this Forum should be run from now on.

Harold Sherman (1898–1987) earned his living as a creative writer. He wrote hundreds of short stories for boys, several juvenile sports books, adult novels, Broadway plays, radio and television scripts, Hollywood screenplays, and self-help books. He was a student of ESP (extrasensory perception) and metaphysics. Many of his books are still printed and sold today. Sherman believed that he had a mission to perform for humanity that was connected to his writing. His wife, Martha (1898–1998), was his partner, best friend, and soul mate. They had two daughters, Marcia and Mary.

Initially the Shermans were very close to Sadler and Christy (Lena had passed away three years earlier, in 1939). They had dinners together and the two Sadler men shared stories about celestial communications. In September 20, 1942, the Forum began a re-read of the Urantia papers starting with the first, "The Universal Father." The Shermans described this paper as magnificent in hearing it for the second time because it meant "much more" due to the background they had from reading the entire book on their own. The next few papers they also found very inspiring.

The Shermans wrote that the Sadlers hosted Forum members at meetings every Sunday and Wednesday as well as every other Monday. It was a busy household both day and night. In 1942, the Forum meetings were still on Sundays from three to five in the afternoon. The group called the Seventy met every other Monday night. Bill Sadler's class met every other Wednesday night. The every other Wednesday meeting was an open discussion.[25]

Attending the Forum was a positive experience for the Shermans into 1943. They noted in their diary on March 7 of that year after hearing Paper 25, "The Messenger

Hosts of Space," that "The latter part of this paper is especially interesting and beautiful, and will take much study, but fills one with an humble appreciation of the loving
care and guidance that is planned for each individual in all the superuniverses."[26] In
October of that year they read Paper 48, "The Morontia Life," which described the
worlds we go to after our life on Earth. The Shermans liked the paper's description
of how the universe was designed to help humans on their journey: "where there will
be new creatures needing the wisdom and experiential knowledge of these spiritualized mortals, now members of the finaliter corps ... that they in turn may start the
sublime Paradise ascent." The Shermans found this extremely moving, but thought
the beautiful panoramic picture that the Urantia papers painted was in fact "beyond
words."[27] The following week brought another paper, "The Inhabited Worlds." In the
discussion, Bill answered a question about physical handicaps slowing spiritual growth
in a manner that the Shermans found magnificent and inspiring. William Sadler
followed by saying that regardless of what man did on this planet, if he showed one
glimmer of interest in spiritual survival, he would "be ticketed for the next world."[28]

The evolution of the Urantia papers is noted in *The Sherman Diaries*. On April 18,
1943, Bill read Paper 31, "The Corps of the Finality." The Shermans found this paper
challenging to follow but thought the ending was "profoundly impressive" because it
disclosed that the author of the paper was an Ancient of Days in the superuniverse of
Orvonton. They believed the paper had been revised three times: once in the early part
of the Forum before 1934, again in 1934, and this final time in 1943. On December
12, 1943, Mr. Kellogg read Paper 57, "The Origin of Urantia." In the Q & A, Sadler
explained that they noted twelve planets even though only nine were known at the
time the paper was written in the mid- to late 1920s. Ceres was discovered in 1801,
Pluto in 1930, and Eres in 2005. All three were designated minor planets in 2006.
This designation is still debated.[29] Another example is from January 2, 1944, from
Paper 58, "Life Establishment on Urantia." Sadler told the Forum that the paper
included new material about how much the heat of the sun would cost the people
of Chicago if they had to pay for it in terms of kilowatt hours. It was a huge sum
for that time—a hundred million dollars. The Shermans believed this information
to be false and suspected that Sadler himself had supplied the statistics. They felt it
was too materialistic for higher intelligences to be the author.[30]

The Shermans continued to question the subject matter and the portrayals they
heard read in the papers. On March 26, 1944, they felt that Paper 70, "The Evolution
of Human Government," was not written from a spiritual perspective and contrasted
with the more sublime earlier stories of human development. They believed that it
reflected William Sadler's superior attitude toward humanity.[31] In October 1944,
the Shermans wrote that several of the papers they heard were not particularly

inspired and sounded as if a human had written them.[32] This attitude shifted 180 degrees when Papers 99 through 102 were read in 1945. They were "profound," the Shermans wrote, the "most inspiring, convincing, and soul-satisfying papers in the entire Book of Urantia. It seemed to us that the knowledge revealed in it was alone enough to lift the whole spiritual comprehension of humanity."[33] Their comments for Papers 103 were mixed. Those that had the greatest impact were on the Thought Adjuster, which *The Urantia Book* describes as the fragment of God that lives within our mind to lead us to perfection. They considered Paper 108 "Mission and Ministry of Thought Adjusters," Paper 110 "Relation of Adjusters to Individual Mortals," and Paper 111 "The Adjuster and the Soul" the most sublime literature on Earth because they appealed to a deeper sense of spiritual logic. These papers were read again after the summer break in September and the Shermans noted that a great deal of material had been added. The Shermans wrote that it appeared that some editorial license was being taken because the new material they heard had degenerated to "mere human expression."[34]

In September 1942, Harold and Martha Sherman became two of the main adversaries for Sadler. They challenged Sadler's approach in managing the Urantia papers project. At this time, weekly Forum attendance was between thirty and fifty persons. Harold Sherman became disturbed by Sadler's organization and publication plans for the revelation, fearing it would develop into another church, and began to voice his frustrations to other members. Many of them agreed with Sherman's points, and after several private meetings between Forum leaders, a petition was drawn up by Clyde Bedell and agreed upon by the others, stating their concerns and asking for more input on the decision-making process. Forty-eight members signed the petition, which a team of three Forumites—Luther Evans, Dent Karle and Elsie Baumgartner— presented to Sadler.[35]

Not surprisingly, Sadler was furious at this challenge to his leadership after eighteen years on the project. He called each signer individually into his office for a private conversation, and one by one they each withdrew their names from the petition. Sadler apparently told them that they were going against the revelators if they did not do so and would be classified as "rebels." This was too intimidating to ignore. The Shermans were never given the opportunity to remove their names. Although the Shermans remained members of the Forum until 1947, from that time on Sadler kept them at a distance.[36] Sherman's methodology and timing were flawed. The Forum had been working as a group for almost two decades with Sadler as its leader. Even though many Forum members agreed with the petition, none of them could maintain that attitude when Sadler questioned them.

The Shermans reported that Sadler told the Forum that the Contact Commissioners

no longer had to pick up the papers at the contact's home because the midway creatures were now materializing them in the Sadler residence at 533 Diversey Parkway.
Sherman wrote that Sadler had told them that "a year and a half elapsed before the
Jesus story started to come through, and then the papers began to appear which were
unsigned, it being indicated that they were being written by midwayers."[39]

Sherman became suspicious that Sadler was editing the text, and a conversation
with Christy only served to increase his suspicion. On June 3, 1942, Harold mentioned
to Christy that there was no mention of psychic phenomena in the Book of Urantia,
as he called it. Christy responded, "Harold, you know a lot about these things. Why
don't you write up an explanation of the way you think it ought to be and let us submit
it? Maybe the Angels of Progress will okay it for the book."[39] Sherman wrote in his
diary that he was shocked by Christy's response. It caused him to wonder whether
Sadler was writing up ideas on different subjects, asking the celestials for permission,
and then adding them to the book. His suspicions were fueled when Clyde Bedell
discovered that passages in the 1943 midwayer message resembled parts of Emery
Reves's book *A Democratic Manifesto*, published in 1942.

According to Urantia Foundation's files, Wilfred Kellogg started writing the
register of copyrights in October 1932 to obtain information on copyright laws.
Initially, for copyright purposes, Wilfred Kellogg was designated as the author of
*The Urantia Book* but transferred authorship to the Urantia Foundation when it was
created on January 11, 1950.

On February 5, 1937, the printer R. R. Donnelley & Sons had given W. C. Kellogg
a contract for ten thousand copies of "A Book on Psychology" of either 6 x 9 inches
at 2,496 pages or 7 x 10 inches at 1,780 pages. On April 23, 1942, the proofing of
Part I had been completed and the galleys returned so that changes could be made
from Kellogg's notes. The typesetting for the book was completed in 1948.[40]

On September 21, 1952, Bill Sadler read a message from the celestials that came
to be known as the Publication Mandate. It stated that they could publish the book
if they heard nothing from the revelatory beings by January 1, 1955. The message
had several parts:

> We regard *The Urantia Book* as a feature of the progressive evolu-
> tion of human society. It is not germane to the spectacular episodes
> of epochal revolution, even though it may be apparently timed to
> appear in the wake of one such revolution in human society. The
> book belongs to the era immediately to follow the conclusion of
> the present ideological struggle. That will be the day when men
> will be willing to seek truth and righteousness. When the chaos of

the present confusion has passed, it will be more readily possible to formulate the cosmos of a new and improved era of human relationships. And it is for this better order of affairs on earth that the Book has been made ready.

You must again study the times of Jesus on earth. You must carefully take note of how the kingdom of heaven was inaugurated in the world. Did it evolve slowly and unfold naturally? Or did it come with a sudden show of force and with spectacular exhibition of power? Was it evolutionary or revolutionary?

You must learn to possess your souls in patience. You are in association with a revelation of truth which is a part of the natural evolution of religion on this world. Over rapid growth would be suicidal. The book is being given to those who are ready for it long before the day of its world-wide mission.[41]

When there was no word from the celestials by January 1955, negotiations began with Donnelley to print the ten thousand copies at a cost of $45,700. The book was published and arrived at the Sadlers' home on Wednesday, October 12, 1955, a momentous day for the Forum members. Finally, after seventeen years, they could hold the book in their hands and take it home to read. Christy, who would be the last surviving Contact Commissioner, told the Forum members that:

We have been called to the great work of taking the first step of offering to mortal man a new light, a new revelation, of the love of God. The easy jog-trot religion of former days no longer suffices to meet the challenges of today. Following Jesus' way of life calls for an act of complete commitment, a dedicated intention, a resolute purpose, a trumpet call to a life that will not compromise.[42]

Now that the book had been published, Christy explained, a new era of answering God's call had arrived. It was time to envision how they could better the world, understand that God could speak to them, use their talents in a particular place of service, and be used to fulfill God's vision for them.

Sadler said that he did not actually believe the revelatory power of the Urantia papers until 1936, when he read the descriptions of the apostles' personalities and character in paper 139. As a psychiatrist, he felt that no human could have written the essays. This was eleven years after the process had begun and after the first drafts of all the papers had been received. Sadler wrote to his friend Jacques Weiss in 1964 that the people in the Forum were validating the process and most importantly his "job" had contributed to his belief in the papers:

> I have steadfastly refused to be diverted from *The Urantia Book* and the Urantia revelation. That is my job.
>
> One of the first communications we had from our midwayer friends at the time of the organization of Urantia Foundation warned us that efforts would be made to divert our attention and to get us occupied with irrelevant movements, cults, phenomena, etc.; that many matters would be brought to our attention to attempt to confuse, occupy, and bamboozle us. And the midwayers' instructions to us said pay no attention, stay on the main line of Urantia revelation, and avoid all of these sidetracks. And that is what we are trying to do. But listen Brother Weiss, the Urantia revelation has nothing to do with all this mixed up and muddled human psychology. We have been given a bigger and better job which ought to keep us busy—which is surely keeping me busy and happy. The fact that your mind and my mind were open to receive the Urantia revelation suggests that this same openmindedness, if it weren't dedicated to a single job, could be completely sidetracked by all this psychic phenomena which (interesting as it may be) has nothing to do with the important work that we have been given to do.[43]

With the book published, the Domestic Extension Committee of the Urantia Brotherhood spent weeks compiling a list of famous people to whom to send copies of the book:

- Edward Teller (physicist, father of hydrogen bomb)
- Arthur Compton (physicist, worked on the Manhattan Project, taught at University of Chicago)
- Philip Wylie (nonfiction author, Hollywood screenwriter, and director of Leaner Marine Laboratory off Miami)
- Stuart Chase (American economist, theorist, and writer)
- Ralph Bunche (UN diplomat, political scientist, first African American to win Nobel Prize)
- Sholem Asch (Polish-born novelist and playwright, an American citizen)
- Jerald C. Brauer (dean of the University of Chicago's Divinity School)

- C. S. Lewis (novelist, poet, academic, author of *The Chronicles of Narnia*)

- Walter Beldell Smith (U.S. Army general, Eisenhower's chief of staff in 1944 and 1945)

- Charles P. Taft (founder of the World Council of Churches, son of President William Howard Taft, mayor of Cincinnati, Ohio)

- Anne Morrow Lindbergh (author, poet, aviator, wife of Charles Lindbergh)

- Justice Felix Frankfurter (Associate Justice U.S. Supreme Court, helped found American Civil Liberties Union)

- Pearl S. Buck (American author and novelist, 1932 Pulitzer Prize winner)

- Eleanor Roosevelt (American politician, First Lady of the United States 1933 to 1945)

- Dwight D. Eisenhower (thirty-fourth president of the United States (1953–1961), U.S. Army general)

- Adlai Stevenson II (intellectual, governor of Illinois, presidential candidate in 1952 and 1956)

What these illustrious individuals thought of the book, if they even saw it, is not known. Nothing was heard from any except Pearl Buck's secretary, who returned the book. From this point on, the Domestic Committee agreed that if someone had established a personal relationship with a famous person they would send the individual a book.[44] This experiment confirmed what the celestials had told the Sadlers: that their best option would be a quiet strategy—person to person, no advertising, no church or material structure—and that it would take hundreds of years for the angels to bring those who were ready to the teachings.

---

[1] Built in 1908, their home at 533 Diversey Parkway (now Urantia Foundation headquarters), is listed in the American Institute of Architects Guide to Chicago. It is a large, impressive, beautifully ornamented three-story building on a corner. It was designed by the firm of Frommann & Jebsen. Emil Henry Frommann (1860–1950) and Ernst Jebsen (1850–1917) founded their firm in 1882. They were also the architects of the Humboldt Park Receptory and Stables in 1895–1896, Schlitz Company Brewery corner taverns (they designed all of the buildings in Schlitz Row, one being Schubas Tavern at 3159 North Southport built in 1903). The architects were noted for their high degree of craftsmanship in traditional masonry. The AIA Guide describes the building this way: "Light years from the firm's turgid, tourelled stone-front houses on Fullerton Ave. is this grand flat, the star of this graceless south-side stretch of Diversey Parkway. Lavish ornament grows out of the wall organically, recalling Art Nouveau and Jugendstil masters. The integration of the metal railing with the stone balcony is the jewel in the crown of this sculptured façade. The building's total square footage of 11,736 square feet with a coach house in the rear with two floors totaling 1,108 square feet."

[2] Carolyn Kendall, "The History of The Urantia Book Revelation," draft manuscript, July 14, 2012, p. 6.

[3] Part of a history represented to have been written by Sadler and used in the case Maaherra v. Urantia Foundation (http://www.urantia.org/urantia-foundation/history#forum).

[4] Sadler, A History, 7.

5   Kendall, "History," 6.

6   Ibid.

7   The Phase 4 date should moved back because that the final type wasn't approved until July 1951. It appears there was more editing of Part IV than oral history holds. This source of the revised date is from printing invoices and contracts located at Urantia Foundation Archives.

8   Part of a history represented to have been written by Sadler and used in the case *Maaherra v. Urantia Foundation*. http://www.urantia.org/urantia-foundation/history#forum. Forum Pledge: We acknowledge our pledge of secrecy, renewing our promise not to discuss Urantia Revelations or their subject matter with anyone save active Forum members, and to take no notes of such matter as is read or discussed at the public sessions, or make copies or notes of what we personally read. (Copy of pledge text found in William S. Sadler, "History of the Urantia Movement," draft typed by Marian Rowley (June 16, 1960) in author's collection).

9   Kendall, "History," chapter 4, 3.

10   Ibid. Chapter 2, 1.

11   William Sadler, *Mind at Mischief*, 382–83.

12   Kendall, "History," chapter 2.

13   Ibid., Chapter 2, 4.

14   Ibid., Chapter 4.

15   Sadler, 1960 history draft, in author's collection

16   Kendall, "History," chapter 3,

17   Ibid., 3

18   Sadler, A History, 9.

19   Ibid., 8.

20   Carolyn Kendall, e-mail to author, April 10, 2013. In author's collection. Carolyn Kendall, Clarence's daughter, described his attendance: He attended meetings regularly all of 1925, and most of 1926. He only attended six meetings in 1927 due in part to his sister, Irene Rydell, coming to Chicago. Twelve meetings in 1928, twenty-five meetings in 1929. Fifteen meetings in 1930. Three meetings in 1931 (he got married that year and moved to Defiance, Ohio). No meetings in 1932 (the year I was born in the depth of the Depression). One meeting in 1933. His attendance at the Forum was very limited in the 1930s and early 1940s. He often met with his friend Albert Dyon and learned the latest news about the Forum. Our family moved to Chicago in August 1943, and after this move his attendance at the Forum increased. By 1945 he was going to all the meetings on Sunday, and re-reading all the papers so he could join the Seventy. I came down with polio in August 1946, which kept the family at home for a few months. He attended all meetings he could until he retired in 1956, and every meeting afterward until his death in 1959.

21   Kendall, "The First Urantia Papers," 4.

22   Saskia Raevouri, e-mail to author, May 9, 2013. The original Sherman diaries are available online: http://archive.org/details/TheOriginalUrantiaNotebooksOfHaroldAndMarthaSherman.

23   Praamsma and Block, *The Sherman Diaries*, vol 1, vii-viii.

24   Praamsma and Block, *The ARA Messages*, introduction, 4.

25   Praamsma and Block, *The Sherman Diaries*, vol. 2, 223–24, 287.

26   Ibid., vol. 3, 81–82.

27   Ibid., vol. 3, 319.

28   Ibid., vol. 3, 326.

29   As of 2013, there are eight planets and three dwarf planets, totaling eleven.

30   Praamsma and Block, *The Sherman Diaries*, vol. 4, 1.

31   Ibid., vol. 4, 62.

32   Ibid., vol. 4, 148.

33   Ibid., vol. 4, 248.

34   Ibid., vol. 4, 248–338.

[35] "The Petition," *Urantia Book Sources and Resources*, http://www.squarecircles.com/UrantiaMovementHistory/petition.htm.

[36] Saskia Praamsma and Matthew Block have published five volumes of these diaries. See vol 1, vii–ix.

[37] Harold Sherman's letter to Sadler, July 29, 1942, in Praamsma and Block, *The Sherman Diaries*, 71–81.

[38] Ibid., vol. 5, 27.

[39] Ibid., vol. 2, 29.

[40] Urantia Foundation, R.R. Donnelley & Sons Printing Files, Chicago, IL

[41] "The Publication Mandate," copy in author's collection.

[42] Kendall, "The Future: Divine Plans" (unpublished manuscript, 2012), 3.

[43] Letter, William S. Sadler to Jacques Weiss, April 20, 1964.

[44] Kendall, e-mail correspondence with author, April 2–6, 2014.

# 6

❖

# CELESTIAL COMMUNICATION

*You humans have begun an endless unfolding of an almost infinite panorama, a limitless expanding of never-ending, ever-widening spheres of opportunity for exhilarating service, matchless adventure, sublime uncertainty, and boundless attainment. When the clouds gather over-head, your faith should accept the fact of the presence of the indwelling Adjuster, and thus you should be able to look beyond the mists of mortal uncertainty into the clear shining of the sun of eternal righteousness on the beckoning heights of the mansion worlds of Satania.*

—*The Urantia Book*, 1193-1194

TO GRASP THE CELESTIAL COMMUNICATIONS INVOLVED with the Urantia papers, it is helpful to see how God reaches down to humankind from Paradise. According to *The Urantia Book*, there are many spiritual influences in the universe and in reality they are all one. A vast and almost innumerable number of celestial beings are described in the book. To begin, Paradise is the center and the master pattern of the universe. It is spoken of as the dwelling place of God, an infinite place outside both space and time. To assist his evolving children, *The Urantia Book* explains, God created spirits that downstep to coordinate with humans as they ascend to Paradise. In fact, according to *The Urantia Book* the whole of creation as designed to bring all God's creatures to perfection through this downstepping.

One example of these coordinate spirits is angels, who were created to stand by and personally guide us through earthly existence to eternal life. The Universe Mother

93

Spirit creates angels a little above humanity. Seraphim live in homes, work in pairs, and are referred to by female pronouns. Seraphim have powers far beyond human comprehension. They work on Earth through the social, ethical, and moral environments to support higher human ideals. It is noted that frequently when people have the urge to pray it is due to angelic influence. The vast detail on celestial beings is one of the unique aspects of *The Urantia Book*. Angels are a group of solely female beings. In 1934, *The Urantia Book* asserted five hundred million pairs of seraphim on Earth. Angels are devoted to the ministry of individual humans and assist them in attaining spiritual perfection.

> Seraphim are the traditional angels of heaven; they are the ministering spirits who live so near you and do so much for you. They have ministered on Urantia since the earliest times of human intelligence.[1]

*The Urantia Book* describes seraphim as mind stimulators—they don't invade the mind but seek to influence humans in "every possible manner consistent with the dignity of [the] personality; under no circumstances do these angels interfere with the free action of the human will. Neither angels or any other order of universe personality have power or authority to curtail or abridge the prerogatives of human choosing."[2] Angels love human beings, retain records of human life as it was lived on Earth, can acquire knowledge as we do, can work individually but on higher circuits in pairs, do not have material bodies, are fairly uniform in design, possess powers far beyond human comprehension, and act as the sure heavenly guides of mankind. *The Urantia Book* also clarifies the belief that angels have wings:

> The erroneous idea that angels possess wings is not wholly due to olden notions that they must have wings to fly through the air. Human beings have sometimes been permitted to observe seraphim that were being prepared for transport service, and the traditions of these experiences have largely determined the Urantian concept of angels. In observing a transport seraphim being made ready to receive a passenger for interplanetary transit, there may be seen what are apparently double sets of wings extending from the head to the foot of the angel. In reality these wings are energy insulators—friction shields.[3]

Some angels serve as seraphic transports, are part of a corps of angels who carry personalities that are unable to transport themselves between planets—or spheres. There are different orders of the beings—some have an energy range that is only suitable for the local universe, other more powerful beings are able to assume energy while in flight for longer journeys. *The Urantia Book* notes that angels cannot transport flesh and blood bodies. When we die, our bodies remain on earth and our spirit is placed in the watchful care of our guardian angels, until it is placed in a new body on the mansion worlds.[4]

Some members of the Forum recounted seeing a seraphic transport. At the time the Sadlers were told by the revelators that a "train" of seraphic transports carrying survivors of a destroyed world would be passing through our atmosphere on the way to a new planet that was being readied for them. The Sadlers, the Kelloggs, and a few other family members rose early and walked to the end of Diversey Parkway to Lincoln Park on Lake Michigan. They saw thousands of transports that stretched all the way across the horizon on a north-south axis. Bill told his daughter Pat about this event and took her to the place in Lincoln Park where they saw the train. Pat told a friend that this occurred shortly before sunrise when the sun was still below the horizon, and they could see the transports backlit.[5]

Angels act as guardians of destiny for humans at the time of mortal death. When a person dies, angels conserve their records, identity specifications, all other values related to future existence, everything that constitutes the individual and the human soul. After gathering this information, our angels go to the first mansion world to await their charge:

> It is indeed an epoch in the career of an ascending mortal, this first awakening on the shores of the mansion world; there, for the first time, actually to see your long-loved and ever-present angelic companions of earth days; there also to become truly conscious of the identity and presence of the divine Monitor who so long indwelt your mind on earth. Such an experience constitutes a glorious awakening, a real resurrection.[6]

Another traditional concept of spiritual communication redefined with new terminology in *The Urantia Book* is the Thought Adjuster, which is described as a fragment of God that dwells in the human mind. The mission of Thought Adjusters is to act as an equal partner with the human mind to foster the growth of their soul. They are described as the greatest evidence of the "love of God." Thought Adjusters constantly communicate with their human charges, not with a voice per se but instead through "picturizations of destiny" in the subconscious. Thought Adjusters' communication is described as a "continuous stream of spiritual intelligences to the human mind."[7] The celestials warned that the voice of the Adjuster is seldom "heard" by people. Adjusters contact the human subconscious when their charges are asleep to effect spiritual transformation. They are important to this history because William Sadler believed that within his mind was something eternal and divine that would guide his path. His faith would serve him to be the architect of his eternal destiny in his belief that his Adjuster was the pilot of his mind and his will was the captain.[8] His Thought Adjuster would have served to sharpen his understanding of the cosmic mind. Sadler did not just surrender his mind to the Adjuster—he chose to follow his Adjuster's guidance because it matched "the desires and impulses" of his natural thinking. Adjusters can be thought of as fostering spiritual ideas within human minds after the person has opened themselves up to spiritual growth.

The contact with the celestial beings who indited the Urantia papers was an active part of the Forum from start to finish. Those celestials were known as the Revelatory Commission. Sadler wrote in his 1960 history draft,

> The midwayers were very real to us—we frequently talked with them during our varied "contacts." We quite fully understood that the secondary midwayers supervised the contacts .... During the early years the Contact Commissioners received many instructions and directives verbally and in writing. They were instructed to destroy by fire most of the written messages upon the appearance of the Urantia papers in print, apparently to prevent the appearance of "Apocrypha," subsequent to the publication of *The Urantia Book.*[9]

Sadler noted that the celestials "spent upwards of two decades in extending our cosmic horizons, enlarging our theologic concepts, and expanding our overall philosophy."[10] All the Urantia papers, he said, appeared in written form. The oral contacts were concerned with instructions and with miscellaneous information about the universe and affairs on Earth—known as "the messages."[11]

The main points that the celestials wanted to communicate in the Urantia papers revolved around three themes. First was the Fatherhood of God. Second was the brotherhood of man. Third was that all people are ever-ascending citizens in an eternal universe. In the first theme the celestial beings described as "faith son of God," as one who lives their life more fully because of their faith in the Fatherhood of God. They trust in God's goodness despite experiencing bitter disappointment and crushing defeat. Faith sons and daughters are conscious of eternal life, a belief that brings them real freedom of mind through earthly challenges. The second theme guides believers in the direction of social service. These are people who live to create a civilization encompassed by love. The third theme is that all things in the universe are designed to work together for eternal life. Salvation is a free gift from God that believers can take for granted. All that is needed is faith, accepting divine forgiveness, and a hunger for truth. All the papers indited by the celestial beings expanded on and supported these themes.

According to oral history of the Forum, the celestial beings were invisible to human eyes. No one claimed to have seen any celestial visitors—except for a few members of the Contact Commission and other family members who said they saw a seraphic transport over Lake Michigan (described previously). Forum members believed that the celestials were present and were conversing with the Contact Commissioners. They knew that they had superhuman beings watching over them and the project as it unfolded. This was the mysterious and wonderful part of their experience. In their minds, 533 Diversey Parkway was the home to a project of epochal significance that God was "out-working on our planet." Some Forum members felt immediately that this was true but others were more skeptical. Those who stayed believed that they were assisting celestial beings in bringing new truth to Earth.[12]

The story passed down from the Forum days was that superhuman beings intended to bring the fifth epochal revelation to Earth for hundreds of years. Urantia historian Mark Kulieke asserts that during the Middle Ages the United Midwayers, described shortly, petitioned for new revelations along the lines of *The Urantia Book*. The evidence he cites is that the earlier petition had been acknowledged or granted on February 11, 1924, four months after the Forum had begun, when Machiventa Melchizedek told the Contact Commission that the plan was to write the Urantia papers with the assistance of the Forum members. Kulieke notes that the celestial contact started seventeen to twenty-five years before the Melchizedek's formal announcement. Apparently, in the early twentieth century, the midwayers were watching three groups of people as possible candidates. One was said to be in Omaha, Nebraska. After observing all the candidates, they chose the Sadlers in Chicago. The early Forum members believed that the Contact Commissioners were brought together by unconscious celestial guidance to perform this service for humankind.[13]

In the origin stories and the diaries of Bowman and Sherman, three celestial beings were described. One was Machiventa Melchizedek, who visited the Contact Commissioners on February 11, 1924, to announce the fifth epochal revelation to Urantia. Melchizedek is described in *The Urantia Book* in paper 93, as the being who brought the third epochal revelation on Earth. Melchizedek was known as the Sage of Salem when he lived in Palestine almost two thousand years before Jesus was born. He lived on Earth for about a hundred years, teaching that there was "one God, a universe deity, a heavenly creator, a divine father." Emphasis was placed on this teaching to appeal to man's adoration and to prepare the way for the fourth epochal revelation, the subsequent appearance of Jesus as the son of the same Universal Father.[14] After Melchizedek departed the planet, he became the Vicegerent Planetary Prince of Urantia, who acts as a planetary minister representing Michael.[15]

Tabamantia is the second celestial mentioned that visited the Contact Commission on September 13, 1924. Tabamantia is described on page 1189 of *The Urantia Book* as "sovereign supervisor of all life-experiment planets in the universe of Nebadon." Christy took shorthand during this visit. Tabamantia made comments about the backward status of Earth, calling it a "strife torn, grief-stricken, and disease-stricken world" that would benefit from the Thought Adjusters, who through their "exquisite unselfishness" and "understanding ministry" are "divinely faithful" to the souls on this "confused planet."

The third celestial was a midway creature known as a-b-c. Midway creatures are described in *The Urantia Book* as our nearest of kin in the universe, "nearer men than angels" that function between angels and mortals thus the name midway.[16] In certain circumstances, they are able to reveal themselves to mortals. The book doesn't mention that this is visual to people on Earth. Midway creatures are permanent residents of Earth. They continually work to enhance the planet's spiritual growth to bring people into what *The Urantia Book* describes as a "settled status of light and life." Midway creatures played a central role in the creation of the Urantia papers as well as in the spiritual evolution of human beings:

> The entire organization of high spirits, angelic hosts, and midway fellows is enthusiastically devoted to the furtherance of the Paradise plan for the progressive ascension and perfection attainment of evolutionary mortals, one of the supernal businesses of the universe—the superb survival plan of bringing God down to man and then, by a sublime sort of partnership, carrying man up to God and on to eternity of service and divinity of attainment—alike for mortal and midwayer.[17]

According to Bowman's diary, celestial messages were read to the Forum periodically in 1924 and 1925. On December 14, 1924, Sadler read revelational messages from a midwayer, a-b-c, and Melchizedek that Bowman described as "wonderful." The celestial communications became a regular occurrence as the papers began to be transmitted. On January 11, 1925, Sadler read accounts from supervisors of Series 606 (Earth's planet number), including celestial visitors from the universe of Nebadon. On Sunday, January 18, 1925, Sadler read answers to 181 questions from a-b-c. that Forum members had asked. On January 24, Bowman wrote, "Went to Dr. Sadler's forum. He read some more messages from some of the extra-planetary beings." The messages continued throughout March and April until the Forum ended for the summer. Bowman's last entry for 1925, on December 13, read, "Went out to Dr. Sadler's forum. Mrs. Sadler read Machivalla's message of 02/11/1924."[18]

The Shermans noted several times when celestial messages were read to the Forum. In January 1943, Forumites and Seventy members Bob and Ruth Burton told the Shermans about a message Dr. Sadler had read to the group on December 20, 1942, after the Shermans had gone home. It was an earlier report from "higher intelligences" that he had been given in 1933, in which they were told that 1933 marked the beginning of great changes on Earth because a "new angelic host arrived with instructions to take over." This new group was called the Angels of Economic and Social Progress and assumed the duties of the Angels of Nations. The Burtons explained that the angelic beings were in charge of the social development of men since the early days of the clan structure of human beings and the widening of the clan saw nations develop. These angelic beings sought to positively influence human-kind whenever they had the opportunity, and that that was their role on Earth.[19] On March 5, 1944, Bill mentioned that he heard the chief of secondary midwayers addressing his group of associates, which the Shermans thought implied contact with the human instrument.[20]

Sadler reported celestial communications in regard to how to deal with the rebel-lious Shermans as well. Two weeks after the Forum petition was presented to Sadler, Christy called the Shermans and asked them to come across the street so that Sadler could speak with them. Sadler explained that he had been in turmoil for two weeks trying to decide whether he should tell them about a communication he had with a midway creature before he had met them. The Shermans wrote about what Sadler said about the conversation:

> I'm referring to the communication I received which I feel pertains
> to you people. Since this message came through during one of my
> personal talks with a midwayer when no one else was present, which
> is the only way they would carry on a personal conversation with
> us, it represents the notes I took that night and wrote out in full the
> next morning. As nearly as I can figure the time, this came through
> about a week or two before Jo Davis phoned me and introduced
> you to me from Marion, Indiana. This is undated as we were not
> permitted to date such messages or to identify from whom they
> came. I have now determined to read this communication to you
> on one condition, that you permit Christy to hear what is said here

and that you say nothing to anyone about this message. The Doctor then read them the message which he called not a warning, but a "pre-enlightenment."[21]

Harold Sherman called the message Sadler read a "contrived and fictionalized psychoanalytic report on us." Sadler indicated that the midway creatures had told him it was up to him whether to accept or reject the "couple" and that the midway creatures would "go along with him on the decision."[22] Sadler had allowed the Shermans to join the group because he was impressed with them.

The celestial messages were read to the Forum after being typed. No Forum member other than the Contact Commissioners ever saw the original handwritten manuscript of the messages or the Urantia papers. The messages were the most direct connection the participants had to the spiritual beings involved with the materialization of the papers. The messages were used to give information to the group about political situations in the world and to give perspective to the members of the Forum. Carolyn Kendall, a Forum member, wrote in her unpublished manuscript "The History of *The Urantia Book*" that these messages appeared orally to the Contact Commissioners or as handwritten messages and were kept by Christy in her office. She describes all the written and oral messages as having the following criteria:

- They came to the same group of persons known as the Contact Commission who received the Urantia papers.
- They arrived by the same technique as the Urantia papers.
- They were provided by the same celestial beings who provided the text of the book.
- Whether oral or written, they were presented in the same voices or handwriting over the forty-five-year period.
- They reveal events that would occur after the completion of *The Urantia Book*.
- They were not intended to be part of *The Urantia Book*.
- They were time limited, but are not generally out of date at the present.
- They were intended to inform or guide current and future leaders of the Urantia organizations in the early years.
- They are consistent with the teachings of *The Urantia Book*.[23]

The messages were read to the Forum periodically from 1924 to 1942. Some of the main messages were as follows:

- *Protection of the name Urantia and copyright of the text.* This message came through in August 1942. The revelators informed the Contact Commissioners that they needed to take steps to protect the name Urantia.

- *The publication mandate.* "We regard *The Urantia Book* as a feature of the progressive evolution of human society. It is not germane to the spectacular episode of epochal revolution, even though it may apparently be timed to appear in the wake of one such revolution in human society. The Book belongs to the era immediately to follow the conclusion of the present ideological struggle. That will be the day when men will be willing to seek truth and righteousness. When the chaos of the present confusion has passed, it will be more readily possible to formulate the cosmos of a new and improved era of human relationships. And it is for this better order of affairs on Earth that the book has been made ready." Publication of the book was not being postponed to the (possibly) somewhat remote date. An early publication was being provided so that it might be in hand for the training of leaders and teachers. Its presence is also required to engage the attention of persons of means who may be thus led to provide funds for the translation into other languages."

- *Instructions from the new regent of the acting planetary prince.* On November 22, 1951, a message told the Contact Commissioners that certain decisions had been made on how *The Urantia Book* should be managed.

- The 1943 peace message. This message was read to Forum members at the picnic in June 1943. It turned out that Emory Reves's book *A Democratic Manifesto* was the source for this message. The message, as *The Urantia Book* does when using sources, sequentially follows the text.

- *The 1946–1950 Communism messages.* In January 1946, a series of messages arrived describing the current political state of the world, with comments about the end of the World War II and the Korean War and prospects for peace.[24]

Another message heralded changes in the superhuman government on Earth that were instituted on August 21, 1950. Another Melchizedek Son, named Norson, became the personal regent to the vicegerent Planetary Prince of Urantia. In a message generated in May 1952, the celestials admonished the Forum to pay attention to the following advice as they directed the Contact Commission to move forward and publish the book:

You are called to a great work and yours is to be a transcendent privilege to present this revelation to the peoples of this strife-torn world.

Supercilious scientists will ridicule you and some may even charge you with collusion and fraud. Well-meaning religionists will condemn you as the enemies of the Christian religion and accuse you of defaming Christ himself.

Thousands of spiritually hungry souls will bless you for the message you bring, and thousands of others will condemn you for disturbing their theologic complacence.

Are you ready for your baptism of joys and sorrows which will certainly attend upon the early distribution of the Urantia Revelation?[25]

In 1963, Christy asked readers of *The Urantia Book* to assume the responsibility of

becoming so saturated with the fragrant truths of this revelation that all persons coming in contact with us will feel that we are truth lovers and spiritual explorers, that we are all cosmic citizens engaged in the fascinating adventure of searching for God and dedicated to the supreme passion of doing his divine will.[26]

A 1966 letter written by Christy to the field representatives of Urantia Brotherhood explained that just as their "unseen friends" had warned, people would want to know the origin of the book. This letter asked the representatives to reaffirm their pledge of secrecy by signing and returning a card to Urantia Brotherhood office. The memo was considered strictly confidential (noted in all capital letters). It quotes a celestial message dated 1945:

You must begin the rehearsal of your attitude as it is to be manifested at the time of publication of *The Urantia Book.* You, as individuals and as a group, are only concerned with the teachings of the book. The origin of the book is the concern of the Contact Commissioners.

At the time of the appearance of *The Urantia Book* a solemn oath will be required of you to the end that you shall remain silent concerning aught you may chance to know about the origin of *The Urantia Book* throughout the remainder of your life.

Only may the Contact Commissioners give out information concerning the origin of the book .... And they will be duly instructed
as to how they shall conduct themselves regarding these matters.

Your troubles will be greatly lessened if you avoid all discussion of
the origin of the book. Be determined to know but one thing—the
soul-saving message of the book.[27]

Christy was seeking to "quash all of the weird stories that come to you regarding
the origin of *The Urantia Book*." She asked the representatives to learn a lesson from
Jesus, "the greatest of all teachers," who when besieged by his apostles to perform
another miracle he did not succumb to their urgings. Finally, she reminded them that
if the celestials wanted an origin story to be told, "we would have been given one."[28]

Sadler died at age ninety-three on April 26, 1969. Celestial communication continued to be received by Sadler until he passed away. Before he died, he was given
a vision of the mansion worlds (where we wake up after we die). Christy reported
what Sadler said to her the night before he died:

The transition from this world to the next is very easy. There is no
pain. It is easy to leave the pains of this world for the pleasures of
the next, and I am going to enjoy every moment of it. I am very
conscious of everything that is going on here tonight. I could go on
visiting with you for hours, but it would be no use. The chapter is
closed. The last lines have been written; the book is finished. This
world is very real, but the next one is much more real.[29]

*The Urantia Book* describes the mansion worlds as numbering seven. Upon waking in the resurrection hall, survivors will see their angelic companions for the first
time. Here they are given a new body, learn the language of these spheres, and are
given ten days to visit those who preceded them in death. Still more material than
spiritual, the mansion worlds are the place where the evolution from the results of an
unwholesome environment, hereditary problems, and unspiritual planetary tendencies
are eradicated. It is the place where a "creature of gross animal nature begins their
journey to a perfected spirit." Sadler heard about these worlds for decades from the
celestials and was given a glimpse of them by his superhuman friends before his death.

---

[1]   *The Urantia Book*, 1241.

[2]   Ibid., 1245.

3   Ibid., 438.

4   Ibid., 426–32.

5   Carolyn Kendall, e-mail to author, May 5, 2013.

6   *The Urantia Book*, 1246–248.

7   Ibid., 1191, 1207.

8   Ibid., 1134–135, 1217.

9   Sadler, *A History*, 4.

10   Ibid.

11   Ibid., no page number

12   Kendall, *A History of The Urantia Book*, chapter 4, 7.

13   Kulieke, "Birth of a Revelation," 3–5.

14   Paper 93, "Machiventa Melchizedek," *The Urantia Book*, 1014–26.

15   Ibid.

16   *The Urantia Book*, 864

17   Ibid., 867.

18   Kendall, "How the Forum Began," 2–3.

19   Praamsma and Block, *The Sherman Diaries*, vol. 3, 12–13.

20   Ibid., vol. 4, 47.

21   Ibid., vol. 2, 245–47.

22   Ibid.

23   Kendall, "Organizational Messages."

24   Ibid., appendix 5, 1–3.

25   William Sadler, "Consideration of Some Criticisms."

26   Christensen, "A Talk by Christy."

27   Urantia Brotherhood field representatives memo.

28   Ibid.

29   Sprunger and Kulieke, "Memorial Service for William S. Sadler."

# 7

♦•♦

# BURNING WORDS

*To the traveler from Britain he said: "My brother, I perceive you are seeking for truth, and I suggest that the spirit of the Father of all truth may chance to dwell within you. Did you ever sincerely endeavor to talk to the spirit of your own soul? Such a thing is indeed difficult and seldom yields consciousness of success; but every honest attempt of the material mind to communicate with its indwelling spirit meets with certain success, notwithstanding that the majority of all such magnificent human experiences must long remain as superconscious registrations of such God-knowing mortals.*

—*The Urantia Book*, 1475

SADLER'S SKILL OF FUSING AND BLENDING others' thoughts with his own would be a good background for his channeling a book as complex and intricate as *The Urantia Book*; especially if we hold to the idea that his cosmic consciousness would expand when he was connected to the cosmic circuit. Then his writing superseded his normal style becoming far more literary. For his popular published books, he replied on his polymath nature in science, philosophy, and religion. When he compiled information for his Chautauqua lectures, it would be based on his reading in the subject area and later the lecture would be turned into a book. Before he turned forty, Sadler was reported to stay up one night a week dictating to two secretaries.[1] He probably learned this method of writing from John Harvey Kellogg. Kellogg's biographer, Richard Schwartz, noted several characteristics of Kellogg's writing style:

105

- his books were produced in an extremely short period of time by dictation to secretaries;

- he used a brief written outline and then wrote from memory;

- his literary style was simple and direct—being easy to follow but was repetitive and discursive; and

- as he told his wife after forty-five years of writing, he "did not think it was necessary to get new material or even a new method of treatment or style when writing a new book. One needed only to give the appearance of a new volume through changing the wording, chapter order, and headings." He "often incorporated entire sentences and paragraphs from earlier works."[2]

Sadler addressed his own writing methodology in *The Mind at Mischief* in 1929:

> On the majority of occasions when I am dictating, the ideas seem to be all fully formulated in my mind. I visualize the material in paragraphs, with all the punctuation clearly recognized. In the majority of instances, when I am dictating to my secretary, as I have often expressed it, I am merely redictating what I see passing before my own eyes, as I would look upon the titles of a moving picture flashed upon the screen.
>
> My experience in writing is sometimes so marked in this respect that I could easily be persuaded that I was under the control of some external power, that my mind was being used by another author, and I am sure that if I were a devotee of spiritism, I could even persuade myself that much that I write is indited by spirits separate and apart from my own mind and body.[3]

Religious threads consistently appeared in Sadler's writing, from his first known notebook in 1891, through his tome *Theory and Practice of Psychiatry* in 1936. His concepts matured over time. One of his main themes was to proclaim that religious faith was "superpsychiatric," meaning that in his eyes the teachings of Christ were the greatest known destroyers of doubt and despair. In his books, pamphlets, and articles, he argued that if religion were freed from fear it could provide a higher purpose in living that could help one meet the difficulties in life; it also promised eternal salvation. Sadler would testify that he saw distraught psychiatric patients transformed when they gained what he called God-consciousness. Once touched by God, he observed, "the patient set about to face the realities of living, superbly motivated by a new and transcendent concept of universe citizenship."[4] For him, this meant that religion could activate a person into a new, creative, and dynamic life.

The earliest example of his known writing is a small brown notebook dated February 10, 1891. It includes ten questions, each of which he answered with a biblical quote related to the importance of prayer. One question was "Why is it necessary to ask God for all these things?" His answer was "Every good gift and every perfect gift is from above and cometh down from the father of lights with whom is no variableness within a shadow of turning: James 1:17." Then he added a few of his own reasons:

> From this text some may be led to question the utility of prayer if the Father does not change. "Why then" one may ask, try to change his mind by our prayers? It is true that praying to God does not change his mind; that is not the design of prayer. It is the petitioner who is to be benefited [*sic*] by his prayer. God is ever ready to bestow on his children the blessings they need. When they place themselves in that relation to him where he can consistently favor them. His sending Christ to die for the world without any request from man shows his willingness to help. He also says he is not willing that any should perish. Peter 3:9.[5]

In the December 1903 issue of *The Life Boat* (a Seventh-day Adventist magazine that Sadler founded), he described how prayer helped him start the publication. In 1897, Sadler and his co-editor David Paulson had been searching "for a periodical containing the milk of the gospel, suitable for spiritual babes," but they could not find one. They were looking for a "modest little sheet devoted to the simple gospel story."[6] Sadler believed in providence and wrote about how God showed him he was in favor of the undertaking:

> It was midnight; we had just returned from the evening's soul-saving effort and the matter of a gospel paper weighed heavily upon our minds. Once more we sought God to know certainly if He had laid this work. I felt so utterly incompetent to carry it forward and so helpless in knowing how to begin that I almost hoped the Lord would lay the burden upon someone else. I dropped upon my knees, and as I prayed the conviction deepened in my mind that we must arise and build. I promised God to devote mind and energy and whatever ability His grace might bestow, and then laid on a chair before me five dollars—all the capital I had in the world. When I

arose from my knees at that midnight hour I could never doubt that God had set me at the task.

When I arose the next morning *The Life Boat* was an assured thing in my mind. The energies I had devoted in seeking to know the way of Providence I now spent in cooperating with Providence.[7]

*The Life Boat* sold for five cents a copy. Sadler's sales skills became evident as well: the first month's circulation was five hundred, the first year's five thousand. The figure jumped to one hundred thousand in 1903 when Sadler left and went to the West Coast to open the San Francisco Medical Mission and to study medicine.[8]

Like other Seventh-day Adventist institutions, the San Francisco Mission offered a variety of services to skid-row dwellers: a free medical dispensary, free baths, free laundry, evening school for Chinese, a visiting nurse's service, diet service, free obstetrical care, and religious services in cooperation with the Pacific Garden Mission. Three days a week the baths and laundry were reserved for women and children.[9] A penny lunch was served first on Sundays and then daily, where five hundred to six hundred people ate bean soup and Zwieback crackers. The meals were discontinued after a year because the number of diners grew to fifteen hundred, and funds ran out. In the first four years Sadler worked at the Mission, more than thirty-eight thousand baths and twenty-six thousand treatments were given, along with seventy-five thousand penny dinners.[10]

In addition to the articles for religious periodicals, Sadler wrote numerous articles for popular magazines and more than forty books. His writing sought to popularize academic ideas for a lay audience and he was one of the first doctors to write for the popular press. In 1911, an associate editor of the *Ladies' Home Journal* was a patient of Sadlers. The associate told him that the editor of the magazine, Merle Croswell, was interested in Sadler writing articles for them. A meeting was arranged and Croswell convinced Sadler to write for the Journal.[11] When a picture was requested for the article, Sadler became concerned that he would lose his membership in the AMA and the ACS. Because "no doctor had ever had his picture in a magazine or newspaper without losing his membership in the American Medical Association, it was necessary that the way be cleared for such an unprecedented move, before Mr. Crowell's request could be met." He decided to approach both professional associations to ask them for advice. Medical professionalism being the priority at the time, both associations agreed it was time to allow physicians to educate the public on preventive medicine and hygiene. Sadler's photograph appeared with the article.

Another way Sadler spread his teachings was by selling his books at the Chautauqua lectures. He arranged with the Chautauqua management to donate all the profits from his books to the local Chautauquas. At the time, Sadler had book contracts with publisher M.C. McClurg for a series of health books, which included his most popular lectures on the Chautauqua Circuit. One of these was "Americanitis," on which he lectured for twenty years before the book was written.[12] Thomas Rockwell and American Publishers gained the rights to the Sadlers' previously released books and published them under the house names.[13] These books were not footnoted. Although some sources were mentioned in the main text, Sadler had a habit of not acknowledging some of the authors from whom he borrowed ideas—including himself.

From 1899 to 1901, Sadler wrote more than sixty articles, sermons, and reports in *Advent Review & Sabbath Herald* and *The Youth's Instructor*, both Seventh-day Adventist publications. Many of Sadler's nondenominational articles were written for *American Magazine*, launched in 1906 when journalists Ray Stannard Baker, Lincoln Steffens, and Ida Tarbell left *McClure's* to start the new periodical. Originally focused on muckraking, it evolved to feature human-interest stories, social issues, and fiction. After 1915, the magazine focused more on a female audience, which helped double its readership. Some of its notable contributors included Agatha Christie, Will Durant, Amelia Earhart, F. Scott Fitzgerald, Henry Ford, Dashiell Hammett, Franklin D. Roosevelt, Upton Sinclair, and H. G. Wells. Sadler himself contributed nearly thirty articles between the mid-1920s and 1930s. The subjects of his articles were health and behavior related with titles such as "Ways to Work Out Your Own Mind Cure," "Six Fundamentals of Happiness," "Watch Out for Health Fads," and "What You Can Do about Your Heredity: Putting to Rout the Bugaboo of Inherited Bad Traits Is Largely a Matter of Confidence and Discipline."[14]

In the introduction to his first book, *Soul Winning Texts, or, Bible Helps for Personal Work*, published in 1909, Sadler wrote that he had been "collecting and arranging texts" for fifteen years. As the "compiler," as he called himself, Sadler had engaged in a "soul-winning effort" as a student, evangelist, teacher, and medical missionary.[15] This book began a pattern that would carry on throughout Sadler's life: he would read abundantly in a field, lecture about it, and then write a book using sources and citing sources in some cases and in others taking others' thoughts and using them sequentially. *Soul Winning Texts* was Sadler's only purely religious book. It was a pocket-sized volume with a small font so the book would be portable. Sadler wrote that his motive in writing it was to promote the study of the "Word of God," which Sadler asserted was "the richest blessing of all forms of Christian service."[16] He chose scriptures to assist those in all classes of society who faced challenges in their lives. The experience Sadler had in "inquiry rooms, camp meetings, cottage meetings, slum mission work, personal visitation, pastoral work, in the medical missionary dispensary, teaching missionary students, hospitals and sanitariums" with the scriptures helped him narrow the passages down to those that most resonated with people.

The first chapter, "A Personal Word with Personal Workers," outlined Sadler's beliefs at this point in his life. For him, the greatest blessing of Christian life was being actively engaged in personal service. He lectured his students on their qualifications: they must have a personal experience with God; know their Bible; ask God to give them a burning love for souls; trust the wisdom and power of the Holy Spirit; and remember that "the measure of your responsibility is determined by your opportunity." They were given hints to help their success, practical suggestions, and a section titled "Dealing with Different Temperaments," in which Sadler divided people into seven distinct types and included tips on how best to handle them.

The book's sections begin with thesis statements and accompanying scriptural quotes. For example, part 1, "Good Texts for Anxious Seekers and Those Who Want to be Saved," begins with the question, "What Must I Do to be Saved?" and is answered by the statement, "Believe God's word and accept Christ as your personal Savior," followed by a quote from Acts 16:25–32, the story of the prison guard being saved by the words of Paul and Silas after an earthquake, "And they said, Believe on the Lord Jesus Christ, and thou shalt be saved, and thy house."[17]

The publisher of the book was The Life Boat Mission, an imprint of the Seventh-day Adventists. Independent researcher Matthew Block noted the reflection of Seventh-day Adventist belief system in *Soul Winning Texts*. Sadler relied on the teachings of Ellen Gould White, the prophetess of the SDA church. The book stresses the importance of evangelizing one-on-one, to build on the beliefs of their contacts rather than attack them, to hold discussions with people to draw them out, and to note the difference between faith and feeling. Block argued that Sadler never lost his reliance on the Bible even though his religious philosophy evolved. He pointed out that in his *Theory and Practice of Psychiatry* published in 1936, Sadler stated that reading the Bible daily would give a patient increased strength, faith, and courage.[18]

Many of Sadler's books were republished several times. His second, *The Science of Living*, was initially published in 1910 and went through five printings through 1914. In 1930, it was republished by a new publisher in Chicago, Thomas S. Rockwell/Health Press. His third book, *The Cause and Cure of Colds*, was first published in 1910, reprinted six times, published as a new edition in 1930 and last published in 1938, with Lena as coauthor. His fourth book, *The Physiology of Faith and Fear; or the Mind in Health and Disease*, was published originally in 1912 by McClurg, which issued eight printings through 1920 and a new edition in 1927. Rockwell/Health published the final edition in 1930.[19]

Sadler's twenty-second book, The *Mind at Mischief: Tricks and Deceptions of the Subconscious and How to Cope with Them* was first published in 1929.[20] The intention of the book as stated in the preface was to illuminate abnormal psychology so that the layman could understand these matters more fully. Sadler wrote that he wanted a book he could place in the hands of his patients or friends to "aid him in his effort to reconstruct his intellectual life and bring his mental workings into more normal channels."[21] Both a psychologist and a neurologist wrote introductions to the book. Robert Gault, a professor of psychology at Northwestern University, wrote, "The author of this book has done a real service to science and to the general public by means of his searching investigations into the nature and operations of neurotics, hysterics, and psychics, and no less by publishing his results in untechnical form."[22] The neurologist, Meyer Solomon, wrote:

> It so happens that Dr. Sadler is eminently well fitted to present the subject matter of this book. He is well grounded in the theoretical and practical aspects of medicine and surgery. Day in and day out he is meeting with the practical problems of nervous disorders of a functional nature (that is, of emotional origin). Being a thorough student of whatever he undertakes, while at the same time of a practical bent, he has combed the best literature and practices in this field and has put them to the acid test of every-day clinical experience. He is, I am happy to say, a free lance. He belongs to no set school or dogma. Like the bee flitting from flower to flower, he has taken whatever of value he could find from the best students in abnormal psychology (Janet, Prince, Freud and his followers, McDougall, and others) and combined them, with additions of his own, into a very valuable presentation of the phenomena of the subconscious.[23]

Solomon's description of Sadler's writing style—to comb the best literature, compile the best ideas, and then write a book weaving his own ideas into the mix—has been controversial to present-day scholars, who believe he was plagiarizing. Since 2004, Block has conducted studies of Sadler's books and found sources and a pattern he deemed similar in *The Urantia Book*, discussed later in Chapter 9. Block charted Sadler's habit of using others' ideas and experiences as his own in his writing.

Block's work on paralleling chapter 4 in *The Truth About Spiritualism*, "The Physical Phenomena of Spiritualism," discovered eight source books.[24] Paralleling is demonstrated with two columns of text. The source text is in the left column while the book text is in the right column making the comparison easy to decipher. The pattern is always the same: the sequence of words and ideas in the source text are followed in Sadler's own work. One troubling if infrequent aspect is that Sadler claimed many of the experiences as his own. The most glaring example is the verbatim use of Harry

Houdini's "Ghosts That Talk—By Radio" (1922), Joseph McCabe's "A Chapter of Ghostly Accomplishments" (1922), and David Abbott's "Spirit Writing and Slate Tests" (1906). Block notes that Sadler failed to explain that he used these books as sources, instead he presented himself as the expert based on firsthand experience and other rarely cited sources.

Block discovered five sources for chapter 18 of "Automatic Writing," in *The Mind at Mischief*.[25] The study was of the entire work, but only this chapter is discussed. Chapter 18 uses two of Sadler's earlier books as sources, *The Physiology of Faith and Fear* (1912) and *The Truth About Spiritualism* (1923). Sadler quotes his previous books verbatim at times and other times lightly reworked. Again, Sadler described experience with psychics and mediums from uncited sources. Block's parallel charts demonstrate that Sadler followed the source point-by-point sequentially within his own writing. This is an important distinction: Sadler always wove the sources into the text rather than borrowing them directly. His discussion on the automatic writers W. Stainton Moses and Andrew Jackson Davis is representative. The source text for these is McCabe's *Is Spiritualism Based on Fraud?* (1920). The other sources for the chapter show similar point-by-point use. In the section titled "Dissociation," Sadler used some sentences verbatim from Hart's book *The Psychology of Insanity* but included no citations or bibliography.

Reviewers seemed to notice Sadler's habit of fusing others' thoughts with his own. *The Mind at Mischief* received mixed reviews. *The Bookman Advertiser* stated that the book was a hybrid because it fused "the psychology of complex-formation" and "the control of the subconscious, wishes and sublimation as does any medico-literary member of the Viennese clique" with the way psychiatrists handle neuroses and minor psychoses. The fusion is used to explain automatic writing, telepathy, hypnotism, spiritual mediums and other manifestations of the supernatural. The reviewer noted that because of his blend of themes, Sadler invited comparisons with "Adler, Jung, and Freud (not to mention many others who are inferior to Dr. Sadler)."[26] *The American Journal of Public Health's* review was decidedly negative: "In the language of science, it constitutes just another portion of psychiatric hash—and not very good hash at that."[27] And this:

> As far as those parts of the book are concerned which represent Dr. Sadler's own thinking, there is little to recommend. His premises often are sketchy, his deductions frequently weird, and this thinking is shallow. *The Mind at Mischief* is just about the sort of effusion one has come to expect from enthusiastic and probably well-meaning authors whose training in psychiatry is negligible or, at least meager.[28]

This review illustrates an issue that plagued Sadler with educated reviewers—he never used the terminology that psychiatrists learned and used in graduate school. In academe, writing and speaking are done in the language of the realm of one's peers. Any other will be criticized. Sadler was a self-taught psychiatrist and never fit neatly into any professional school. He thought for himself his entire adult life after he broke away from the Seventh-day Adventist church.

The Sadlers' 1937 book *Psychiatric Nursing* was co-authored with Anna Kellogg. In a review in *The American Journal of Nursing*, reviewer Gladys Stilson, who was a registered nurse, found that the book had serious weaknesses in its language in that it used catchy phrases, included errors in terminology, and on the whole was didactic. She did find the suggestions on how to practically manage a mental patient to be helpful to a psychiatric nurse.[29]

The Sadlers' *Living a Sane Sex Life* (LSSL) was first published in 1938 as a two-volume set, followed by one volume of the same name later that year.[30] In the 1944 and 1946 versions only William Sadler was listed as author because Lena had died in 1939. Block noted in his studies that the 1940s was a bad time for sex education. Due to new restrictions, revisions were made in four of the twenty chapters of the earlier books. The changes included deleting information on birth control and "graphic descriptions of sex activities."[31] In the preface, Sadler stated that their intention was "to speak freely, to tell in plain English those facts which should be known about sex and sexual relations."[32] Only one reference is given to any source author in the preface and in the index, and that is to Havelock Ellis for his "modern, helpful, and scientific manner of looking at sex problems."[33] *Living a Sane Sex Life* has two parts: The first, Sexual Hygiene, includes chapters on sexual anatomy, biology, sexual impulses, masturbation, sexual deviations, sadism, masochism, exhibitionism, homosexuality, and venereal disease. The second, Marriage, covered love-making, marriage, sex problems, contraception, and menopause. In the final chapter, Sadler argued that women who indulge in sex before marriage "will wake up in their late twenties deserted and alone,"[34] an attitude that reflected popular thinking of the time. Sadler continues by stating that unless we devise a plan for early marriage, hedonistic liberty will continue to plague society. "It has a debasing and cheapening effect upon the temperamental life," he noted, "to engage in these relations in parked automobiles, in wayside cabins, and in tawdry city hotels. This is not the environment in which to nourish, sustain, and ennoble human love."[35]

Block fully paralleled the last chapter, which uses several source books in a way that Block describes as "rampant paraphrasing." The introduction uses Havelock Ellis's *Psychology of Sex*. Section 1 is drawn from Paul Popenoe's book, using every sentence consecutively but changing them slightly by adjusting sentence structures and substituting synonyms while maintaining Popenoe's meaning. Section 2 goes back to Ellis. Section 3 uses Everett, which was used throughout *LSSL* and never cited. Sections 4 and 5 are from a *Reader's Digest* article on the dangers of premarital sex. Block argued that the opinions Sadler expressed in the book were in fact from *Reader's Digest*. In fact, just about all of the information in this *Living a Sane Sex Life* is from other sources. In Block's opinion, Sadler was a master creative writer.[36] *LSSL* includes no bibliography or sources but the sources appear and reappear specific to each topic. The sources are occasionally quoted word for word, but most frequently the pattern of words and ideas are what can be traced to the source texts. Sadler's pattern was to follow the general ideas of the source. The most striking aspect of Block's discovery is the sequence of ideas and words Sadler used.

By far the largest, most complex, and most impressive of Sadler's books is the massive *Theory and Practice of Psychiatry (TPoP)*, published in 1936. The book was intended to be "a psychiatric textbook for neuropsychiatric specialists and general practitioners of medicine," and "a reference handbook for psychologists, sociologists, pastors, and other professional readers."[37] Sadler stated in the preface that he wanted to "contribute something which will assist the medical profession in divesting mental hygiene of many of its psychiatric mysteries." The book includes seventy-seven chapters in five parts, a thirty-five page glossary, and a thirty-seven page index. It begins with a forty-three page historical introduction that surveyed the background of the psychiatric profession from the beginning of medicine to the 1930s.

The book is described as fitting into the American School of Psychiatry. Nevertheless, Sadler wrote that he drew from all schools of psychological thought. He outlined the trend of the book to be along the lines of "present-day genetic-dynamic concepts of psychiatry which have contributed so much to making human behavior, normal and abnormal, more understandable."[38] The use of sources is also discussed, Sadler noting that he drew upon his own notes at the Chicago Institute of Research and Diagnosis as well as from permanent and periodical literature. To assist the reader, he acknowledged in the preface several volumes as being "of great help," and added specialized bibliographies at the end of each chapter and a larger bibliography at the end of the book.

In closing, Sadler noted that because his purpose was to assist the other professionals he concentrated on various neurotic, emotional, and personality disturbances rather than on the insanities which were more institutional in nature. His hope was to "contribute in some way to the furtherance of the curative and prophylactic efforts of the medical and associated professions in the management of personality disturbances, the psychoses, the neuroses, and allied nervous disorders."[39]

The book received many favorable reviews. *Southern Medicine and Surgery* reviewed it in August 1936:

> It may well be doubted if there is to be found between the lids of any other book so much instruction of every day usefulness to the doctor of medicine, for it is a remarkably good textbook of normal and abnormal psychology.[40]

Ira Wile reviewed the book for *The Survey* in September 1936, titled "Those Neurotics":

> In an excellent exposition of the theory and practice of psychiatry with particular emphasis upon the neuroses, Sadler offers well organized material, with a broad and eclectic approach, discussed without overemphasis on unnecessary technicalities. Recognizing the fundamental master motives as the life urge, the sex urge, the urge for power, the social urge and the urge to worship, he develops his schemes of human activity in a practical manner and in a style that promotes interest as well as readability.[41]

Religious journals liked the fact that Sadler wrote favorably of spirituality. Norman Richardson, who reviewed the work for the *Alumni Review, Presbyterian Teachers Seminary*, in Chicago, in October 1936 wrote, "For a psychiatrist to put his patient into sympathetic and life-giving touch with God, knowing that here is the highest source of curative vitality, is to suggest to ministers the presence of a new ally in their work for world redemption." Richardson called it a "monumental" volume of "remarkable extensiveness or scope" and that the author, "is on the very forefront of those creative students and practitioners who are applying the basic principles of mental therapy to the vast multitude of persons who need help but who with the skilled counsel of a dependable psychiatrist who sees life as a whole, can manage his own psycho-neuroses without commitment to an institution for mental diseases."[42]

*Psychology* magazine in December 1936 had this to say about the text:

> Cast on a desert isle for a goodly period of time and with Dr. William S. Sadler's new book as his sole companion, a person totally unacquainted with psychology, sociology, psychiatry and various other subjects known to professional readers, could quite plausibly, emerge with a very fair working knowledge of all of them.[43]

Many other psychiatrists shared the *New York State Journal of Medicine's* opinion that Sadler's argument that the practice of mental hygiene could be broadened. The reviewer, A. E. Soper, found Sadler "neither a radical nor an ultra conservative but is rather an exponent of the American School of Psychiatry." He saw him as belonging to the "middle-of-the-roaders." Soper believed that the book would not please every reader but thought there was use for the book for physicians and others interested in the welfare of nervous and mental patients.[44]

Foreign journals reviewed the book as well. One of the strongest came from *The Medical Press* in 1937. A Canadian magazine, launched in 1839, was still going strong when this review was published.

> Among the more important universally known psychiatric treatises rare are those which present a view of an ensemble so vast, comprehensive, and clear as the work of Professor Sadler of Chicago. It follows the general concepts of the American School of Psychiatry, which is of particular interest, but the author, with meritorious independence, borrows conceptions and methods from other schools of psychology and psychiatry, permitting him to produce a work which is from every viewpoint practical and of high clinical value. The orientation adopted is based upon present-day ideas, which aids one to understand the human personality, not as an entity of detached parts, but as an indivisible whole where the phenomena are interdependent. These ideas are given to indisputable progress in the interpretation and in the treatment of the neuroses, the psychoneuroses, and the properly called mental maladies.[45]

Sarask Lal Sarkar wrote the review of *TPoP* for the *Journal of the Indian Medical Association* in May 1937:

> [It] was meant to be a broad-minded text, not committed to any special school of psychiatric practice. It is meant to contain the common-sense treatment of mental, nervous, emotional, and personality disturbances rather than the insanities."
>
> The book in general follows, what the author denominates the psychiatric concepts of "The American School of Psychiatry." But the views of this school of psychiatry have not been clearly indicated by comparison and contrast with other sectarian psychologic schools as those of Freud, Adler, Jung, Watson, McDougall, and Gestalt.

The author of the book gives a reason for this as "The American School of Psychiatry is evolving and with passing of each decade, more and more of its practitioners are coming to agree upon certain fundamentals of psychiatric procedure." By this, the learned author admits that the eclectic attitude of American psychiatrists is not yet fully developed, and we have to wait and see what ultimate shape it takes. The American School of Psychiatry as dealt with in this book, appears to be a kind of modification of the psychoanalysis of the Freudian School by a new critical approach, which may not be bound by the dogmatic beliefs and the author has denominated this attitude of American psychiatrists as "middle of the roaders." The author has tried to work out this attitude in his book.[46]

Other reviews were mixed. Harold Palmer, wrote in the July 1937 issue of *Mental Hygiene*, the magazine of the National Association of Mental Health:

> The catchy phrase-making in which the author indulges does much harm to the more valuable contents of the book. There are inadequacies and errors of terminology. The therapeutic aspects of the book are inadequate.
>
> The book is a detailed presentation which, up to the point of departure from scientific thinking, seems to be a thoroughly useful and commendable book.[47]

Another American reviewer, Regina Westcott-Wieman, a source author for chapter 60, was quite critical. Her review in *The Christian Century* in 1936 noted that the *TPoP* was "genially expansive and chatty, yet disorganized." It appeared, she remarked, that "the material had been set down pretty much in the order it happened in the mind of the writer," and that "no consistent plan for presenting the material under the lesser headings" was evident. She also questioned Sadler's use of religious thought in a psychiatric volume. Sadler wrote, "I am rather disposed to accept the equivalent of the cosmic doctrine of the Universal Mind as a basis for some of the phenomena commonly described as telepathy." He had also stated that:

> The concept of man indwelt by a spirit entity enables us to construct a philosophy of living for the now and the hereafter which is at one and the same time consistent with the progressive phenomena of evolution, in the material sense, and consonant with man's high ethical, moral, and spiritual potential of personality development.

Statements such as these did not sit well with academic psychiatrists. Westcott-Wieman differed in opinion with Sadler on many topics in his book but agreed that the reader could still "glean serviceable material" from the book.[48]

Block recently began to study the sources of *Theory and Practice of Psychiatry.* He has completed a parallel of chapter 60, "The Physician as a Personal Counselor." He found one source was Henry Nelson Wieman and Regina Westcott-Wieman's *Normative Psychology of Religion*, which was published in 1935.[49] In neither the chapter nor the book's bibliography, however, does Sadler list either of the two. The parallels Block notes are words, phrases, and flows of thought that are typical of Sadler's use of sources in his other works. This chapter, like the book, appears to be the work of years of reading and uses a vast number of sources.

Why didn't Sadler source his material? One reason was that he was never trained to use notes. The colleges he attended were not leading research universities and may not have instructed him on their importance. Footnotes in the early twentieth century were primarily used in writing for an academic audience. Sadler did write for professional journals, but his primary audience was the general public. In an exchange with Princeton history professor Anthony Grafton, author of *The Footnote: A Curious History*, and this author about the history of notes in books, Grafton responded that even university presses did not insist on notes when a book was aimed at a large readership in the early 1900s to the mid-1950s. He gave the example of Palmer's *Twelve Who Ruled: The Year of the Terror in the French Revolution*, published by Princeton University Press in the 1950s, which sold about ninety thousand copies. The university did not require citations. Grafton believes that Sadler was following standard practice in not sourcing his material.[50]

Second, Sadler may have thought he did not need to note citations because he considered his books to be compilations of his own thinking. As mentioned earlier, many of his books were derived from his Chautauqua lectures. He dictated them after the fact and may have thought that the use of sources was not important given the general audience. As far as the research indicates, he was never cited for any kind of copyright infringement or plagiarism. Regardless, Block has pointed out that the way Sadler used sources would be considered plagiarism by today's standards. There is no excuse, however, for Sadler's using others' clinical experiences as his own.

Sadler saw a need to clear up the great confusion that existed in the religious world. As a practical man, he saw that a new spiritual ideology that validated both the Old and New Testaments—meaning it would recognize the basic truths in each—might at the same time portray that divine truth is living and expanding, "always growing and increasingly illuminating the pathways of human development." Thirty years later, *The Urantia Book* would explain in its foreword that it intended to ease this "conceptual poverty associated with so much ideational confusion" in the "minds of the mortals of Urantia" and it coordinated the "highest existing concepts of planetary knowledge" to reveal a coherent revelation of divine truth to humankind. Given Sadler's photographic memory, his skill as a compiler, his belief in prophecy, and his connection to the cosmic mind, he was a good candidate to be the scribe of *The Urantia Book*.

[1] Meussling, "William S. Sadler," 31.

[2] Schwartz, *John Harvey Kellogg*, 88.

[3] Sadler, *Mind at Mischief*.

[4] Sadler, *Theory and Practice*, 1073, 1088.

[5] Notebook is in the collection of Carolyn Kendall, Chicago, Illinois.

[6] Sadler, "The Story of the Life Boat," vol. 335.

[7] Ibid.

[8] Letter, Clough to Magan, October 14, 1931.

[9] Ibid., 9.

[10] Ibid., 10.

[11] Meussling, "William S. Sadler," 36–37.

[12] Ibid., 37–39.

[13] Manning, *Source Authors*, 335–36.

[14] For a list of Sadler's book and articles, see Manning, *Source Authors*. For more on muckraking, see Weinburg, *The Muckrakers* (2001); Jenson, *Stories That Changed America* (2003); Brady, *Ida Tarbell* (1989); and Zinn, *A People's History* (1999).

[15] Sadler, *Soul Winning Texts* (1909).

[16] Ibid., 1.

[17] Ibid., 18.

[18] Matthew Block in reprint of *Soul Winning Texts*, xi–vx.

[19] Manning, *Source Authors*. This pattern of several editions held for *Worry and Nervousness; Personality and Health; Constipation and How to Cure Yourself; Americanitis--Blood Pressure and Nerves; The Elements of Pep; How You Can Keep Happy; The Truth About Mind Cure; and Living A Sane Sex Life*.

[20] Sadler, *Mind at Mischief*.

[21] Ibid., vii.

[22] Ibid., x–xi.

[23] Ibid., xv.

[24] Block, "Work in Progress."

[25] Sadler, *The Physiology of Faith and Fear* (1912); *The Truth About Spiritualism* (1923); Hart, *The Psychology of Insanity* (1916); Prince, *The Unconscious* (1914–1921); McCabe, *Is Spiritualism Based on Fraud?* (1920).

[26] "Notes on New Books, Philosophy and Psychology," *The Bookman* (December 1929): xii–xvi.

[27] Pratt, review, 139.

[28] Ibid.

[29] Stilson, review in *American Journal of Nursing* vol.–38, no.5.

[30] Block, "Some Source Parallels." http://www.squarecircles.com/urantiabooksourcestudies/index.htm

31  Ibid.

32  Sadler, *Living a Sane Sex Life*, vi.

33  Ibid., vii.

34  Ibid., 322.

35  Ibid., 320.

36  Block, "The Sadlers on the Modern Sex Problem," 1. Block discovered the following sources for *Living a Sane Sex Life* (1938): Everett, *Hygiene of Marriage* (1932); Fielding, *Sex and the Love-Life* (1927); Van de Velde, *Ideal Marriage* (1926); Wright, *Sex Factor in Marriage* (1937); Ellis, *Psychology of Sex* (1938); Hamilton, *A Research in Marriage* (1929); Wiggam, *Fruit of the Family Tree* (1924); Keyserling, "Proper Choice of Partners" (1930); Popenoe, *Preparing for Marriage* (1938); Lindsey, "An Answer to the Critics" (1930); Exner, *Sexual Side of Marriage* (1932), Butterfield, Marriage *and Sexual Harmony* (1938); Dickinson and Beam, *A Thousand Marriages* (1931); Hamilton and Macgowan, *What Is Wrong with Marriage* (1929); Eddy, "The Problems of Marriage" (1930); Cooper, *Technique of Contraception*, (1928); Popenoe, "Broken Homes" (1930); Banning, "The Case for Chastity" (1937); Sadler, *Theory and Practice* (1936) and *Mind at Mischief* (1929).

37  Sadler, *Theory and Practice*, frontspiece.

38  Ibid., viii

39  Ibid., ix.

40  Reviews of *Theory and Practice of Psychiatry*, Kellogg Archives #26415.

41  Ibid., #26414.

42  Ibid., #26411.

43  Ibid., #26406.

44  Ibid., #26399.

45  Ibid., #26404 .

46  Ibid., #26393.

47  Palmer, review, XX.

48  Westcott-Wieman, review.. Westcott-Wieman was the wife of Henry Nelson Wieman, a clinical psychologist who taught at the University of Chicago and was coauthor of *Normative Psychology of Religion*, a source book for *The Urantia Book*.

49  Block, "Work-in-Progress Parallel Chart."

50  Anthony Grafton, e-mail correspondence, June 27, 2010.

# 8

———◄•►———

# THE URANTIA BOOK

*There is in the mind of God a plan which embraces every creature of all his vast domains, and this plan is an eternal purpose of boundless opportunity, unlimited progress, and endless life. And the infinite trea-sures of such a matchless career are yours for the striving!*

*The goal of eternity is ahead! The adventure of divinity attainment lies before you! The race for perfection is on! Whosoever will may enter, and certain victory will crown the efforts of every human being who will run the race of faith and trust, depending every step of the way on the leading of God's spirit and on the guidance of that good spirit of Jesus, which so freely has been poured out upon all flesh.*

—*The Urantia Book*, 365

AN INTRODUCTION TO THE URANTIA BOOK can demonstrate its extraordinary nature. *The Urantia Book* is a 2,097-page volume with four parts divided into 196 papers. It provides detailed descriptions of human and animal origins, nature, history, and destiny. It claims celestial authorship by describing itself as a "composite presentation by many beings."[1] Briefly, it teaches that human beings were created in the image of God, endowed with free will, are imbued with a frag-ment of God that serves as a guide toward eternity, and by their faith they traverse the universe until they reach Paradise, eternal life. The book states that it is the fifth epochal revelation to earth and defines its purpose and goal to "expand cosmic con-sciousness and enhance spiritual perception." *The Urantia Book* page numbers are cited

121

in parentheses. (1).[2] According to the book, there have been five epochal revelations in the earth's history. These revelations are stated as confirming the plan of "progressive development for a world of mortal habitation." They are described as follows:

- *The Dalamatian Teachings* occurred five hundred thousand years ago when a Planetary Prince was established to uplift the primitive tribes on earth.

- *The Edenic Teachings* were forty thousand years ago in the era of Adam and Eve, supermaterial beings sent to earth to uplift the planet biologically and culturally.

- *Melchizedek of Salem* lived four thousand years ago and was sent to earth to sustain the belief in one God in order to prepare the way for Jesus.

- *Jesus* lived two thousand years ago and came not to start a new religion but to teach us that we are all God's children. According to *The Urantia Book*, it was to reveal God to man and man to God in a way that better reflected Jesus' true teaching. He brought the Spirit of Truth who seek to change the world even today in positive ways.

- *The Urantia Book.* The purpose of the book is to expand humans' cosmic consciousness, concept of the cosmos, and awareness of their supreme duties as citizens of the universe.

*The Urantia Book* contains many ideas familiar to Christianity in that it incorporates a great deal of material from both the Old and New Testaments. This chapter will describe the teachings of the book, albeit very briefly, and it will highlight some of the ways *The Urantia Book* differs from the Bible. This chapter cannot fully depict the scope or breadth of *The Urantia Book* or illustrate the consistency of its themes. In the future religious scholars will best decipher the teachings of *The Urantia Book* by comparing its teachings to other sacred texts. I can demonstrate that the book delineates the vast plan of the Paradise Deities for universe children—to know God, find him, and evolve to become more and more like him.

In his unpublished 1958 history, Sadler wrote sixteen ways that Urantia teachings changed his and the Forum members' concepts of cosmology and philosophy. This two-decades-long "class" from their superhuman friends expanded their understandings by explaining that Earth was part of a far-flung cosmos containing trillions of inhabited worlds. The universe is really a giant school, where humans evolve to eternal life by fusing with their Thought Adjusters and becoming "finaliters" who will have a home on Paradise. The fragment of God, a Thought Adjuster, lives inside each person's mind to help spiritually guide him or her to a more spiritual life. *The Urantia Book* introduces scores of different celestial personalities. Sadler noted that he spoke with several of them during the Papers' manifestation. The Urantia teachings also told of the special reasons for Jesus' bestowal on earth.

Sadler wrote a series of workbooks to guide students of *The Urantia Book* in their study. These workbooks are evidence of Sadler's mastery of the similarities and differences of the teachings of the Bible and *The Urantia Book*. Seventeen workbooks were completed:

- *Urantia Doctrine*
- *The Theology of The Urantia Book, Part I, Part II, Part III & Part IV*
- *Worship and Wisdom*
- *The Short Course in Doctrine*
- *Summary of The Theology of The Urantia Book*
- *Science in The Urantia Book, Volume 1 & II*
- *The Teachings of Jesus*
- *Topical Studies Vol. I & II*
- *The Urantia Book and the New Testament*
- *Analytic Studies Vol. I & II*
- *Diagrams and Maps*

Sadler completed the workbooks in concert with feedback from members of the Seventy who met at his home on Wednesday nights. The workbooks were intended for use by the Urantia Brotherhood School which began in September 1956. In the volume Bible Study, Sadler noted that the Bible and *The Urantia Book* emphasized Jesus' religion differently. According to *The Urantia Book*, Christianity is the "religion *about* Jesus as differentiated from the religion *of* Jesus." To support the point that the Bible never claims infallible authority, he quoted Paul's statement in Timothy 2, 3:16. "All Scripture is inspired by God and profitable for teaching, for reproof, for correction, and for training in righteousness." In addition, Sadler pointed out that even though Jesus frequently quoted Scripture, he never alluded to it as being inspired. Jesus never called Scripture the word of God.[3] Therefore Sadler concluded that, strictly speaking, the Bible should not be called the word of God. "Inasmuch as God may be speaking in and through the Bible, it would be qualifiedly the divine word." In this sense, he opines that *The Urantia Book* was spoken of as "The Word Made Book." Sadler regarded the Bible as an incarnation, the union of the human and the divine. In his eyes the higher criticism of the Bible had about run its course in the mid twentieth century. Now, he saw an era of common sense where "the time is ripe for the real interpretation of *The Urantia Book* to appear," and in his mind it did.[4]

Reviews of *The Urantia Book* noted that it is an exceptional work. One said, "*The Urantia Book* is one of the most impressive literary achievements of all time. The fourth section alone, perhaps the most detailed rendition of the life of Christ, is stupendous. The rest of the book, which basically is a cosmology that expands far beyond the skimpy mythology of the Bible, is a masterpiece of storytelling and metaphysical speculation."[5] The Let Us Reason Ministries—a group that seeks to "Deliver, Define, and Defend" the gospel and the truth of "the word"—wrote, "The book consists of deep and profound philosophical ramblings and shrewd conglomerations of Bible stories and history, as well as other religions. It certainly has the air of being given by a higher intelligence, one that is able to manipulate words and concepts far beyond any human being."[6]

The authors of *The Urantia Book* begin the text with a description of the complex and infinite universe and end it with the simple and the finite life of Jesus, because this method—complex to simple—is the best way to attain "spiritual wisdom" rather than "generic knowledge." This method allows for human destiny to be revealed rather than just our origin. A celestial being called a Divine Counselor of Uversa explains in Paper 19 that to study any reality problem, human or divine, terrestrial or cosmic, we must do a "full and unprejudiced study and correlation of three phases of universe reality: origin, history, and destiny" (215). The Foreword and four parts of the book are:

**The Foreword.** Is intellectually dense and challenging. The Foreword was authorized by the Ancients of Days and "presented" by a Divine Counselor, a being of very high rank. Five of the authors are described as one-time mortals who had achieved Paradise and become "trinitized" beings who are now assigned to special service of the superuniverse rulers. A Mighty Messenger, who is a trinitized being and the author of Paper 22, describes the act of trinitization as being a secret, "I cannot fully unfold to the material mind the experience of the supreme creative performance of perfect and perfected spiritual beings—the act of trinitization. The techniques of trinitization are among the secrets of Vicegerington and Solitarington and are revealable to, and understandable by, none save those who have passed through these unique experiences. Therefore is it beyond the possibility of any being successfully to portray to the human mind the nature and purport of this extraordinary transaction" (249).

**Part I.** "The Central and Superuniverses" this group of papers is "Sponsored by a Uversa Corps of Superuniverse Personalities, acting by authority of the Orvonton Ancients of Days." These thirty-one papers begin with a description of God and the central universe of divine perfection. It describes God as the source of all true love, our Creator Father who places a fragment of himself, called the Thought Adjuster, in our minds to act as a spirit guide as we evolve toward Paradise. God is the source of all that is good, beautiful, and true.

**Part II.** "The Local Universe" contains twenty-five papers that are "sponsored as a group by a commission of Nebadon personalities numbering twelve and acting under the direction of Mantutia Melchizedek." This series of papers describes how the universe evolved, explains the celestial personalities who serve in the local universe including angelic corps, describes how the local universe is governed, details the mansion worlds where we go after we die and then narrates our universe career as evolving spirits, and tells the story of Lucifer and his rebellion.

**Part III.** "The History of Urantia" like Part II, is sponsored by a group of personalities acting under the direction of Mantutia Melchizedek. These sixty-three papers depict the history of how life was established on Earth all the way until Jesus' arrival. It explains the origin of Earth; how Life Carriers (they wrote Papers 57-65) are beings who implant and institute life on planets using life plasm; how humans evolved; the story of Adam and Eve (highly advanced celestial beings brought to Earth to upstep the genetic life of human beings on the planet); how religion, government and marriage evolved; and who and what angels and Thought Adjusters are.

**Part IV.** "The Life and Teachings of Jesus" is based on a narrative by a secondary midwayer (celestial beings nearer human than angel who operate on Earth) who was assigned to the superhuman watchcare of the apostle Andrew. The exception is the first paper which was indited by a Melchizedek. The papers are "sponsored by a commission of twelve Urantia midwayers acting under the supervision of [this] Melchizedek revelatory director." These seventy-seven papers portray the life of Jesus from before his birth to his death. *The Urantia Book* enlarges the view of traditional Christianity because Michael is described as the divine Son of God who created the part of the universe where we live. In other parts of the grand universe there are other Sons of God who have created their own universes just like Michael. Michael came to earth as Jesus so he could experience life on earth as a human in order to become more understanding and loving as our sovereign and to teach us to live the religion of Jesus rather than the religion about Jesus.

The first two parts of *The Urantia Book* are the densest, containing the most unique concepts and the most original propositions. The second two parts are original in their presentation but rely more heavily on books written in English and published between 1880 and 1942. *The Urantia Book* describes the religion of revelation as evolutionary and always progressive. Revelation's purpose is to expand truth, to present cosmic data to assist in illuminating spiritual teachings, to clarify knowledge, and to allure people to seek the God of love. It intends to accomplish this by portraying teachings that are not too advanced from the thought and reactions of the age in which they are presented—in this case, the early twentieth century. "The Gift of Revelation" in Paper 92 argues that "revelatory religion is propounded by the real spiritual world; it is the response of the supernatural cosmos to the mortal hunger to believe in, and depend upon, the universal Deities. Evolutionary religion pictures the circuitous gropings of humanity in quest of truth; revelatory religion is that very truth" (1007). Sadler stated that "Jesus was the greatest of all revelations—the incarnation—but he preached a simple gospel: the Fatherhood of God and the brotherhood of men." In answer to a question about why there was no "startling" new institution based on the teachings of *The Urantia Book*, Sadler said:

> *The Urantia Book* is an attempt to unify present-day scientific knowledge and religious truth. The main purpose of the Urantia papers is to help the average person to a better understanding of Jesus' religion. This means an emphasis on the religion of Jesus as contrasted to the religion about Jesus.
>
> *The Urantia Book*, while presenting many new concepts, devotes much attention to the exaltation of much that is old—the home, education, and social equity.
>
> Remember, it is not the purpose of *The Urantia Book* to start a new church. The book condemns sectarian religions. The book is a gift to all religions, including Christianity.[7]

Highlights from the Foreword and each of the four parts of the book can only begin to illustrate the depth and sweep of material covered.

## Foreword

The Foreword and Part I contain the most intellectually difficult papers in the book. Bill Sadler, Jr. gave a series of topical talks about *The Urantia Book* in the late 1950s and early 1960s in California and Oklahoma City. Few people have written or spoken with the same intimate knowledge of *The Urantia Book*. His explanations helped those in the early study groups understand some of the more challenging concepts in the book. He gave a talk about the Foreword on June 12, 1961, which remains one of the most accessible descriptions of this complex paper. Several excerpts follow:

> I would like to communicate to you my feeling for the intent which is behind the Foreword. The Foreword starts out with an apology, it says that our language isn't very good (and indeed it isn't) and it says … we want to help you understand. You see, the secondary

purpose of *The Urantia Book* is the illumination of the human mind. Its primary purpose is the salvation of human souls, but the Book makes an intellectual appeal because the Book is in English, therefore it's got to enter our consciousness through mind. The Foreword tips its hat, in two paragraphs, to the human desire to start from man and proceed to God. You'll recall in one of the papers where they first talk about Trinity Teacher Sons, they tell why they wrote the Book the way they did, starting from God and proceeding outward and downward to man. They point out that if you start from man and go to God … this might be a certain way of grasping fact, but the truth would elude you. You don't start with consequences, you start with causes, you start with sources, and so they start this book talking about God, but there are two paragraphs here (that start on page one at the bottom) which very quickly accede to the human yearning to start from the simple and proceed to the complex. In the last two paragraphs on page one they very quickly start with our world and go right into *Paradise* and then they add a few comments:

"Your world is one of many similar planets which make up the local universe of Nebadon. This, with similar creations, makes up the Superuniverse of Orvonton, from whose capital, Uversa, our commission hails. Orvonton is one of the seven evolutionary superuniverses of time and space which circle the never-beginning, never-ending creation of divine perfection—the central universe of Havona. At the heart of this eternal and central universe is the stationary Isle of Paradise, the geographic center of infinity and the dwelling place of the eternal God."

I submit that's quite a paragraph, isn't it? In just eight or nine lines of type, they start here and take you swiftly into the center of all things. This is their concession to the human desire to start from the simple and go into the complex. I think it's very significant that the Foreword starts with a discussion of Deity and divinity.

Deity they define as a word which is larger than the word God, because God means a *personal* aspect of Deity. Deity can be other than personal, as well as personal.

It's quite foreign to orthodox Christian theology it is not only foreign to Western philosophy. The concept of a finite God is encountered in western philosophy, but usually when you encounter that concept, it is to the exclusion of an infinite God. Only in this

Book do I find the two concepts associated. In the evolutionary Supreme Being, the Universal Father who inhabits eternity and pervades infinity, is escaping from the terrible limitation of absolutes. Through the Supreme Being, the Universal Father vicariously can have the experience of having an origin, of having a time of growth, of knowing what it is to struggle.

How could an infinite God know struggle, except through a finite expression of that infinite God? As you see, God's love, His purpose, His energies, broadside throughout the finite level, in creation and evolution, then consider a bringing back together of all these things, and that is the supreme function of deity.

This section goes on to discuss divinity, and it points out that there are many different kinds of divinity, qualities of divinity, but that the one thing which is characteristic of divinity is it is the *cement* that holds all the acts of deity together. If something is related to deity in any way, shape or form, it manifests qualities of divinity. Elsewhere in the papers, the comprehensible elements of divinity are defined as truth, beauty and goodness. We are told that these are unified in living personalities, as love, mercy and ministry.

They sum up, at the end of this section, the functioning entity of a human being: body, mind, spirit, and soul. The body, our life mechanism. The mind, which we think with and confuse ourselves with. The spirit, which invades the mind, just as sperm invades the womb, and the soul is the embryo that comes into origin as a result of that cosmic conception. The human mind is the material womb of the soul. The spirit that comes from the Father is the invader, and when that invasion takes place, in about the fifth year of mortal life, something new begins to grow, and this is the embryonic soul that evolves within the womb of the mind, and this is the soul which has the capacity to survive death.

## Part 1. The Central and Superuniverses

*The Universal Father*—God has created planetary systems populated by numerous beings who can know God, receive divine affection, and love him in return. Human beings are part of this divine creation and are on a long journey to understand God's divine nature and realize his supreme mandate, which is "Be you perfect, even as I am perfect" (73). This quest for God is the supreme universe adventure for all the inhabitants of the worlds of time and space. "Ever bear in mind that these profound truths pertaining to Deity will increasingly clarify as your minds become progressively spiritualized during the successive epochs of the long mortal aspect to Paradise" (21–72).

In his June 12, 1961, talk about the Foreword, Bill explained how *The Urantia Book* expands upon the concept of God:

> The word God has more than one meaning in these Papers, the word God is used with seven different meanings. We are familiar with the first three, God the Father, God the Son, and God the Spirit. We're not familiar with God the Supreme, this is the emerging Deity of the finite level of existence. This is evolutionary Deity. This is God in time, not God in eternity. This is God in space, not God in infinity. God the Supreme is a consequence of the acts of infinity. God the Sevenfold is an association of Deity. Our encounter with God the Sevenfold is in the bestowal of Jesus, a very real encounter. When Jesus said, "He who has seen me has seen the Father," he spoke as God and for God and this is the truest illustration that we can apprehend concerning the function of God the Sevenfold. God the Sevenfold is God anywhere in time and space. God in action, in the imperfect evolutionary domains. To us, the only God that we can comprehend is in the human bestowal of Jesus, and this is God the Sevenfold in action. God reaching out from Paradise to fellowship with any creature at any level of existence, even mortal creatures at the lowest level of existence. What God the Supreme is to the finite level, God the Ultimate is to the super finite, the absonite level, that level which, (always like the ham in a sandwich, if the lower piece of bread is finite and the upper piece of bread is absolute and infinite, then the ham would be absonite, transcendental separating the finite from the absolute). God the Absolute would be the final expression of Deity. God the Absolute would be the final experiential or comprehensible expression of the Father, as the Eternal Son is the existential expression of the Father.[8]

*The Eternal Son*—This is the aspect of the Universal Father that relates to time-bound mortals. He is the Second Person of Deity (the third person of Deity is designated as the Universe Mother Spirit whose spiritual presence is known as the Holy Spirit) of the existential Trinity from eternity. This Son is the associative co-creator with the Universal Father of all universes and things. He is devoted to bringing the love of God to the universes of universes—to execute spiritual aspects to the Father's eternal purpose (73–89). Bill explained the Eternal Son as follows:

> The Eternal Son is the pattern personality. All personality is fashioned after the similitude of this absolute pattern in varying degrees. The Father simply steps aside from the absolute personality. In so doing, he possesses himself of Father personality. I can best understand that by thinking, "If he can be father of the absolute person, he can be father of any person." At the same time, he builds the absolute machine. He builds it for the same reason that men build machines: to act as a material governor, to perform repetitive acts. This absolute machine is the Isle of Paradise. It's the only machine which the Father ever built personally. It is just as much a revelation of the Father, or of God, as is the Eternal Son. The Father is the source of Paradise as he is Father of the Eternal Son. The Eternal Son, then, is the Universal Father minus everything which is non-Deity, extra-divine, and other-than-spiritual.[9]

*The Infinite Spirit*—Is the Third Person of Deity, also known as the Infinite Reality, the Universal Organizer, or Personality Coordinator of all aspects of God. The Infinite Spirit can be thought of as love and mercy to ascending creatures such as humans. The Spirit guides humans through their evolution toward God. In their lowliest form they minister to people as angels. This Spirit also ministers to the human mind through the Adjutant Mind Spirits of our local universe. As the Conjoint Actor, the Infinite Spirit is the source of mind for human beings to "constitute a living ladder whereby mortal man climbs from chaos to glory" (90–107).

*The Paradise Trinity*—Is the Universal Father, Eternal Son, and Infinite Spirit. "The original and eternal Paradise Trinity is existential and was inevitable. This never-beginning Trinity was inherent in the fact of the differentiation of the personal and the nonpersonal by the Father's unfettered will and factualized when his personal will coordinated these dual realities by mind. The post-Havona Trinities are experiential—are inherent in the creation of two subabsolute and evolutional levels of power-personality manifestation in the master universe" (15). *The Urantia Book* states that Jesus taught the apostles the truth about the Trinity but they thought he was speaking figuratively. "Not since the times of Jesus has the factual identity of the Paradise Trinity been known on Urantia (except by a few individuals to whom it was especially revealed) until its presentation in these revelatory disclosures" (1145). They are equal to each other and they are one. *The Urantia Book* teaches that we can only have a partial understanding of the Paradise Trinity because we are imperfect beings. Even though we are limited in our understanding we are reminded that "The mortal mind can immediately think of a thousand and one things—catastrophic physical events, appalling accidents, horrific disasters, painful illnesses, and worldwide scourges—and ask whether such visitations are correlated in the unknown maneuvering of this probable functioning of the Supreme Being. Frankly, we do not know; we are not really sure. But we do observe that, as time passes, all these difficult and more or less mysterious situations always work out for the welfare of the universes" (108–17).

*The Isle of Paradise*—Sadler through his celestial contacts learned the proposition that "The Father, in eternalizing the Original Son, simultaneously revealed the infinity potential of his nonpersonal self as Paradise." Paradise is the eternal center of the universe of universes and the abiding place of the Universal Father, the Eternal Son, and the Infinite Spirit and their associates. Its spiritual beauty, the magnificence of its physical perfection, superb intellectual accomplishments of its inhabitants are considered to be beyond mortal comprehension. It is from eternity—outside the time and space realm. It is the most "gigantic organized body of cosmic reality in all the master universe. This is where God lives—he is personally, literally, and actually present. And from him, an infinite being, flow the flood-streams of life, energy, and personality to all universes (118–27). Paradise is the goal of spiritual evolution for all ascending mortals, "Every God-knowing mortal who has espoused the career of doing the Father's will has already embarked upon the long, long Paradise trail of divinity pursuit and perfection attainment. And when such an animal-origin being does stand, as countless numbers now do, before the Gods on Paradise, having ascended from the lowly spheres of space, such an achievement represents the reality of a spiritual transformation bordering on the limits of supremacy" (127).

*Havona*—Is the name of the central and divine universe—the center of all creation. The Paradise Havona system is the perfect and eternal nucleus of the master universe. "*The Paradise-Havona System*, the eternal universe encircling the eternal Isle, constitutes the perfect and eternal nucleus of the master universe; all seven of the superuniverses and all regions of outer space revolve in established orbits around the gigantic central aggregation of the Paradise satellites and the Havona spheres." (129) It contains one billion worlds of unimaginable beauty and "superb grandeur" that are settled, perfect and established. The layout of the worlds is in seven concentric circles that surround the three Paradise satellite circuits. We evolve through these worlds with definite goals of intellectual, spiritual, and experimental achievements. It is part of our universe schooling—study worlds. We are told that each of the worlds on Havona is an original and unique creation that contains a variety of surprises for us mortals. "Havona is the pre-Paradise training goal of every ascending mortal, the portal to Paradise and God attainment" (140, 152–63).

The Seven Superuniverses—Are the seven superuniverses of creation, a giant ellipse that swings around the central universe, Havona. They are organized, and each location and number of every inhabited world is known and ministered to lovingly by a multitude of spiritual beings. There are superuniverse circuits and local universe circuits that serve as the two energy-circuit divisions. When a local universe gains enough spiritual harmony, physical stability and spiritual loyalty, it becomes settled in light and life and may be eligible for admission into the "spiritual confederation of the perfected union of the supercreation" (164). Each one of the seven superuniverses has a special function and a unique nature. Earth, Urantia, is part of the seventh superuniverse, known as Orvonton. *The Urantia Book* explains that Earth is planet number 606 of 619 in the Satania system. "Your planet is a member of an enormous cosmos; you belong to a well-nigh infinite family of worlds, but your sphere is just as precisely ministered and just as lovingly fostered as if it were the only inhabited world in all existence" (182–83).

The Corps of Finality—Is the spiritual destiny of human beings. The corps are made of "perfected and ascendant beings of time and space," who will have as yet unrevealed opportunities for universe service. "Evolutionary mortals are born on the planets of space, pass through the morontia worlds, ascend the spirit universes, traverse the Havona spheres, find God, attain Paradise, and are mustered into the primary Corps of the Finality, therein to await the next assignment of universe service. The author of this paper, a Divine Counselor and One without Name and Number, tell us we are free to theorize with them the mystery of our ultimate destiny of the Paradise Corps of Finality.

## Part II. The Local Universe

*Evolution of Local Universe*—The local universe is the creation of a Creator Son of the Paradise order of Michael. This series of twenty-four papers was "sponsored" by a Nebadon Corps of Local Universe personalities acting under the authority of Gabriel of Salvington. All these beings are of local universe origin. The local universe contains one hundred constellations and one hundred systems of inhabited worlds. The local universe is evolutionary in physical, intellectual and spiritual natures. Even though this universe was created and is administered by Michael and his assistants, God is actively present through his ordained agencies and personalities.

> There is great and glorious purpose in the march of the universes through space. All your mortal struggling is not in vain. We are all part of an immense plan, a gigantic enterprise, and it is the vastness

of the undertaking that renders it impossible to see very much of it at any one time and during any one life. We are all part of an eternal project which the Gods are supervising and outworking. The whole marvelous and universal mechanism moves on majestically  ·  through space to the music of the meter of the infinite thought and the eternal purpose of the First Great Source and Center (364).

*The Life Carriers*—Life does not appear spontaneously in the universes. The vital spark of life is bestowed through the Life Carriers, not by them. The Universe Mother Spirit supplies the essential factor of the living life plasm. The Life Carriers design and carry life to the planets, implant it, and foster its development. Life Carriers are a type of Universe Son. "They are the carriers, disseminators, and guardians of life as it appears on the evolutionary worlds of time and space" (399).

*The Ministering Spirits of the Local Universe*—The seraphim are the angelic corps of a local universe. The Universe Mother Spirit creates seraphim in pairs who will work together. They do not have bodies—they are of spirit nature and origin. Seraphim are described as being a trifle ahead of human beings in the scale of creature existence in nature and personality endowment. One of their purposes is to serve as guardians of destiny. As mortals evolve seraphim are assigned in accordance to the intellectual and spiritual nature of the individual. Once assigned, they serve for the rest of the mortal's life. Angels work in the social, ethical, and moral environments to assist human beings in ascending spiritually. Seraphim function as teachers by urging the mortal mind into paths of new and progressive experiences. They do not manipulate. Angels respect the dignity of the human personality and act to make the best possible use of the course chosen (418-425, 1245-1246).

*The Lucifer Rebellion*—Lucifer was a created being—a Lanonandek Son of Nebadon. Considered one of the most brilliant personalities of his kind. He succumbed to the urge of self rebelled against the divine plan. Lucifer wrote a manifesto declaring that God did not exist, that the local universe should be autonomous instead of Michael acting as the sovereign leader; and argued against training mortals in the principals of universe administration because they were unsound. The Lucifer Rebellion caused many other worlds to rebel with him and Satan. The arch-rebels were removed of administrative authority but were not adjudicated until Jesus came to Earth on his bestowal mission over 2000 years ago (601-612).

*The Seven Mansion Worlds*—The seven satellites of world number one in Jerusem (headquarters of Satania, our local universe). These seven worlds are where mortals go after they die to resume their lives just as they were before death. The journey begins on the first mansion world where mortals are resurrected in a new body with the "mortal-mind transcripts," and "active creature-memory patterns" become spiritualized and the transition toward Paradise continues. The mansion worlds are where mortal survivors transition into higher spiritual attainment or a true Paradise ascender (530-540).

*The Morontia Life*—Morontia is a level of existence (or a condition) between the material and the spiritual. *The Urantia Book* proposes that after humans die they don't just enjoy endless bliss and eternal ease. The goal of transcendence is achieved by evolving through a series of worlds where we have the opportunity to grow spiritually. "The mortal-survival plan has a practical and serviceable objective; you are not the recipients of all this divine labor and painstaking training only that you may survive just to enjoy endless bliss and eternal ease. There is a goal of transcendent service concealed beyond the horizon of the present universe age. If the Gods designed merely to take you on one long and eternal joy excursion, they certainly would not so largely turn the whole universe into one vast and intricate practical training school, requisition a substantial part of the celestial creation as teachers and instructors, and then spend ages upon ages piloting you, one by one, through this gigantic universe school of experiential training" (558). Morontia Life is what life on the seven mansion worlds is called. Human beings evolve ever higher by making spiritually fruitful decisions which grow their soul. Morontia Life is "one of the stages of their agelong progress from animal to angel and from angel to spirit and from spirit to God" (558). Mortals assume a morontia body when they wake up on the mansion worlds. Jesus' resurrected body was a morontia body.

## Part III. The History of Urantia

Part III tells of the origin of Earth, Urantia; the evolution of animals, plants, and human beings; Adam and Eve and their default; government, marriage and religion; how seraphim (angels) act as guardians of destiny; and explains God the Supreme. The papers in Part III have a broad subject matter that reflects the science of the early twentieth century.

*Colored Races*—*The Urantia Book* describes the evolutionary races of Earth in terms that reflect the thinking of the early twentieth century. It describes many peoples who lived on Earth until the six Sangik races emerged in one family five hundred thousand years ago. The races are named: red, orange, yellow, green, blue and indigo. The story describes migration of these racial groups migrated and their characteristics. Although *The Urantia Book* makes it clear that all people are equal spiritually, it does point out many negatives about the defective and degenerate strains in all the races.

*Adam and Eve*—In current biblical scholarship, the story of Adam and Eve is considered folklore. Contemporary liberal theologians refer to the story as not being historical fact but a method to present spiritual truths. Adams and Eves, in *The Urantia Book,* represent an order of superhuman beings designed as "biologic uplifters" to the human race. When a planet evolves to the point where natural evolutionary tendencies have stagnated, an Adam and Eve is sent from the local universe to bring new, higher genetic blood strains into the indigenous people. "The Material Sons and Daughters always serve together. It is the essence of their service at all times and in all places never to be separated. They are designed to work in pairs; seldom do they function alone." (828) The overall plan is for the Adam and Eve to have many children of their own and that then these pure "Adamites" mate with the local inhabitants to bring superior evolutionary traits, such as greater disease resistance. *The Urantia Book* describes Adam and Eve as vegetarian, having bodies that shimmered in the sunlight (this is how the concept of halos originated), eight feet tall, and with superior eyesight and senses. They were able to see the angelic hosts and other orders of beings on the planet. They were to reproduce their own kind until their numbers were around a million before bestowing themselves on the evolutionary peoples, but they defaulted. Eve grew impatient with the progress of their mission and had a child with the leader of one of the more advanced races, hoping thereby to hasten their task by prematurely giving the world a line of Adamic blood. Adam, despondent, chose to share Eve's fate and did the same with a woman who bore him an Adamic child. The Melchizedeks stopped the enterprise because Adam and Eve erred by deviating from the divine plan (850-851).

*Religion*—The definition of religion in *The Urantia Book* is a human being's personal relationship with God. Religion is man's liberator:

> The purpose of religion is not to satisfy curiosity about God but rather to afford intellectual constancy and philosophic security, to stabilize and enrich human living by blending the mortal with the divine, the partial with the perfect, man and God. It is through religious experience that man's concepts of ideality are endowed with reality (1116).

Bill's description of his experience of God:

> Listen, even in this life, you can get a feeling for it, you know? I live with a feeling of the flavor of God. Not having been raised in a church, I may impress you characters as being a very un-pious guy. It's simply because my experience with God doesn't happen to flow in normal channels. I can taste the Universal Father. And,

to me, that's a very ordinary thing. And it amazes me that most people don't have this flavor. But, to me, that's just as common and ordinary a thing as the fact that I can feel gravity acting on the mass of my body to give me the feeling of weight. You know? Just as ordinary. To me, God is just as plain and simple as dried apples and rainwater. And why make a big fuss about it? This is a normal, natural human experience. And I'm continually surprised when I find lots of people say they don't have this experience.

Now, if no other human being agreed with me, I would decide I was paranoid, but I wouldn't change my conviction. I can't. I got that feeling before I ever read these papers. And I got it just before I was introduced to them.

One day I sat down and wrote my mother a long letter, asking her what she and father believed. And when I started that letter, I wasn't sure; and when I finished that letter, I knew, and I've known ever since. And I didn't have any cold sweat or anything else. I can't tell you at what point in writing the letter I discovered that I knew. It was a very common discovery, completely free from emotion.

This realization was not born during the simple writing of that letter. I discovered it. There had been a-borning I suspect for about a year before then.[10]

_The Thought Adjusters_—These are the fragments of God that lives within human minds:

> The Adjusters are the actuality of the Father's love incarnate in the souls of men; they are the veritable promise of man's eternal career imprisoned within the mortal mind; they are the essence of man's perfected finaliter personality, which he can foretaste in time as he progressively masters the divine technique of achieving the living of the Father's will, step by step, through the ascension of universe upon universe until he actually attains the divine presence of his Paradise Father. (1176)

Thought Adjusters constantly communicate to their mortal charges to evolve through enlightened thinking and action. They don't speak per se, in fact, _The Urantia Book_ advises that we are unable to distinguish between the Thought Adjuster's communications and our own intellect until we are more spiritually advanced. They are always near to mortals. They do not speak directly to us; they assist us in spiritualizing our minds with "picturizations of destiny" that become more vivid as we ascend heavenward. Once people achieve the requisite cosmic growth they "fuse" with their Thought Adjuster and attain immortality (1203–14). Sadler wrote that "The Adjusters are on loan for the time being—but it is intended that they become 'one with us.'" (26.5) Bill spoke about his relationship with his Thought Adjuster this way:

> I'm interested in getting as much help from my partner [Thought Adjuster] as I can. I feel rather diffident about discussing my problems with an infinite God, even though in my mind and heart I know he's got all the time in the world for me. But somehow it seems presumptuous. He's running a big universe. And it seems to me that there are so many other things that he could more profitably spend his time on.
>
> But I don't feel this way about this Thought Adjuster. Because this Thought Adjuster is God individuated for me. And I am his business. For this particular assignment, I am his principal concern. He may have some peripheral activities going on, but they're definitely secondary to me. Just as you are primary to the function of your Thought Adjuster.
>
> I have no hesitancy about discussing anything with this Thought Adjuster. I have a feeling of comradeship for him. And let me explain. I've never heard him say anything to me. If I ever did, it would probably scare me quite out of my wits, and I would immediately feel this is paranoia, you know? And I would put the whole thing on ice and think about it for quite a number of weeks or months, until my human judgment could evaluate it, or until a little time passed.
>
> And yet I've never doubted that this is a dialogue. It's a dialogue between two conscious beings, one of whom is deaf. I can talk, but I can't hear. And I don't let my deafness impair my faith in the least. I keep asking my partner for help in certain directions: How can I be more useful? How can we do a better job about coping with my ego? This belligerent self that I'm not sure I've conquered at all. And if I were sure, then I'd be afraid of that concept, too—I'd fear this was spiritual pride, you know, which goeth before a hell of a crash.
>
> I try to tell my partner about what life is like down here. There's a whole lot that he doesn't get out of this world, because he doesn't have eyes, you know? He doesn't have ears. He has a sensory mechanism, but it's quite different from mine. I know he's trying to tell me

about Paradise. I tell him about this world—what it means to me.

When we go to a new city, I kinda let him see the city through my eyes. We talk about this. I probably spend more time talking to him in the privy than any other single place on earth, because there's the one place I'm sure to be alone. It's when I occasionally ride trains—in the bedroom—one is alone. But that's not just because I love my Thought Adjuster. I happen to be a creature who needs periodic solitude. This is temperamental.

I think if I'm going to be able to live more of this, he's got to help me. He's got to help me be less of a mammal, and more human. The heck with being more spiritual. This is for the future. I'm content if I can just become less mammalian, and more human. I'm not trying to be a frog. I can think about frogdom, but I'm a tadpole now. I'm not trying to get out on dry land, I wouldn't live. I've got to live in water. I'll wake up on dry land.

I ask my partner, "How can I be of more service?" Because in my religion, there's none of this. My religion is very, very simple. Somewhere, at the center of all things, is the boss. And these odd critters I bump into down here on earth are the boss's kids. And they should be treated accordingly. That's my religion. I can say it in three sentences. My partner's interested in this, because he comes from the boss. He understands that these are the boss's kids, and I'm sure he'll help me in every way he can. I have no doubts about this.

The thing that dismays me is my own inconstancy. This mammalian inertia. Not that I do evil or sinful things, but I don't do enough. It's not that I dwell on sinful thoughts, but that I forget to deal with the Boss and my Partner. Yet, the book tells me that God can look on the inside of me and see that dismaying and dismal picture which I know about, and he still loves me.[11]

*Personality Survival*—Earth is where the divine adventure begins. With a Thought Adjuster as a guide, mortals evolve through successive stages of growth until they fuse with their Thought Adjuster and become immortal. Personality is bestowed upon human beings as a potentially eternal gift from God. It is changeless. As mortals evolve it helps unify the changing realities they experience and helps coordinate all relationships. Here is an excerpt of how Bill described the journey after mortal death:

You know, this isn't going to be quite as bad as you think.

When you fuse with your Thought Adjuster, one of the contributions which the Adjuster will make to the new being is past-eternal memory. Now, I don't believe that your human consciousness will be able to absorb that past-eternal memory beyond the limits of achieved comprehension.

*Audience:* Will it vary with the individual?

I think it will vary with your life span. In other words, when you have lived on the mansion worlds ten thousand years, the Adjuster will be able meaningfully to communicate to you ten thousand years worth of past time. And when you have lived a billion years, the Adjuster will be able to communicate to you in those terms. And when you have lived a trillion, trillion years, you'll be able to go quite a ways back. I've got an absonite (level of reality closer to God) number very handy. This is a second floor number.

When you have lived a jillion years, the Adjuster will be able to do quite a lot with you. Do you follow me? If your soul were mature, you wouldn't wake up on the mansion worlds, because these are incubating worlds, designed to do for premature souls just what an incubation job does for a premature birth in a hospital. Let's go back to resurrection morn. And let's take inventory of precisely what happens. Let's say that—to simplify matters—let's say that you have a personal seraphim, so you make it on the third day. I just don't want to have to deal with a mass of people, see? And you are waking up in one of the private resurrection rooms off the main amphitheaters. And they are getting ready for you; they got three days' warning. So the proper authorities go over to the morontia quartermaster department, and they draw out of issue one standard GI form, first stage morontia, suitable for the type of being that you were.

*God the Supreme*—This is the aspect of God that operates on the experiential worlds of time and space, such as Earth. The Supreme is the avenue on which God's love outflows to all creation. God the Supreme is the catalyzer and focus for all human growth—it pours understanding and insight to a creature's limit to help it connect with eternity. As Jesus was a living channel from humanity to divinity because he personally experienced the complete universe path of progression, the Supreme Being functions as the "actual embodiment and personal epitome of all creature evolution, progression, and spiritualization" (1281). Mortals grow from a material creature to a spiritual one through the strength, power, and persistence of their own decisions and as their Thought Adjuster reaches down to assist the soul in its growth. The Supreme expands as his mortal children evolve—human beings are partners with this aspect of Deity because they are co-creators in the Supreme's immortalization (1282).

## Part IV. The Life and Teachings of Jesus

This part describes Jesus as a Creator Son known as Michael of Nebadon, one of a series of beings who bestow themselves in the universes of time and space to earn their sovereignty over their own (self-created) part of the universe. This bestowal experience helps them become intelligent, understanding and wise leaders of their own universes. Jesus coming to Earth was his last—seventh—bestowal. In 1935, a commission of twelve Urantia midwayers sponsored this series of seventy-seven papers. The introduction to the Jesus papers, as they are known, describes the source of this narrative as a secondary midwayer who was assigned to the superhuman watchcare of the apostle Andrew.

*The Urantia Book* is consistent with biblical theology in that they both maintain the importance of the spiritual realities of love, faith, and eternal life. However, *The Urantia Book* goes beyond what the Bible offers in how it details Jesus' life year by year, in the intricacies about the eternal career of human beings, and the spiritual and biologic life on Earth. Life in this universe consists of interlocking activities between celestial beings and divine spirits who labor to honor God and to help his humans advance to higher spiritual realities (54). Divine truth is living, expanding and always growing to assist mortals on their survival of life after death.

*The Atonement Doctrine*—The atonement doctrine, the text asserts, is an insult to Deity. It is rejected because it misrepresents God's love for his children. God would never require the sacrifice of Jesus to heal the sin of Adam and place humankind back into grace. It was evil men, not our Heavenly Father, who crucified Jesus. Even if God was a stern monarch, he would never be satisfied with the childish scheme of substituting one innocent sufferer for a guilty offender. The whole concept of ransom and atonement is incompatible with the teachings of Jesus. Jesus taught that God is a true and loving Father, not an offended monarch who delights in punishing his children. The crucifixion does have some positive significance because his death greatly illuminated the path to salvation for the whole universe, not just those on earth. The cross stands for sacred service to yourself and the welfare and salvation of your fellows. *The Urantia Book* suggests that we look at the cross as the final manifestation of the love and devotion of Jesus to his life's mission—to stimulate our realization of God's eternal love and his Son's unending mercy—across the universes of time and space (2017–19).

*Original Sin*—Original sin is rejected. The definition of sin in the book is "a purposeful resistance to divine reality—the conscious choosing to oppose spiritual progress—while iniquity consists in an open and persistent defiance of recognized reality and signifies such a degree of personality disintegration as to border on cosmic insanity" (754). In other words, when we make a spiritually fragrant decision—choosing to be unselfish—we grow our soul. If we repeatedly make decisions that violate the loving nature of the universe than we don't grow our souls. *The Urantia Book* affirms that Jesus' attitude toward sinners was one of eternal and loving salvation not condemnation. "Love is truly contagious and eternally creative" (2018). Jesus went beyond a higher quality of justice to prove that "divine love does not merely forgive wrongs; it absorbs and actually destroys them" (1746). True love destroys hate. For Jesus taught that God's love is rehabilitation—eternal survival.

*The Twelve Apostles*—The complete history of the twelve is written. *The Urantia Book* greatly expands upon what is revealed in the Bible in Matthew 10:2–4; Mark 3:13–19; and Luke 6:12–16. The apostles were laymen. They had not been to rabbinical school nor had they had what we could call higher education but they had enjoyed separate experiences on how to live. *The Urantia Book* describes each apostle individually and in great depth. Sadler was quoted as saying the descriptions of the apostles were what made him believe *The Urantia Book* was a revelation.

*Nature of the Resurrection*—After Jesus was entombed the chief of the archangels on Earth summoned the council of the resurrection of sleeping humans to see if they could restore Jesus to life. They realized that they did not have the power to resurrect him. As a Creator Son he had laid down his life and would pick it up again when he made that choice to do so. Jesus came forth from the tomb in his morontia (in between material and spiritual) body. His body of flesh remained in the tomb. His morontia body was just like ours will be when they are resurrected on the mansion worlds. Morontia bodies do not have blood that circulates and do not partake of ordinary material food—but they are real (2029). The celestial hosts then disposed of his Earth body by accelerating time to have the body of Jesus return to dust sooner. So when the Bible reports that the tomb was empty it was because of the special dissolution by the celestial hosts. Jesus appeared to others in this morontia body. His first appearance was to Mary and the women who went to the tomb to anoint his body with embalming lotion. The tomb was empty, and as the women sat down outside the tomb puzzling at the missing body, Jesus appeared. The morontia body is quite different from a human body so the women did not recognize him at first. But when he spoke to Mary, she immediately knew it was Jesus' voice. The book informs the reader that the women could see Jesus with their mortal eyes in this spiritualized state because of the work of the transformers and the midwayers (2020-2028).

*The Urantia Book* restates that the power that Jesus has—to endow life—was what allowed him to rise from the dead and it is the same as the gift of eternal life that he bestows on believers. Human beings will arise on the mansion worlds in a new body in the same way Jesus did on Earth. Jesus made nineteen morontia appearances on Earth before he ascended to Edentia (2029–58). It is noted that as Jesus ascended to the Father his apostles gradually started to change his message. Instead of the religion *of* Jesus they certainly changed it into a form of religion *about* Jesus (2051).

*Pentecost*—The Spirit of Truth arrived as Jesus had promised after he ascended. It brought the believers a new sense of spiritual joy, security and confidence. It was a new consciousness of spiritual strength. This new bestowal of the Son's spirit in the form of the Spirit of Truth made certain that all normal human beings would be able to accept a Thought Adjuster. In this manifestation it helps mortals have an enhanced fellowship with Jesus, helps people understand Jesus' message as well as to "illuminate and reinterpret his life on Earth." The Spirit of Truth is bestowed to "lead all believers into all truth, into the expanding knowledge of the experience of the living and growing spiritual consciousness of the reality of eternal and ascending sonship with God" (2061).

"The first mission of this spirit is, of course, to foster and personalize truth, for it is the comprehension of truth that constitutes the highest form of human liberty. Next, it is the purpose of this spirit to destroy the believer's feeling of orphanhood. Jesus having been among men, all believers would experience a sense of loneliness had not the Spirit of Truth come to dwell in men's hearts" (2060).

In Paper 194, the book informs that the apostles in their joy after the Spirit of Truth was bestowed, focused on the fact of Jesus' resurrection—not on his message. In this they stumbled into an error of substituting some of the facts of the gospel for the gospel message itself. *The Urantia Book* affirms that Jesus' message is: "The fact of the Fatherhood of God, coupled with the resultant truth of the sonship-brotherhood of men. Christianity, as it is developed from that day, is the fact of God as the Father of the Lord Jesus Christ, in association with the experience of believer-fellowship with the risen and glorified Christ" (2059). They began to preach a new gospel about Jesus in place of the former message of the Fatherhood of God and the brotherhood of man.

*Faith of Jesus*—The last chapter of *The Urantia Book* describes Jesus as a man with a "sublime and wholehearted faith in God," who experienced ups and downs but never doubted God's watchcare and guidance. This faith was not "traditional or merely intellectual," it was "personal and purely spiritual." Jesus did not originate the idea of God as a Father, but he did achieve a new revelation by stating that every mortal creature is a child of this Father of love, a son of God (2087).

Jesus did not cling to faith in God as would a struggling soul at war with the universe and at death grips with a hostile and sinful world; he did not resort to faith merely as a consolation in the midst of difficulties or as a comfort in threatened despair; faith was not just an illusory compensation for the unpleasant realities and the sorrows of living. In the very face of all the natural difficulties and temporal contradictions of mortal existence, he experienced the tranquility of supreme and unquestioned trust in God and felt the tremendous thrill of living, by faith, in the very presence of the heavenly Father. And this triumphant faith was a living experience of actual spirit attainment. Jesus' great contribution to the values of human experience was not that he revealed so many new ideas about the Father in heaven, but rather that he so magnificently and humanly demonstrated a new and higher type of living faith in God. Never on all the worlds of this universe, in the life of one mortal, did God ever become such a living reality as in the human experience of Jesus of Nazareth (2087).

*The Urantia Book* is vastly more detailed about Jesus' life than the New Testament. The New Testament describes twenty-nine days in Jesus' life. *The Urantia Book* dedicates 689 pages to his year-to-year activities for all of his thirty-six years.[12] As in the Bible, the Jesus of *The Urantia Book* is both human and divine and serves as a mediator between human beings and God. The book explains that we have mistakenly assumed that Jesus was the Second Person of Trinity. The reality of the situation is much more complex. At the dawn of eternity the Isle of Paradise and the Central Universe were created along with a plan for finite evolutionary worlds within their own local universes. The Universal Father (God) and the Eternal Son originated an order of Michael Sons—Creator Sons—(of which Jesus was one) who would create this own universe such as the Milky Way. Michael, according to *The Urantia Book*, coming to Earth as Jesus, is both the creator and savior of our own part of the universe.

In the prologue of John, Paul in Col. 15–16, and the writer of Hebrews 1:2 noted that Jesus was a creator. Although this statement puzzled theologians, *The Urantia Book* authors expand that concept in a detailed manner. All of these Creator Sons are unique beings in their nature and personalities. Each of them is considered the "only begotten Son" of their universe. The book describes Jesus as the local universe personification of the Universal Father and the Eternal Son in his own universe. As with the biblical Jesus, *The Urantia Book* Jesus brings mortals up to the Father through his benevolent ministry. This is reflected in the Bible in John 12:32, "I, when I am lifted up from the Earth, will draw all men to myself." In both the Bible and *The Urantia Book*, the Spirit of Truth is bestowed on the planet after Jesus ascends to heaven.

*The Urantia Book* also takes leave of the Bible in the areas of scriptural infallibility. The attitude of *The Urantia Book* is that all things that pass through human minds cannot be the Final Truth. It makes no claims of infallibility—in fact it states that it is not inspired and that much of the science contained in the book will be outmoded. It came from God in that it brings new revelational truth but that revelation only becomes complete when mortals achieve the Father, because the Father is the source of all truth. *The Urantia Book* asks its readers to honor the sacred texts of all religions because all contain truth but at the same time to understand that the truth they contain is only partial. God is the source of truth, not a book, because it can only serve as a road map to truth—it is not the truth.

*Eternal Life*—Salvation is not when you die on Earth and wake up in heaven as a full-fledged spiritual being. Instead, the plan for mortal attainment of eternal life is a vast scheme of universe education. Humans ascend toward Paradise—the goal of destiny for all spirit personalities—by growing spiritually through a succession of worlds where they become less material and more spiritual by their decisions. All people who know God and choose to do the Father's will have embarked on the journey to Paradise. The journey is portrayed as "an endless unfolding of an almost infinite panorama" of "exhilarating service, matchless adventure, sublime uncertainty, and boundless attainment" (1194). The adventures ascending humans will experience will be based upon their own choices. The possibilities as hinted at in *The Urantia Book* appear to be unlimited—what your soul desires will be experienced.

Another theme running throughout *The Urantia Book* is the importance of service to one's fellows. Bill explained service this way during one of his lectures:

> I read this book, of course I want to read it all, but I want to live it. I don't want just the words just to come in and know it intellectually. I want to live it. How? How do you start? It's a very good question. I think you—I think you—I can't speak for anybody but myself. This is too intimate. What in essence you have asked me is, "What is your religion—not your theology or philosophy?"
>
> I think there is a possibility of developing, from this blue book, a religion the like of which this world has never yet seen. A religion that's full of good humor. A religion which is full of the joy of existence. A religion which is totally devoid of fear on the theological or spiritual nature.
>
> A religion which people wear casually and yet earnestly. A religion which is gracious in its tolerance, in its leashed strength. A religion

which has nothing to do with any one day of a week. A religion which pervades the whole of a human life, twenty-four hours a day. A religion which is dealt with in a familiar, friendly way. A religion which is a part of a human being.

A religion which is inseparable from philosophy, from ethics, from morality, from economics, from political thinking, and everything else. A religion which seeps down through all the levels of a human personality until it becomes indistinguishable from the whole social fragrance of that human being.

This, to me, is religion which appeals. And this, to me, is a religion which you don't find very much of in human history.

This is a religion which you're good-natured about. This is a religion where you don't pick it up gingerly, you know. You breathe it, like you breathe air. You drink it like you drink water. It's a normal part of living. It's real. It's not something that's dissociated, compartmentalized, or set off. It's something which your—it's so much a part of your life that you're casual with it. It's a familiar thing. You're casual with it like you're casual with clothing that's well broken in—an old suit of tweeds. It's a friendly, familiar, warm thing. It's nothing which you feel either ashamed of or heroic about. It's something which you just are.

The text of *The Urantia Book* is comprehensive, detailed, internally consistent, and edifying to believers. It proclaims that it is the fifth epochal revelation of truth to our world. It describes a friendly universe created by God who is also a loving Father, with whom we can have a personal relationship now and in eternity. The book urges and encourages us to seek truth wherever it may lead us. "Truth is relative and expanding; it lives always in the present, achieving new expression in each generation of men—even in each human life" (757).

I personally found my spiritual world was briefly turned upside down by my research discoveries for this book. As Rufus Jones stated in his 1904 book, "There are few crises to compare with that which appears when the simple, childhood religion, imbibed at mother's knee and absorbed from early home and church environment, comes into collision with a scientific, solidly reasoned system. However after thinking it through I came to a place where I understand that facts are different than truth. Sacred texts are not history books; they are books of faith. Facts have no quarrel with faith. Faith is a confidence in the validity of a spiritual consciousness. For me it is the most powerful method for living a life of buoyancy. After all, facts don't have a quarrel with religious faith as theories do. If the religious value of a text is dependent on it being factually correct, then it has little value. But if readers find that the book's teachings lead them to a place of greater spiritual insight then its value is immeasurable."[13]

Two important elements that *The Urantia Book* shares with other sacred texts from the Bible to the Koran are, first, it seeks to re-enchant its readers and bring them back onto their own spiritual path through its teachings; and second, the achievement of authority and authenticity comes from a creative figure, in this case a group of celestial beings that spoke through a human channel. *The Urantia Book* differs from other sacred texts in several meaningful ways as well. First, it claims celestial authorship rather than inspiration from an angelic being or God. Second, it was written over a period of two decades with hundreds of people asking questions of a group of celestial beings rather than being channeled by a person in a shorter period of time or written by a multitude of human authors over centuries. Third, the people behind its writing never sought any financial gain or fame from doing so. Fourth, there is no authoritative body supporting an Urantian religion based upon the teachings of the book. *The Urantia Book* neither favors nor desires an organized religion. Instead it calls upon its readers to have a religion based upon their personal relationship with God:

> The purpose of religion is not to satisfy curiosity about God but rather to afford intellectual constancy and philosophic security, to stabilize and enrich human living by blending the mortal with the divine, the partial with the perfect, man and God. It is through religious experience that man's concepts of ideality are endowed with reality. (1116).

In one of his lectures about spreading *The Urantia Book*, Bill described how to be useful to one's fellow man:

> This book is not religion. This book is a cosmology, a philosophy, a metaphysics, a theology. Anything which is in written language is not religion. It's intellectual. That should be very, very clear.
>
> But this book is attempting to make an intellectual approach, a philosophic approach, to the religious nature of man. And if you encounter a person who is not philosophical, don't rub his nose in Part One of this book, and the Foreword, and everything else. Give him the spiritual heart of this book. I don't think he has to know anything about the Trinity of Trinities to qualify for the first mansion world. It says you have to accept sonship with God, that's all.
>
> But there are a lot of people who are curious. I am. As the papers point out, one of the things that's wrong with Christianity is

that—from a philosophical standpoint—it's a pretty sterile religion. Pretty sterile. You want to know something? Mahayana Buddhism offers a great deal to a thinking God-seeker which Christianity does not offer. It's a much broader religion, with a richer philosophy.

Arnold Toynbee well says that the two best religions on earth today are Christianity and the Mahayana form of Buddhism. And I think he's very discerning when he further says, in his judgment, neither of them are good enough.

If you find a person who is hungry to understand more about the universe, to take the findings of science and attempt to reconcile them with the spiritual longings of his heart—and this is the function of philosophy—then you better either know this book and be able to discuss it with him, or pass him on to one of your philosophic-minded colleagues who can do this.[14]

The origin story of *The Urantia Book*—how it came to be—echoes both terrestrial and eternal realities of other sacred texts. It is a story of how humans seek to illuminate the larger mysteries of the universe to better understand the reason for their lives. The pattern for most religious texts is that they claim a supernatural origin that scholars later discover to be grounded more in myth than in fact. For example, in the later nineteenth century, critical studies of the Bible became the genesis for Christianity to divide itself into liberal, conservative, and fundamentalist camps. This was because nineteenth-century science declared that many of the Bible's descriptions of the physical world were false. The Bible described grass, land plants, and trees as being created before the sun. We know that this is not possible. As this debate raged, Christian scholars had to decide how to interpret the Bible based upon what they believed. How should they explain these discrepancies to the laity? Was the Bible infallible or not? These questions led liberal religionists to appreciate the fact that symbolic language in the Bible can represent spiritual truths, while at the same time the text is full of science "stories." The same can be said of *The Urantia Book*. It is a text that is filled with stories that reveal new spiritual truth but as with earlier sacred texts, it relies on myth to teach while reflecting the era in which it was written. *The Urantia Book*, because of the breadth and depth of its teachings, remains an unparalleled religious achievement in the 20th century.

---

[1] *The Urantia Book*, 1008

[2] All page number references are from *The Urantia Book*. The previous four epochal revelations are found on page 1007: (1) the Dalamatian Teachings: Prince Caligastia's staff revealed the true concept of the First Source and Center; (2) the Edenic Teachings, Adam and Eve portrayed the Father of all to the evolutionary peoples; (3)

Melchizedek of Salem, an emergency Son of Nebadon who taught the cardinal precepts of trust and faith; and (4) Jesus of Nazareth, the essence of his teachings were love and service.

3  http://www.urantia.org/bible-study/1-bible-authority-and-significance

4  http://www.urantia.org/bible-study/5-interpretation-bible

5  See Amazon.com reviews, http://www.amazon.co.uk/Urantia-Book-Foundation/dp/0911560513

6  "*The Urantia Book*," Let Us Reason Ministries, 2009, http://www.letusreason.org/Cults17.htm

7  William Sadler, "Consideration of Some Criticisms," 14.

8  *The Urantia Book* Workbook, Foreword and Part I, 27

9  http://urantiabook.org/archive/readers/doc611.htm

10  http://urantiabook.org/archive/readers/doc701.htm

11  http://urantiabook.org/archive/readers/doc714.htm

12  Much of the information in this section comes from Meredith's Sprunger's essay "Urantia Book Deviations from Traditional Christian Beliefs" (http://www.urantiabook.org/introductions/urantia-book-differences.htm).

13  Jones, Social Law.

14  http://urantiabook.org/archive/readers/doc713.htm

# 9

———◄•►———

# THE ARCHITECTURE OF REVELATION

*On the majority of occasions when I am dictating, the ideas seem to be
all fully formulated in my mind. I visualize the material in paragraphs,
with all the punctuation clearly recognized. In the majority of instances,
when I am dictating to my secretary, as I have often expressed it, I am
merely redictating what I see passing before my own eyes, as I would
look upon the titles of a moving picture flashed upon the screen.*

*My experience in writing is sometimes so marked in this respect
that I could easily be persuaded that I was under the control of some
external power, that my mind was being used by another author, and
I am sure that if I were a devotee of spiritism, I could even persuade
myself that much that I write is indited by spirits separate and apart
from my own mind and body.*

—Sadler, *The Mind at Mischief*

S CHOLARS JAMES R. LEWIS AND OLAV HAMMER study the how the
beliefs and practices of sacred traditions have been handed down through the
generations. In their book of essays, *The Invention of Sacred Tradition*, they note one of
the perennial aspects of religious history is the pattern of the invention of the world's
religious traditions. This means that what religions claim doesn't necessarily overlap
with documented historical evidence. Many religious followers understand their
history based upon texts that scholars have proven to have misattributed authorship.
The Hebrew Bible and the New Testament contain largely spurious attributions of

authorship—defined as meaning the real authors are not the ones listed in the text. Lewis and Hammer draw the distinction between transcendent origins and human transmission of texts to be roughly analogous to that between myth and history.[1]

Lewis and Hammer depict that scholars who study sacred texts portray their authorship in three major ways. One is pseudepigraphic, which describes a book written by someone who attributes it to another person. Mahayana Buddhist texts are an example of this form because they put words into the mouth of the historical Buddha. The second type is anonymous. It begins with a text at the first stage of transmission and later the writings are misattributed to a well-known writer. An example of this second type would be several medieval texts by unknown authors that were later attributed to Aristotle. This went on for centuries because translators and commentators stated that these were in fact part of his writings. The third form is the spiritual texts attributed to people who never existed. An example of this form of authorship is Hermes Trismegistus, a pagan theologian who lived at the time of Moses. His stature during his era was influential in that the documents he authored served to legitimate magic and other religious practices long after scholars proved without a doubt his existence was entirely fictive.[2]

The Bible has several examples of these types of authorship. Einar Thomassen in his essay pointed out that out of the twenty-seven writings that became the New Testament only seven are unanimously accepted by scholars to have been authored by the name of the original author. There are also instances of pseudepigraphy where books were deliberately written in someone else's name. This is due to the fact that special authority was given to texts written by those who were closely associated with the charismatic leader. This is the reason why many of the authors listed in the New Testament are considered those closest to Jesus.[3]

Lewis and Hammer's examination of sacred traditions affirm that nearly every religion has spurious traditions and misattributed texts. They believe this happens because naming certain authors can confer greater legitimacy to the religions' claims and practices in a text. Newly emerging religious traditions typically have a charismatic figure at their center. Scholars Lewis and Hammer attribute this phenomenon to early followers that members of this new religion who witness the astounding feats of their living leader. When the charismatic leader dies, a new leader must emerge who continues the traditions and charismatic leadership evidenced by the original leader. If a new charismatic leader does not emerge then that power needs to be transferred to another medium for the religious movement to continue to exist. Typically this transfer is to tangible signs such as the founder's image, to a place the leader visited, or to the works they composed.[4]

*The Urantia Book* is quite unique in the tradition of sacred texts. Scholar Sarah Lewis noted in her essay, "The Peculiar Sleep: Receiving *The Urantia Book*," that the text is not the result of a previous lost tradition, nor does it claim that the material resulted from any great figure in history. Instead *The Urantia Book* claims that it was indited by higher beings through a human subject. Lewis lists six possible benefits to keeping the identity of the human channel of *The Urantia Book* secret. First, she argued that naming the channel would have provided critics the opportunity to discredit the individual who served as the channel. Since the book was not attributed to a person it could not suffer from an unfavorable review of the human channel. Second, divine authorship holds within it the fact that celestials do not make errors, in which case the book could stand as being infallible—which it doesn't. Third, since leaders, or prophets, of new religious movements tend to be controversial this can overshadow their message. Fourth, Lewis stated that a leader, like Sadler, would want to avoid being the focus of attention because this would help the revelation stand on its own. Fifth, the Contact Commission may have wanted to save the contact and his family from being intruded upon. And lastly, she postulated that Sadler might have kept the channel's identity secret along with the Contact Commission, in hopes that the "colorful myth" would attract attention to *The Urantia Book*.[5]

*The Urantia Book* acknowledges several times within its pages that it is not a completely original work, that it was sourced from human writing:

> Successive planetary revelations of divine truth invariably embrace the highest existing concepts of spiritual values as a part of the new and enhanced co-ordination of planetary knowledge. Accordingly, in making these presentations about God and his universe associates, we have selected as the basis of these papers more than one thousand human concepts representing the highest and most advanced planetary knowledge of spiritual values and universe meanings. Wherein these human concepts, assembled from the God-knowing mortals of the past and the present, are inadequate to portray the truth as we are directed to reveal it, we will unhesitatingly supplement them, for this purpose drawing upon our own superior knowledge of the reality and divinity of the Paradise Deities and their transcendent residential universe.[6]

As is the case with other previously published sacred texts, *The Urantia Book* claims it has a transcendent source. It claims a supernatural origin that scholars may later argue is grounded more in myth than in fact. In the later nineteenth century, for example, critical studies of the Bible became the genesis for Christianity to divide itself into liberal, conservative, and fundamentalist camps. This was largely because nineteenth-century science declared that many of the Bible's descriptions of the physical world were false. For example, the Bible stated that grass, land plants and trees were created before the sun. We know that this is impossible scientifically because the former need the latter to exist. Another fallacy in the Old Testament was identified by Israeli Bible scholar Noam Mizrahi, who in the last few years used radiocarbon dating to prove that camels were not in Israel until the last third of the tenth century BC—centuries after the kingdom of David, further evidence that the narration in the Bible is not always reliable history.[7]

As these debates of historical accuracy raged, Christian scholars had to decide how to interpret the Bible based on what they believed. How should they explain these discrepancies to the laity? Was the Bible infallible or not? Such questions led liberal religionists to appreciate that symbolic language in the Bible can represent spiritual truths, but that at the same time the text is rife with false science. In other words, the Bible is fallible despite the essential spiritual truths it relates. The same can be said of *The Urantia Book*. It is a text filled with stories that reveal new spiritual truth to its readers but, just as the sacred texts before it, the traditions and origin story were created over time. Much of its content reflects the era in which it was written.

*The Urantia Book* identifies the celestial author at the end of each paper. The most striking acknowledgment occurs in the Foreword, "Indited by an Orvonton Divine Counselor, Chief of the Corps of Superuniverse Personalities assigned to portray on Urantia the truth concerning the Paradise Deities and the universe of universes:"

In formulating the succeeding presentations having to do with the portrayal of the character of the Universal Father and the nature of his Paradise associates, together with an attempted description of the perfect central universe and the encircling seven superuniverses, we are to be guided by the mandate of the superuniverse rulers which directs that we shall, in all our efforts to reveal truth and co-ordinate essential knowledge, give preference to the highest existing human concepts pertaining to the subjects to be presented. We may resort to pure revelation only when the concept of presentation has had no adequate previous expression by the human mind.

Successive planetary revelations of divine truth invariably embrace the highest existing concepts of spiritual values as a part of the new and enhanced co-ordination of planetary knowledge. Accordingly, in making these presentations about God and his universe associates, we have selected as the basis of these papers more than one thousand human concepts representing the highest and most advanced planetary knowledge of spiritual values and universe meanings. Wherein these human concepts, assembled from the God-knowing mortals of the past and the present, are inadequate to portray the truth as we are directed to reveal it, we will unhesitatingly supplement them, for this purpose drawing upon our own superior knowledge of the reality and divinity of the Paradise Deities and their transcendent residential universe.

We are fully cognizant of the difficulties of our assignment; we recognize the impossibility of fully translating the language of the concepts of divinity and eternity into the symbols of the language of the finite concepts of the mortal mind. But we know that there dwells within the human mind a fragment of God, and that there sojourns with the human soul the Spirit of Truth; and we further know that these spirit forces conspire to enable material man to grasp the reality of spiritual values and to comprehend the philosophy of universe meanings. But even more certainly we know that these spirits of the Divine Presence are able to assist man in the spiritual appropriation of all truth contributory to the enhancement of the ever-progressing reality of personal religious experience—God-consciousness.[8]

*The Oxford English Dictionary* defines indite as "1. To utter, suggest, or inspire a form of words which is to be repeated or written down; 2. To enjoin as a law, precept, or maxim; b. To dictate to, enjoin (a person). 3. To put into words, compose (a poem, tale or speech, etc.); to give a literary or rhetorical form to (words, an address); to express or describe in a literary composition."[9] From Sadler's comment that the contact both spoke and wrote the celestial communications, any of these definitions could be correct. It is also possible that Sadler dictated the words and his secretaries transcribed them, or that he had some kind of other-worldly experience over decades that created the content of the book in partnership with celestial beings. It remains a mystery.

## Scholarly Findings

One way of proving authorship of written works today is done through computer-statistical analysis. The most famous example is *The Federalist Papers*. John Adams, Alexander Hamilton, James Madison, and John Jay wrote *The Federalist Papers* in 1787 and 1788. It was known that John Jay wrote five of the eighty-five papers;

Alexander Hamilton wrote fifty-one; John Adams wrote fourteen; and that Madison and Hamilton had collaborated on another three. The authorship of the twelve remaining papers was disputed until the middle of the twentieth century.

In 1964, the scholars Frederick Mosteller and David L. Wallace used statistical analysis to prove that Madison was the author of the disputed twelve papers. Their conclusion was tested by Robert A. Bosch and Jason A. Smith in 1998 and by Glenn Fung in 2003 and found to be correct. An extremely simplified explanation of the methodology is to measure the quantity and pattern of how function words such as a, all, also, the, so, have, when, which, who, would, and your, are used in a writing sample. These function words are used with a regular pattern by authors and can be graphed through computer analysis, and compared against other writing samples to see if the patterns match. If they do, it is likely that the same person wrote them.

Two attempts were made to test authorship by scholars Aaron Walker and Christopher Smith, using linguistic computer tools. They compared Sadler's writings against other authors to the writing of *The Urantia Book*.

Walker, who at the time was a PhD candidate in linguistics at the University of Southern California, tested the following selections: in Part I (pages 17 and 32); Part II (Paper 39); Part II (paper 88); and Part IV (Papers 130, 160, and pages 1319 and 1343). His results are presented in Table 1:

| Table 1. Authorship Test, Walker | |
|---|---|
| Papers Analyzed | Conclusion |
| 88 and 160 | Strong probability that Sadler was not the author (99 percent) |
| 39 | Strong possibility Sadler was the author |
| Foreword and acknowledgments, pages 17, 32, 1319, and 1343 | Strong possibility Sadler was the author |
| 160 and source for 160, Henry Wieman's *Issues of Life* | Strong possibility that either Sadler or Wieman was the author—Sadler slightly favored by data |
| S130 (130-2-7 through 130-2-10 - no title; 130-4 Discourse on Reality; 130-7 Discourse on Time and Space; 132-1 True Values; 132-2 Good and Evil; 132-3 Truth and Faith; 133-5 Discourse on Science; 133-6 Discourse on the Soul; 133-7 Discourse on Mind) versus the source for 130, Flewelling's *Creative Personality* | Stylomentric fingerprints suggest either Flewelling or Sadler. Given Sadler's pattern of heavily borrowing from other authors and greater involvement with *The Urantia Book*, it is most likely that Sadler was the author |

The results of these tests showed statistical significance (a 99 percent chance) that Sadler's use of function words made him the probable author of the Foreword, the acknowledgments, and Papers 88, 130, and 160.[10] At the same time, the tests Performed on Paper 39 indicate that Sadler was not the author. Walker concluded that Sadler was the author because he was the common denominator in the history of the text, unlike Wieman and Flewelling, who were not members of either the Contact Commission or the Forum. Subsequent research proved that this method—even when correct ratios are used—is not a reliable one to prove the authorship of sacred texts because by their nature they are compiled works.

Another scholar, Christopher Smith, a graduate student in theology at Claremont Graduate School, was hired to do further testing on the authorship of *The Urantia Book*. Smith used writing samples from Sadler, Lena Sadler, and Bill Sadler, Jr. The four control authors were Smith, Sigmund Freud, and the biblical writers Matthew and Luke (from the King James version of the Bible).[11] Of the 105 control samples he used, 75 percent were attributed to the correct author. Smith found this to be highly significant. Smith found that "sequence and genre were exogenous variables that correlated highly with authorship."[12] He concluded that the extent to which authorship was the measured variable was an open question. As for *The Urantia Book*, ninety-one of the papers were attributed to Sigmund Freud, seventy-four to himself (Christopher Smith), seventeen to Luke, eleven to William Sadler, three to Lena Sadler, two to Matthew, and none to Bill Sadler.

Smith also discovered that in a number of cases—particularly in the section that narrates the life of Jesus—the individual papers were more similar to the author to whom they were assigned than to the averages for *The Urantia Book* as a whole. This is nonsensical: Sigmund Freud wrote in German and thus cannot be the author and Christopher Smith was not alive at the time the book was written. Smith's conclusion was that the true author or authors of the book were not included in the test. He determined that this method simply is not an accurate way to test authorship of compiled texts, which *The Urantia Book* is. Smith concluded that proof that Sadler was the author had to be based on carefully collated textual and historical evidence. In other words, computer analysis is not a reliable way to test sacred texts because its authorship is usually a compilation of different sources, which is not easily tested.

The proof of such authorship has to rely on other circumstantial evidence. So what is the evidence that Sadler is the contact and/or scribe of *The Urantia Book*? In Part IV, "The Life and Teachings of Jesus," the midwayer author writes,

> The memoranda which I have collected ... embrace thought gems and superior concepts of Jesus' teachings assembled from more than two thousand human beings who have lived on Earth from the days of Jesus down to the time of inditing of these revelations, more correctly restatements .... And, 'I, with the collaboration of my eleven associate fellow midwayers ... have portrayed this narrative

in accordance with my concept of its effective arrangement and in response to my choice of immediate expression ... I have served more as a collector and editor than as an original narrator.'[13]

## Matthew Block's Source Studies

The source material in *The Urantia Book* has begun to be examined because of the discoveries of an independent researcher, Matthew Block. Block began discovering human sources for *The Urantia Book* in the Spring of 1992, when he was browsing though old books on religion in a used book store. Noting very close and unique similarities in the texts and *The Urantia Book*, he began to search for other source books. His research also revealed that Sadler used uncited sources for his other books in similar ways. Occasionally Sadler stated as his own medical cases that were not his because they had been first chronicled by other authors. Although he was never accused of plagiarism during his life, and his books were reviewed in major journals, Sadler's use of other authors' material without acknowledgment would be a breach of modern literary ethical standards.

Nonetheless, Block affirms that much of *The Urantia Book* is original, but that much of it also has a "kernel of already conceived ideas." As an example, he points out that *The Urantia Book*'s "radical" description of "God and the universe, with the Creator in the center surrounded by the created universes and personalities revolving around him, was an old concept." Block explained that Ellen Gould White knew about this pattern of using sources from literature written prior to her visions.[14]

In 1992, Block asserted that Parts I and II of *The Urantia Book* are the most "thoroughly original." Their main source is the Bible and Bible dictionaries. The administration of the cosmos and the roster of angelic orders are also original to *The Urantia Book*, according to Block. Block found that Parts III and IV have much original material, but hypothesized that Sadler may have been inspired by the source materials to write a much more complex and compelling story.[15] Block's research raised several important questions about the authorship of *The Urantia Book* and:

- demonstrated a relationship between *The Urantia Book* and many source books;

- pointed out that Sadler used sources in his own books without citation;

- argued that the way Sadler used sources in his own work is similar in some respects to the way *The Urantia Book* used sources;

- provided evidence that Sadler used other authors' experiences as his own;

- hypothesized that Sadler was the probable author of some or all of *The Urantia Book*.

Block discovered sources for more than one hundred of the 196 papers in *The Urantia Book*. These sources were printed in English, published between 1880 and 1942, and written almost exclusively by white men—including many notable scholars. The question that needs answering is why celestial beings who were writing an epochal revelation for Earth would choose only these texts as sources. A number of believers speculate that the remaining sources will be found in the future.

The sourcing is not proved by a verbatim use of a text. The compelling evidence of sourcing is that the ideas presented in the source books are followed sequentially in *The Urantia Book*. This pattern is found consistently in the portions of *The Urantia Book* that have human sources. Block's research uncovered the following examples of source texts found in *The Urantia Book*.

Paper 1. "The Universal Father"

- Nave, *Nave's Topical Bible* (1896, 1897)

- Knudson, *The Doctrine of God* (1930)

- Matthews, *God in Christian Thought and Experience* (1930)

- Illingsworth, *Personality Human and Divine* (1894)

Paper 68. "The Dawn of Civilization" (and fourteen other papers)

- Keller and Sumner, *The Science of Society* (1927)

Paper 103. "The Reality of Religious Experience"

- Baillie, *The Interpretation of Religion* (1928)

- Garnett, *A Realistic Philosophy of Religion* (1942)

- Knudson, *The Doctrine of God* (1930)

- Lewis, *God and Ourselves* (1931)

Paper 159: "Instruction for Teachers and Believers"

- Weatherhead, *Jesus and Ourselves* (1930)

Block detected these patterns in Paper 159:[16]

- Seventy-five percent of the time, the phrase "summarized and restated" or "summarized and stated in modern phraseology" indicates that the passages that followed were sourced.

- Weatherhead wrote testimonies *about* Jesus. *The Urantia Book* author converted them into instructions given by Jesus.

- The compiling and paraphrasing is "practiced with a rare editorial art that required high intelligence." The acknowledgment in *The Urantia Book* notes, "Although I have sought to adjust the verbal expression the better to conform to our concept of the real meaning and the true import of the Master's life and teachings, as far as possible I have adhered to the actual human concept and thought pattern in my narratives."[17]

- New concepts are blended with the source material. Weatherhead's "Jesus-centrism" becomes Jesus' emphasis on the Thought Adjuster, a previous idea fleshed out in *The Urantia Book*. Block notes, "Indeed, Part IV's references to the Thought Adjuster occur as thematic supplements in many sections which draw from modern source books, whose authors have vaguer notions about our spiritual endowments."[18]

In addition, Block identified "brilliant pruning" occurring between Weatherhead's book and *The Urantia Book*. The author, Block notes, "is as comfortable and skilled in condensing as in elaborating."

Another independent scholar, J. T. Manning, offered the following preliminary generalizations about the source authors of papers 85 through 103 in 2002:

- The books and articles used as sources were published by well-known publishers between 1883 and 1945. They enjoyed wide circulation.

- All source materials were published in English. In cases where the source may appear to be foreign it is an English translation. For example, he cites Emile Hovelaque's *China* as being sourced from the English translations of the originally published French text.

- All source authors were white and all but three—Ellen Gould White, Lena Sadler, and Regina Westcott-Wieman—were men. Most authors were from the United States, followed by England and Scotland.

- The sourced literature reflected current trends of thought. All source authors were recognized as experts in their field by other academics.

- The sourced texts were written for a college student or well-read lay person.

- Almost every author had a college degree at a time when having a one was rare. Most of them earned multiple degrees. Many worked at a variety of institutions before establishing tenure at a highly respected university or church.

- Many knew each other, but it is not known if they knew Sadler.

- Except for Ellen Gould White, none of the source authors claimed to be writing from divine inspiration.

- The authors were passionate about their subjects, believed in the upward progress of civilization, wanted to contribute to that trend, were not revolutionary in their writing, and worked within existing communities.

- Their political views ranged from the far Left to the far Right when judged by the standards of the time. They were not politically active.

- Their views within their fields were diverse, and some openly debated with each other.

- Virtually all believed in God even if they did not belong to any particular religious organization. Almost all belonged to mainline Protestant, Unitarian, Quaker, or Jewish communities. None were Roman Catholic. (Only Ellen G. White and the Sadlers belonged to a non-mainline religion (Seventh-day Adventist).

- Many had learning disabilities or mood disorders. Manning points out that this is not surprising because contemporary psychologists and psychiatrists have found an unusually large number of prominent or creative people have these challenges in their lives.

These facts deepen the mystery surrounding the book's authorship. While some sections of *The Urantia Book* have sources, numerous portions of the papers appear to be original. Even while having hundreds of sources interwoven throughout its pages, *The Urantia Book* remains harmonious. This fact is true, even when the authors of source works argued towards a conclusion different than that in *The Urantia Book*. It is quite an accomplishment to weave original and sourced material into a consistent narrative for over 2,000 pages.

---

1  James R. Lewis and Olav Hammer, eds. *The Invention of Sacred Tradition*, Cambridge University Press (2007): 1-17.

2  Ibid.

3  Einar Thomassen, "'Forgery' in the New Testament," in *The Invention of Sacred Tradition*, edited by James R. Lewis and Olav Hammer, Cambridge University Press (2007): 141-157

4  Ibid.

5  Sarah Lewis, "The Peculiar Sleep: Receiving *The Urantia Book*," in *The Invention of Sacred Tradition*, edited by James R. Lewis and Olav Hammer, Cambridge University Press (2007): 141-157 Ibid, 199-212

6  *The Urantia Book*, 17.

7  Wilford, "Camels Had No Business in Genesis."

8  *The Urantia Book*, 16–17.

9  *Oxford English Dictionary*, http://dictionary.oed.com/cgi/entry/50115483?query_type=word&queryword=indite&first=1&max_to_show=10&sort_type=alpha&result_place=2&search_id=DBat-5V9wDq-9980&hilite=50115483.

10  Walker, "Did Sadler Write Papers 88 and 160?"; "Findings Report: UB130, 132, and 133"; "Findings Report: Stylometric Analysis"; "William S. Sadler and Papers 39, 88, 160."

11  Smith, "*The Urantia Book* as a Test Case."

12  Ibid.,19.

13  *The Urantia Book*, 16–17, 1343.

14  Matthew Block, e-mail correspondence, May 15, 2010.

15  Ibid.

16  Block, "A Source Study."

17  *The Urantia Book*, 1343.

18  Block, "A Source Study of Instruction for Teachers and Believers" 1-22, 2001 http://www.squarecircles.com/urantiabooksourcestudies/pdf/InstructionTeachersBelievers.pdf

# 10

## THE COSMIC MIND CONNECTION

*Q. Do you feel, Dr. Sadler, that you have a particular place in carrying on this work in connection with the book?*
*A. No, I have no such feeling. I think I just happened to be around when this happened.*

—Interview, April 27, 1958

ACCORDING TO *THE URANTIA BOOK*, THE many spiritual influences in the universe are in reality all one. The pattern of the universe is both perfect and infinite, and its shadow can be found on less-than-perfect worlds, such as Earth. *The Urantia Book* further explains that the universal mind is the source of all intelligence and forms the master pattern of reality. The part of the universal that acts in time and space is the cosmic mind. The cosmic mind is or has a circuit that flows from Paradise out into the worlds of time and space containing—or reflecting—genuine intellectual values, divine thought, and perfect ideas. As discussed earlier, God created a spiritual circuit that downsteps to the worlds of time and space to bring people Godward. One example is angels. Another aspect of this scheme reveals that the minds of humans are individualized circuits of the cosmic mind when they evolve spiritually enough to receive the mind-gravity grasp of God as it flows out from Paradise.

Another way *The Urantia Book* expresses this idea of spiritual oneness is that the infinite mind is the spiritual agent that draws all truth-loving souls to return to themselves. Therefore, it can be hypothesized that humans can tap into the cosmic mind circuit to assist in intellectual and spiritual thinking. It is written in *The Urantia Book*

161

that "spirit mind is divine purpose in action" (88). Sadler hypothesized in his own books that he had the experience of tapping into this circuit. He believed that when a person has direct contact with the cosmic mind circuit, they are able to function at their highest possible level because they are permitting the spirit to reign within them.

That said, Sadler wrote that he did not understand how *The Urantia Book* was written in a letter to the Reverend Benjamin Adams on March 17, 1959:

> My own preoccupation with *The Urantia Book* has been along two lines. First, I was concerned as to whether or not this was some fraudulent psychic phenomena or possibly a case of subconscious dissociation on the part of the subject such as I was familiar with in the fields of automatic writing, trance mediums, etc. I was the last of my family to accept the Urantia Papers. I finally decided that the whole thing was beyond my ability to understand.
>
> My next concern had to do with the consistency of the Papers. I finally decided that a fraud could not go on the witness stand for twenty-five years, to be examined and cross-examined by 250, and to give more than a million words of testimony and never once contradict himself. I decided that the subject must be telling the truth in order to discuss such a wide range of topics and not once slip into a contradiction.[1]

Sadler thought like a scientist. He was honest in admitting that science could not adequately explain these so-called spiritual experiences. He surmised that the answer might lie outside science and be part of a spiritual culture. In three of Sadler's books, he wrote about telepathy, which he defined as "the transmission of thought or feeling from mind to mind independently of the recognized channels of sense." In *The Physiology of Faith and Fear* (1912), *The Mind at Mischief* (1929), and *Theory and Practice of Psychiatry* (1936) these identical two paragraphs appear:

> All intelligent beings recognize the existence of gravitation—that universal law of cohesion which holds all things together. If a new world should be created in the universe, untold billions of miles away—so far that hundreds of years must pass before its light could reach Earth—the moment such a new planet was born, our world would feel its pull of gravity. Gravitation is an omnipresent force acting independently of time and space; and even if we were not confronted with the universal religious teaching of a Great Spirit, we could suspect, by analogy from the well-known force of gravitation,

that there might also exist an all-pervading and universal spirit intelligence.

This plausible hypothesis of a Universal Mind completely does away with the transfer of thought from one finite mind to another. There may be a Universal Intelligence whose emanations radiate to all who are in harmony with the Divine Mind. Every soul who is in tune with the infinite would enjoy the possibility of receiving messages and inspirations from this Central Source. If this is the truth, it is not difficult to see that two minds may have the same thought at the same time, just as two wireless telegraph stations which are attuned alike may receive, at the same time, the same message flashed from a vessel far out to sea.[2]

This belief is quite similar to that of John Harvey Kellogg and expressed in his book, *The Living Temple*:

Two minds which are in tune with the Infinite will be in harmony with one another. This fact accounts for the frequently observed simultaneous development of a new truth in many different parts of the world at the same time. God is everywhere. Human nature is essentially the same the world over and its needs are much the same. Hence it is not surprising that kindred gifts from the same source of truth should come at the same time to widely separated portions of the race.[3]

The beliefs about prophecy existing as part of the natural order were always part of Sadler's thinking. In *Mind at Mischief,* he says that he has an open mind to this phenomenon:

I would not deny that we encounter, now and then, a phenomenon which seems to require something analogous to the telepathic process to afford a satisfactory explanation. Separate and apart from the whole question of spiritualism, there may exist laws of a perfectly natural order which are at the bottom of some of these unique experiences. I am willing to continue to look at this phase of occult investigation with an open mind.[4]

In 1936 he wrote:

There is a Universal Intelligence whose emanations radiate to all who are in harmony with the Divine Mind. Every soul who is "in tune with the infinite" would enjoy the possibility of receiving messages and inspirations from this Holy Spirit.[5]

> I have had some personal experiences that would be difficult to account for on the theory of pure coincidence or mathematical chance. Not being a mechanist, I suppose it is easy for me, at least temporarily, to seek for a satisfactory explanation of these experiences in the hypothesis of the cosmic mind—spiritual attunement.[6]

This is the most clearly Sadler ever stated his spiritual experiences, and he repeats it nearly twenty years later in *Mental Mischief and Emotional Conflicts.*[7] Again he suggests that he had personal experience with spiritual attunement with the cosmic mind—the intellectual potential of the grand universe. In *The Urantia Book*, the cosmic mind is defined as the spirit presence of the Infinite Spirit. Another word for this attunement is self-revelation—an innate connection for bringing a technique of clear-reasoning and deep thinking via the cosmic mind circuit. Self-revelation is mentioned as being unlimited recognition of reality. Connection with the cosmic mind brings an instant mental clarity that in turn provides an objective reality to a person's experience with things, meanings, and values. The cosmic mind is innate in all people. It explains that kindred minds and spirits, when human minds are running in "channels of astonishing similarity and in inexplicable agreement," are connected through the cosmic mind.[8] This state of mind occurs when a person "seems to enter an ethereal zone, an inexplicably heightened state of ability." Studies of this phenomena are being conducted in sports and other fields.[9] Academics once dismissive are now more open to the possibility of this phenomenon.

One of the reasons that readers of *The Urantia Book* have scoffed at the suggestion that Sadler wrote *The Urantia Book*, is because the writing in his own books is pedestrian by comparison. As mentioned earlier, reviewers of *Theory and Practice of Psychiatry* found it "chatty," "disorganized," and "inconsistent," and his theories were described as "middle of the road."[10] It is hard for many to believe by looking at Sadler's writing that he is the author of *The Urantia Book*. We must use other criteria to examine whether he is in fact the author. This assessment can be supported by current scholarship on automatic writing, channeling, and creative genius. Scott Dunn's essay, "Automaticity and the Dictation of the Book of Mormon," in *American Apocrypha: Essays on The Book of Mormon*, defined automatic writing as:

> the ability to write or dictate text in a relatively rapid, seemingly effortless and fluent manner with no sense of control over the

content. Indeed except for sometimes knowing a word or two in moments of advance of writing or speaking, the individual is typically not consciously aware of what the content of the writing will be. Channeling is a form of the same phenomenon that allegedly involves a spirit being (or entity) transmitting information through a living medium.[11]

Many people who produce such writing, Dunn remarked, believe that it comes from an outside intelligence. Frequently this external consciousness will have a name and personality all its own. Dunn found that some of these works "exhibit an awareness and writing skills" that far exceed what the individual is capable of doing under normal circumstances. When the subject discovers that they can rapidly produce writing that is superior to their normal skills they attribute it to an outside source. This falls under the term dissociation, which psychologists define as mental activities that occur outside *our range of consciousness* (emphasis added).[12]

Examples of automatic writing can include multiple authorship, use of archaic language, accounts of bygone historical figures, accurate descriptions of times and places apparently unfamiliar to the writer, narratives with well-developed characters and plot, accounts of the ministries of Jesus Christ, doctrinal, theological, and cosmological discussions, and discourses by deity.[13] According to Dunn, automatic writers usually do not use notes or outlines or conduct major reworkings of a text. In some cases, automatic writers produce detailed information they have seen or read but have no memory of doing so. Examples include someone under hypnosis who can speak in a foreign language they heard at age three. Memory quirks such as these are termed cryptomnesia and may explain the style and literary patterns in both the Bible and the *Book of Mormon*. Another example is a woman who, using a Ouija board, produced automatic writing almost word for word of death notices in the local newspaper. She had done the crossword puzzle on the same page and her mind had apparently picked up and stored the material in her field of vision. Her unconscious could produce this information even when her conscious mind was unaware of its existence.

Some evidence exists that Sadler considered that the contact personality was using parts of his subconscious (his superconscious) because he thought this was where the "ministry of spirit forces and beings," spiritual experience, and revelation happened. This is similar to what Dunn argued in that a channeling subject uses parts of their brain outside their normal range of consciousness. Sadler notes a similar possibility in a history manuscript he dictated in May 1958, in which he described ways that *The Urantia Book* did not manifest:

*Psychic Phenomena*
*Unusual activities of the marginal consciousness (subconscious mind)*

- automatic writing

- automatic talking

- speaking in tongues

- trace mediums

- spirit mediums

- catalepsy

- automatic hearing—clairaudience

- hearing voices

- automatic seeing

- dream states—twilight meditation

- visions—automatic dramatization

- hallucinations (shifty "reality" feelings)

- automatic thinking

- automatic fearing—anxiety neurosis

- automatic ideation—mental compulsions

- automatic judgments—intuition, hunches

- automatic association of ideas—premonitions

- automatic guessing—ESP (extrasensory perception)

- automatic deductions—delusions, paranoia

- dominance by marginal consciousness—dreams and hypnosis

- automatic remembering

- clairvoyance—automatic memory associations

- telepathy—mind reading (?)

- fortune telling (largely fraudulent)

- musical and mathematical marvels

- automatic acting

- automatic behavior—major hysteria, witchcraft

- automatic motion—motor compulsions

- automatic overdrives—manic episodes

- automatic walking—somnambulism

- automatic personalization

- automatic forgetting—amnesia

- automatic dissociation—double and multiple personality

- schizophrenia—split personality

- combined and associated psychic status[14]

Sadler added this note: "The technique of the reception of *The Urantia Book* in English in no way parallels or impinges on any of these phenomena of the marginal consciousness."

Below this information, Sadler crossed out a section, which read as follows:

- activities of the superconscious mind

    — ministry of spirit forces and beings

    — spiritual experience, evolution of the soul

    — revelation

    — incarnation

- Prince's staff of one hundred

- Adam and Eve

- Melchizedek

- Michael[15]

The first item of the crossed out section above allows for the possibility (one Sadler never wanted to admit publicly) that *The Urantia Book* could have manifested through his own mind. *The Urantia Book* uses the term *autorevelation* to describe information being revealed to a mortal through the work of the Thought Adjuster (the fragments of God that live within human minds seeking to spiritualize their thinking). The book describes epochal revelation occuring when truth is presented by the work of a celestial agency, group, or personality (such as *The Urantia Book*). Both of these options fit within the last section above which Sadler crossed out. If the information provided in the book came through his subconscious mind he could have concluded that it was his Thought Adjuster acting within the cosmic mind circuit. This idea fit within his belief system. He couldn't prove it; nor would he mention this possibility to others since he probably did not want to open that door for fear it would end his career in psychiatry. We will never know for certain. The precise origin of the newly revealed revelatory truths in *The Urantia Book* remains a mystery even if Sadler appears to be the channel.

What evidence is there that Sadler could be the channel for *The Urantia Book*? Sadler possibly being the author is that he was a biblical scholar. From Block's source studies, we know that the primary source in *The Urantia Book* is the Bible. Sadler authored several biblically-oriented workbooks to train teachers and leaders in the Urantia community: a biblical overview; a history for both the Old and New Testaments; and study guides for both the New and Old Testaments. These three books are cumulatively more than two thousand pages long. In the *History: Part One—A Survey of the Bible* begins with "The Bible: Authority and Significance" followed by "Why the Bible Is Essential to Christianity," the "Harmony of Faith and Scripture," "The Bible and the Church," and "The Bible as the Word of God." In the first section, he notes that the Bible never claims to be infallible but is a tool that is "inspired by God and profitable for teaching, for reproof, for correction, and for training in righteousness."[16] This statement reflects Sadler's Protestant and Adventist views of believing that any individual aided by the Holy Spirit can interpret the Bible. Again, Block discovered that most of the Urantia workbooks were sourced. The workbooks were paraphrased by using articles by George Arthur Buttrick in his twelve-volume series *The Interpreter's Bible* (1951).

Along with his writing about the Bible, Sadler taught "Bible Principles and Methods of Christian Work" at the Chicago Medical Missionary Training School on Wabash Avenue, from 1897 to 1900. The course covered: a) Bible study by books; b) topical study of the Bible with special reference to personal and evangelistic work; c) principles and methods of personal work; and d) methods of mission work, rescue work, street work, cottage meetings, and personal work. Tuition was free to "consecrated Christian young men and women who desire to devote their lives to work for God and humanity."[17]

Sadler also demonstrated his proficiency in the Bible in his paper "Consideration of Some Criticisms of *The Urantia Book*," answering questions as only an expert could. Someone charged, for example, that *The Urantia Book* was a revival of Gnosticism, which the Christian Church repudiated. Sadler listed the teachings that characterized Gnosticism and points out that *The Urantia Book* strikes down the principles of Gnosticism and all other religions that rely on secrets, symbols, slogans, ceremonies, or any other magic techniques of gaining divine favor. He pointed out that *The Urantia Book* proclaims that a person gets to heaven by faith and knowing God, not by the "secret names of intervening demons." *The Urantia Book* declares that souls get to heaven by evolving on Earth; after death they traverse the morontia spheres to rid themselves of deficiencies in order to attain spirit status, and get mustered into the Mortal Corps of Finality be given their assignments for undisclosed service in outer space. Furthermore, in this same article, Sadler lists seventy-four new concepts in *The Urantia Book* that are not found in the Bible.[18]

The Urantia community has always maintained that the book was not a channeled work for the simple reason that Sadler, who maintained the Seventh-day Adventist's narrow definition of channeling throughout his life, denied it. According to the current definition of channeling, *The Urantia Book* is a channeled work. Jon Klimo, professor at the American School of Professional Psychology, describes channeling as:

> … the communication of information to or through a physically embodied human being from a source that is said to exist on some other level or dimension of reality than the physical as we know it, and that is not from the normal mind or self of the channel.[19]

Klimo, who is also the co-director of clinical research at the American School of Professional Psychology, found that channeled material is usually positive and "stresses the reality of a larger, spiritual universe and our own creative self-determination in this lifetime."[20] *The Urantia Book* fits that description as well. Klimo's studies describe the process of those who channel as co-creating with what he refers to as "pre-entity energies" that exist on other realms. People who become channels go through seven stages. Klimo describes them as follows:

> Stage 1, *conceptualization*—the channel begins to experience a nonphysical reality beyond themselves;

> Stage 2, *preparation*—the channel feels that definite contact has been made with a nonphysical reality that causes physiological as well as psychological repercussions;

> Stage 3, *gestation*—the channel begins consciously developing a sense of the physical and nonphysical relationship of energies within their emotional system;

> Stage 4, *recognition*—the channel starts to define and accept the reality of the nonphysical energy system within their own system and gives it a name;

Stage 5, *activation*—the channel makes a choice to participate, the final adjustments are made to fine tune the energies involved. Because this experience can be frightening and puzzling;

Stage 6, *integration*—the final balancing occurs and the channel develops a "trust between the nonphysical energy and the medium" that is comfortable and real; and

Stage 7, *maturation*—the channel becomes a final self-actualized personality, or personalities.[21]

For Klimo, these experiences come from the universal mind and the collective unconscious—the channel's higher self.[22] This is similar to how Sadler described the phenomena of the cosmic mind. If Sadler was the channel, his wife, son, adopted daughter, and brother- and sister-in-law all believed that the channeling was from a celestial source. None of them ever mentioned the possibility that any of them was the sleeping subject. They told the origin story which featured the sleeping subject story whenever they were asked, as did Sadler. This kind of unprovable belief was not unusual. Groups of people around the world have and still believe in channeled materials. The reality of prophecy was part of Sadler's belief system which grounded him in the possibility of celestial connection. Recall that the Urantia phenomena happened over thirty years—a sustained, lengthy, and focused process and the origin story similarly evolved over time.

Dean Keith Simonton is a distinguished professor of psychology at UC Davis in California. He has spent his academic career empirically examining the nature and origins of genius as it manifests in creativity, leadership, talent, and aesthetics. He argues that creative geniuses recombine ideas to produce original works—and they must link these ideas by unusual pathways. Creators need a vivid intuitive imagination, for new ideas are not generated by deduction, but instead by artistically creative imagination. A creative individual is obsessed with certain problems and will not rest until they can find a solution. Due to this drive, creators can insist that the illuminations that solved the problems were largely out of their control—the moment of inspiration is a breakthrough—it departs significantly from what has previously been done. Simonton explains:

A genius is a genius because he can put together such a staggering number of insights, ideas, theories, random observations and unexpected connections that s/he almost inevitably ends up with something great.[23]

Some of Simonton's conclusions echo those of Sadler. Simonton argued that exposure to role models and mentors foster the creative potential of geniuses. Sadler had Lew Wallace, General McNaught, Ellen Gould White, and John Harvey Kellogg as mentors. Firstborns are more likely to get higher degrees and become professionals, which was true of Sadler.[24] Sadler also fit into the genius category from the mentor standpoint. However, he does not validate Simonton's assertion that firstborns are more likely to oppose revolutionary ideas. If Sadler was the author of *The Urantia Book*, a revolutionary text, then he also failed to conform to Simonton's description of genius because firstborns are not usually revolutionaries.

Asked about other ways to test writing samples using archival data analysis to give a more definitive answer or proof that Sadler could be the author of *The Urantia Book*, Simonton replied,

> Authorship questions are very difficult to settle, as I've learned from personal experience with the Shakespeare authorship question. For example, stylometric methods clearly show that the person who wrote the plays and poems attributed to Shakespeare of Stratford could not have been written by the 17th Earl of Oxford, a rival claimant. Yet the Oxfordians cry foul because they consider such comparisons apples and oranges—or rather caterpillar and butterfly, to use their metaphor. The only work definitely by Oxford are early song lyrics, which cannot be compared with the works that they assume came much later (and were completely revised later still). Once the good earl decided to write under a pseudonym (so the explanation goes) he also radically betrayed his style so that even the lyrics are distinctively different between youth and maturity. Who can prove the Oxfordians wrong under those assumptions?
>
> It's not unknown for persons to alter their verbal style in a qualitative manner when changing genres. Muhammed's revelations are quite distinct from his more prosaic pronouncements, for example—one of the reasons why Muslims can believe that the Koran is divinely inspired—or rather dictated. The same holds for Joseph Smith: *The Book of Mormon* is quite unlike anything that the prophet actually wrote. (If you're a Muslim or a Mormon, you will necessarily reject one of these examples, but you can't reject both!)
>
> Perhaps the authorship question you're dealing with is very similar.
>
> Sadler might have gotten into a rather different "ecstatic" state.[25]

One of Simonton's main assertions is that fecundity is the heart of the truly gifted. He believes that the mediocre mind may have a dozen ideas in a lifetime whereas, say, Bach had more than a thousand. Darwin's ideas about evolution slowly evolved over more than two decades and his thinking rate was high. A genius is a genius because he or she can "put together such a staggering number of insights, theories, random observations, and unexpected connections that he almost inevitably ends up with something great."[26] Using this explanation, Sadler could be classified as a genius.

But how could such a rational mind believe that he was in touch with celestial beings? One reason is that Sadler believed in spiritual communication and something was clearly happening that allowed the words to appear in his mind. Michael Shermer argues that our brains are a "belief engine." We form our belief systems for a variety of subjective, personal, emotional, and psychological reasons. These beliefs are part of the environment we live in and society at large. Once our beliefs are formed, we "defend, justify, and rationalize them" with our minds in rational ways to others. Shermer calls this *dependent realism*: what we believe is real depends on the beliefs we hold. In other words, the belief comes first and the reasons for that belief follow. Once we are committed to the beliefs, we develop cognitive biases that distort our perceptions to fit our belief system.[27]

Sadler always demurred when asked to divulge the origin of the Urantia papers and stated that he was "not in a position to do so." In 1959, he answered eighteen questions about *The Urantia Book* in a paper titled "Consideration of Some Criticisms of *The Urantia Book*." When asked "Why should not the person who put the Urantia papers in written English be known?" his response was that:

> The authors of the books of the Bible are known. The book itself tells about how the Urantia papers came to be. The reason given us for not disclosing the identity of the subject employed in this transaction was: We do not want future generations to be concerned with the adoration of a Saint Peter or Saint Paul, a Luther, Calvin, or Wesley. We want no individual to be exalted by the Urantia papers. The book should stand on its own nature and work.[28]

Sadler told the Shermans early in the 1940s that people enjoyed mysteries and that he thought keeping the origin of the Urantia papers a mystery would enhance their value.[29]

Textual studies of the Bible have revealed that it was written differently than tradition held. Scholars have explored how the Bible has been changed throughout the centuries. For example, of the twenty-seven writings in the New Testament, only seven have been accepted by modern scholars to have been written by the stated original author. Scholars have in fact determined that both the Hebrew Bible and the New Testament consist largely of books with counterfeit authors. They argue that the Old and New Testaments should be read as literary documents rather than historical records. This thought has caused contentious debate. Philip Davies has pointed out that authorship is not an issue given the value of the contents. He has divided texts into two types: documentary, which include records, fiscal, commercial, and legal transactions, and chronicles; and literary, which include myths, philosophy, liturgy, and stories ranging from historiographical to novelistic.[30] Reza Aslan in *Zealot*, argues that the gospels were never meant to be a historical documentation of Jesus' life. He describes them instead as testimonies of faith composed by communities of faith. Aslan wrote that it was a foreign concept to the writers of the gospel for whom history was not a matter of uncovering facts, but of revealing truths.[31] Based on these ideas, *The Urantia Book* can be considered, a literary text.

These issues mean that the scholarly analysis of authorship of a sacred text is both open and closed. The existence of God cannot be proved or disproved—it depends on the personal experience of each person. Truth seeking is not for those who are not willing to have their fondest beliefs crushed. As Paul Johnson wrote:

> Christianity, by identifying truth with faith, must teach—and, properly understood, does teach—that any interference with the truth is immoral. A Christian with faith has nothing to fear from the facts; a Christian historian who draws the line at limiting the field of enquiry at any point whatsoever, is admitting the limits of his faith. And of course he is also destroying the nature of his religion, which is a progressive revelation of truth. So the Christian, according to my understanding, should not be inhibited in the smallest degree from following the line of truth; indeed he is positively bound to follow it. He should be in fact, freer than the non-Christian, who is precommitted by his own rejection.[32]

Readers of *The Urantia Book* are undergoing what all religious groups encounter when they discover valid challenges to the origin and veracity of their text. They may find comfort in the opinion of those who traveled before them and found that open-minded truth seeking and faith are the essence of religion. The text is the device that leads them to that place where faith is an expanding and releasing experience and leads the person to sublime peace. It is enlightened reason, religious insight, and the will that believes.[33] None of this can really be measured because it is personal. Johnson points out that faith has no fear—we should actively question our beliefs.

This process helps one come to understand the true nature of religion, which is faith. *The Urantia Book* urges that we should divest ourselves of erroneous ideas of the nature of God as we learn and maintain our faith.

It was initially propagated that for geniuses such as Beethoven and Mozart the music just "came" to them in a stream and they wrote it down. Current research has demonstrated that this is not the case. Both men labored over their compositions. The idea in the 19th century was to romanticize and mythologize artistic endeavors. As with sacred texts, musical scholars examining the documents realized that there was no superhuman miracle occurring—rather it was a genius at work. Sadler fits into the same category. He may have had a connection to the cosmic mind, but he labored for two decades to shepherd *The Urantia Book* to completion. What are the possibilities for Sadler's authorship of the book?

1.  Sadler knowingly assembled the book from sources and from his creative imagination. The evidence for this possibility is that he was a master compiler as is evidenced from the style of using sources—both attributed and not—from examining his forty-three books. He also claimed that when he wrote, the words appeared in front of his eyes as on a screen. If this is the case, he would have done so to make the world a better place. However, by characterizing what he wrote as the work of celestial beings, mandated by the Ancients of Days, stating categorically that the historical facts are accurate, and so on.

2.  Sadler assembled the book from multiple sources but believed that he was being guided in his work by celestial beings. In this case, the charge of delusion might or might not be appropriate, depending on whether he really was guided, but the charge of dishonesty was not.

3.  Sadler did not write the book, and the story of his patient being the channel for the celestial beings authoring the book is correct. However, believing in this scenario becomes more difficult because it does not question the inconsistencies in the origin story. It does not explain why, if the sleeping subject was writing down material from higher beings, he/she would only source books in the English language published at the time the book was written. Why would celestial beings writing a revelation for all humankind only use books written in English between 1880 and the 1940s? It makes no sense that they would only use books written in one language and from one part of the world. It is far more likely that if the book were solely the product of celestials it would be sourced from books from around the globe.

The issue of motive also plays into this query. All indications are that Sadler was respected in all his roles: a Seventh-day Adventist minister, a Chautauqua Circuit lecturer, a teacher, an investigator, a physician, a surgeon, a psychiatrist, an author, and a father. The origin story and Sadler's experience in the writing of the text fits within his belief of prophecy learned from Seventh day Adventist teachings. *The Urantia Book* endures as the pinnacle achievement of Sadler's life but he never claimed ownership of it. After examining all of the evidence, the conclusion that makes the most sense is that Sadler was the channel for *The Urantia Book*. No other person was present, led the group, had the skill set, or spoke about being connected to the cosmic mind as Sadler. The evidence for Sadler being the channel is substantial:

- Sadler wrote in *Theory and Practice of Psychiatry* that he had some personal experiences best explained by the hypothesis of spiritual projection or the cosmic mind. Even though he couldn't really explain the particulars, it appears that he was in a state of superconsciousness, such as the basketball player who "seems to enter an ethereal zone, an inexplicably heightened state of ability in which he is unstoppable."[34]

- Sadler fits Simonton's definition of a genius in putting together a staggering number of insights, ideas, theories, and unexpected connections into the masterpiece that is *The Urantia Book.*

- Sadler called himself a compiler, which is in part how *The Urantia Book* was written. The sourcing patterns between Sadler's work and *The Urantia Book* are also similar. Sadler began his own writing using the Bible as a source, which expanded this skill for writing about medicine for a popular audience. Even though *The Urantia Book* is written at a far higher intellectual level than any of Sadler's work, evidence has shown that people can supersede their known limitations and draw on their subconscious.

- Sadler was a biblical scholar throughout his life and his knowledge of the Bible was extensive. We know this because of all his writings that compare the teachings of *The Urantia Book* with the Bible. According to Block, *The Urantia Book* relies on the Bible and biblical dictionaries as its main sources.

- *The Urantia Book* reflects Sadler's attitudes about eugenics and the prevailing science of the early twentieth century. Why would celestial beings place such spiritually inconsistent and scientifically untrue material in an epochal revelation?

Sadler knew—either consciously or unconsciously from his extensive knowledge of religious history and revelation—not to name himself as author because he knew the kind of scrutiny that would bring. Carolyn Kendall asked Sadler if he ever told any of his medical or seminary associates about the Urantia papers. He replied, "No, none of them would go for anything like this! They are all set in their beliefs; they would scoff at the idea of a new revelation."[35]

The material in *The Urantia Book* has a positive message. It seems unlikely that it would be the result of decades of fraud. Sadler had an experience, an insight into eternal realities that he could not explain, so he let the story evolve and remain a myth, in order to keep him safe in his work.

The brilliance behind *The Urantia Book* can be appreciated on examination. Its pages draw a complex picture, outlining human beings' divine origins and their spiritual growth until they become one with God—an eternal spirit with a home on Paradise. We are reminded in *The Urantia Book* that no revelation short of the "attainment of the Universal Father can ever be complete." The book attempts to bring the whole evolution of early twentieth-century Western science, philosophy, and religion together to achieve the goal of expanding cosmic consciousness and enhancing spiritual perceptions. At its best, it weaves numerous texts into a beautiful, coherent, and edifying narrative that is unique in Western literature. At its worst, the science papers reflect racism and out-dated twentieth-century science. Even taking all this into account, *The Urantia Book* is a masterpiece. It offers proof that Sadler tapped into the divine panorama of the ages.

1   Letter, William Sadler to Benjamin Adams, March 17, 1959, Urantia Foundation Archives, Chicago, IL.

2   Sadler, *Physiology of Faith and Fear*, 464; Mind at Mischief, 271; *Theory and Practice of Psychiatry*, 750

3   Kellogg, *Living Temple*, 475–76.

4   Sadler, *The Mind at Mischief*, 277–78.

5   Sadler, *The Physiology of Faith and Fear*, 464-465

6   Sadler, *Theory and Practice of Psychiatry*, 752

7   Sadler, *Mental Mischief*, 297.

8   *The Urantia Book*, 191.

9   Cohen, "Does the 'Hot Hand' Exist?" D12.

10  Westcott-Wieman, review.

11  Dunn, "Automaticity and the Dictation," 18.

12  Ibid.,19–26.

13  Ibid., 30.

14  Document in authors collection

15  Ibid.

16  Sadler, *Bible Study*.

17  Ad for Chicago Medical Missionary Training School, Third Annual Announcement, The Advocate, vol. 2, no. 04 (April, 1900): 132.

18  Ibid., 2.

19  Klimo, *Channeling*, 2

20  Ibid., 147.

21  Ibid., 132.

22  Ibid., 167.

23  Simonton quotes in Gladwell, "Creation Myth," 44.

24  Simonton, *Origins of Genius*, 125–39.

25  Simonton, e-mail correspondence with the author, May 10, 2011.

26  Gladwell, "Creation Myth."

27  Shermer, *Believing Brain*, 5, 166.

28  http://www.urantia.org/study/consideration-some-criticisms-urantia-book

29  *Sherman Diaries*, vol. 5, 58.

30  Davies, "Spurious Attribution in the Hebrew Bible."

31  Aslan, *Zealot*, 30.

32  Johnson, History of Christianity, viii.

33  *The Urantia Book*, 1122.

34  Cohen, "Does the 'Hot Hand' Exist?" D12.

35  Kendall, "How the Forum Began," (unpublished manuscript in author's possession, 2012), 3.

# BIBLIOGRAPHY

Adams, Henry. *Henry Adams: Novels, Mont Saint Michel, The Education*. New York: Library of Education, 1983.

Abbott, Andrew. *Department and Discipline: Chicago Sociology at One Hundred*. Chicago: University of Chicago Press, 1999.

Abbott, David P. *Behind the Scenes with the Mediums*, 5th rev. ed. Chicago: Open Court Publishing, 1916.

AMWA Archives, Drexel University, Philadelphia, PA.

"The Annual Commencement Exercises of the American Medical Missionary College." *The Medical Missionary*, vol. XV, no. 1, July 3, 1906.

Banning, Margaret Culkin. "The Case for Chastity." *Reader's Digest*, August 1937, 1–10.

Barzun, Jacques. From Dawn to Decadence: *500 Years of Western Cultural Life, 1500 to the Present*. New York: HarperCollins, 2000.

Bateman, Bradley W. "The Social Gospel and the Progressive Era." Divining America, TeacherServe. National Humanities Center. www.nationalhumanitiescenter.org/tserve/twenty/tkeyinfo/socgospel.htm.

Bigelow, Maurice. "A Brief History of the American Eugenics Society." *Eugenic News*, 31 (1946): 49-51.

Black, Edwin. *War Against The Weak: Eugenics and America's Campaign to Create a Master Race*. New York: Dialog Press, 2008.

Blanchard, Charles, ed. Counties of Clay and Owen, Indiana, *Historical and Biographical. Illustrated*. Chicago: F. A. Battey & Co., 1884.

Block, Matthew. "The Sadlers on the Modern Sex Problem." Fellowship Society Administration email list (April 29, 2013).

———. "Some Source Parallels." http://www.squarecircles.com/urantiabooksources-tudies/index.htm

————. "A Source Study of Instruction for Teachers and Believers." *SquareCircles. com*, 2001. http://www.squarecircles.com/urantiabooksourcestudies/pdf/ InstructionTeachersBelievers.pdf.

Bloese, August F. Interview with William S. Sadler, September 15, 1966. John H. Kellogg Papers. Andrews University, James White Library, Berrien Springs, MI.

Boomhower, Ray E. *The Sword & The Pen: A Life of Lew Wallace*, 2nd ed. Indianapolis: Indiana Historical Society Press, 2011.

Boyle, T. Coraghessan. *The Road to Wellville*. New York: Viking Penguin, 1993.

Brady, Kathleen. *Ida Tarbell: Portrait of a Muckraker*. Pittsburgh, PA: University of Pittsburgh Press, 1989.

Brodie, Fawn M. *No Man Knows My History: The Life of Joseph Smith*. New York: Random House, 1945.

Brooke, John L. *The Refiner's Fire: The Making of Mormon Cosmology*, 1644–1844. Cambridge: Press Syndicate of the University of Cambridge, 1994.

Brown, Julie K. *Health and Medicine on Display: International Expositions in the United States*, 1876–1904. Cambridge, MA: The MIT Press, 2009.

Burden, C. A. Obituary in *North Pacific Gleaner*, College Place, Washington. August 13, 1946.

Bushman, Richard, ed. *The Great Awakening: Documents on the Revival of Religion*, 1740–1745. Chapel Hill, NC: Institute of Early American History and Culture, 1969.

Butterfield, Oliver M. *Marriage and Sexual Harmony*. New York: Emerson Books, 1938.

"The Sadler's Popular Health Lectures." Chautauqua Circular , 1915.

Carmichael, Hugh T. "*Theory and Practice of Psychiatry* by William S. Sadler." *Journal of Religion*, vol. 17, no. 1 (January 1937): 119–20.

Chautauqua Managers Association. "Dr. Sadlers Company." Chicago: Lyceumite Press, 1910.

Clee, Paul. *Before Hollywood: From Shadow Play to the Silver Screen*. New York: Clarion Books, 2005.

Cohen, Ben. "Does the 'Hot Hand' Exist? A New Study Says Yes—Sometimes Shooters Really Are 'Feeling It.'" *Wall Street Journal* (February 28, 2014), p. D12.

Cook County Genealogy Records. Chicago, IL. 10220 S 76th Ave, Bridgeview, IL 60455 (708) 974-6150 http://www.cookcountyclerk.com/vitalrecords/pages/default. aspx

Copleston, Frederick C. *Religion and Philosophy*. New York: Barnes & Noble, 1974.

Cronon, William. *Nature's Metropolis: Chicago and the Great West*. New York W. W. Norton, 1991.

Cruden, Robert M. *Ministers of Reform: The Progressives' Achievement in American Civilization.* Urbana: University of Illinois Press, 1985.

Deadrick, Anna V. "The Case of Jack London: Plagiarism, Creativity, and Authorship." Master's thesis, University of North Carolina at Wilmington, 2003.

"The Death of Elder S. H. Lane." *The Advent Review and Sabbath Herald,* September 6, 1906.

Donner, Fred M. *Muhammad and the Believers at the Origins of Islam.* Cambridge, MA: The Belknap Press of Harvard University, 2010.

Dowbiggin, Ian Robert. *Keeping America Sane: Psychiatry and Eugenics in the United States and Canada* 1880–1940. Ithaca, NY: Cornell University, 1997.

Dunn, Scott C. "Automaticity and the Dictation of the Book of Mormon." In American *Apocrypha: Essays on the Book of Mormon,* eds. Dan Vogel and Brent Lee Metcalfe. Salt Lake City, UT: Signature Books, 2002.

E. G. White Estate Archives. Branch Offices: Loma Linda, CA;. Del E. Web, Memorial Library, Loma Linda University, Loma Linda, California 92350 (909) 558-4942 archives@llu.edu

Eisenbach, Eldon J. *The Social and Political Thought of American Progressivism.* Cambridge, MA: Hackett Publishing, 2006.

Engs, Ruth Clifford. *The Eugenics Movement: An Encylopedia.* Westport, CT: Greenwood Press, 2005.

Espejo, Roman, ed. *The Age of Reform and Industrialization,* 1896–1920, vol. 6. New York: Greenhaven Press, 2003.

Evensen, Bruce J. *God's Man for the Gilded Age: D. L. Moody and the Rise of Modern Mass Evangelism.* New York: Oxford University Press, 2003.

Exner, M. J. *The Sexual Side of Marriage.* New York: W. W. Norton, 1932.

*Fifteenth Annual Calendar of Battle Creek College.* Andrews University Special Collections. Berrien Springs, MI: Andrews University, 1890.

Fung, Glenn. "The Disputed Federalist Papers: SVM Feature Selection via Concave Minimization." *Journal of Associating Computing Machinery,* vol. 5, no. N (2003): 42–46.

Furner, Mary O. *Advocacy and Objectivity: A Crisis in the Professionalization of American Social Science,* 1865–1905. Lexington: University of Kentucky Press, 1975.

Galton, Francis. *Hereditary Genius: An Inquiry into its Laws and Consequences.* London: Macmillan, 1869.

———. *Inquiries into Human Faculty and Its Development.* New York: Dutton, 1907.

Gardner, Martin. *Urantia: The Great Cult Mystery.* Amherst, NY: Prometheus Books, 1995.

Gladden, Washington. *Working People and Their Employers*. New York: Funk and Wagnalls, 1894.

Gladwell, Malcolm. "Creation Myth." The New Yorker, May 16, 2011.

Grafton, Anthony. *The Footnote: A Curious History*. Cambridge, MA: Harvard University Press, 1997.

Goldman, Eric F. *Rendezvous with Destiny: A History of Modern American Reform*. New York: Vintage Books, 1952.

Hall, Amy Laura. "The Eugenics Temptation." The Christian Century, vol. 121, no. 22 (November 2, 2004): 24–27.

Haller, Mark H. *Eugenics: Hereditarian Attitudews in American Thought*. Brunswick, NJ: Rutgers University Press, 1963.

Hammer, Olav, and James R. Lewis. *The Invention of Sacred Tradition*. New York: Cambridge University Press, 2007.

Hart, Bernard. *The Psychology of Insanity*. Cambridge: Cambridge University Press, 1916.

Haskell, Thomas L. *The Emergence of Professional Social Science: The American Social Science Association and the Nineteenth-Century Crisis of Authority*. Urbana: University of Illinois Press, 1977.

Hillenbrand, Laura. *Unbroken: A World War II Story of Survival, Resilience, and Redemption*. New York: Random House, 2010.

Hofstadler, Richard. *The Age of Reform: From Bryan to F.D.R.* New York: Alfred A. Knopf, 1959.

James, Janet Wilson. "Isabel Hampton and the Professionalization of Nursing in the 1890s." In *The Therapeutic Revolution: Essays in the Social History of American Medicine*, eds. Morris J. Vogel and Charles E. Rosenberg. Philadelphia: University of Pennsylvania Press, 1979.

Jenson, Carl. *Stories that Changed America: Muckrakers of the 20th Century*. New York: Seven Stories Press, 2003.

Johnson, Paul. *A History of Christianity*. New York: Antheneum, 1976.

Jones, Patricia S., Marilyn M. Herrmann, and Barbara James. "Adventist Nursing." *Journal of Adventist Education* (April/May 2009): 10–14. http://circle.adventist.org/files/jae/en/jae200971041005.pdf.

Justin, Meryl Sallie. "Men, Women, and Women Physicians: The Medical Women's National Association and The Medical Profession, 1915–1945." Unpublished BA thesis, Harvard University, March 1980. AMWA #306-311.

"Keith Vawter, Inventor of the Chautauqua System, and How He Furnishes Bryan, Bands, and Bishops to The Middle West at Four Cents Apiece." *The Lyceum and Talent* (March 1912): 39

Kellogg, John Harvey. *The Living Temple.* Battle Creek, MI: Good Health Publishing, 1903.

———. "The American Medical Missionary College—Its Origin and Development." *Medical Missionary* (August 7, 1906): 54–56.

Kelly, Fred C. "What 20,000,000 People Like to Hear." *The American Magazine*, vol. 87 (1919): 105.

Kendall, Carolyn. "We'll Find a Secretary for You." Unpublished manuscript. August 10, 2012.

———. "The First Urantia Papers." September 8, 1993. Unpublished manuscript.

Kessler, Ronald. *The Bureau: The Secret History of the FBI.* New York: St. Martin's Press, 2002.

Kevles, Daniel J. *In the Name of Eugenics: Genetics and the Uses of Human Heredity.* New York: Alfred A. Knopf, 1985.

Klee, Paul. *Before Hollywood: From Shadow Play to the Silver Screen.* New York: Clarion Books, 2005.

Klimo, Jon. *Channeling: Investigations on Receiving Information from Paranormal Sources.* New York: St. Martin's Press, 1987.

Kulieke, Mark. *Birth of a Revelation: The Story of the Urantia Papers.* Los Angeles, CA: Morning Star Foundation, 1994.

Laughlin, Harry H. *Eugenical Sterilization in the United States. Chicago*: Psychopathic Laboratory of the Municipal Court of Chicago, 1922.

Lewis, James R. and Olav Hammer, eds. *The Invention of Sacred Tradition.* New York: Cambridge University Press, 2007.

Lifson, Amy. "The Book Shook the World." *Humanities Magazine*, vol. 30, no. 6, (November/December 2009).

Longfield, Bradley J. *The Presbyterian Controversy: Fundamentalists, Modernists, and Moderates.* New York: Oxford University Press, 1991.

Loughborough, John N. *The Second Great Advent Movement: Its Rise and Progress.* Nashville, TN: Southern Publishing Association, 1905.

"International Lyceum Association Convention Now In Session," *The Lyceum News*, vol. II, no. 8, (September 1912): 8–10.

Manning, J. T. *Source Authors of The Urantia Book.* Glendale, CA: Square Circles Publishing,, 2002.

Markel, Howard. *An Anatomy of Addiction: Sigmund Freud, William Halsted, and the Miracle Drug Cocaine.* New York: Pantheon Books, 2011.

———. *When Germs Travel: Six Major Epidemics That Have Invaded America Since*

*1900 and the Fears They Have Unleashed.* New York: Pantheon Books, 2004.

McCabe, Joseph. *Is Spiritualism Based on Fraud? The Evidence Given by Sir A. C. Doyle and Others Drastically Examined.* London: Watts & Co., 1920.

McCabe, Marie Belle, ed. "Medical History of Michigan, Michigan State Medical Society," comp. Colonel Bell Burr. Minneapolis, MN: Bruce Publishing, 1930.

Cruden, Robert M. *Ministers of Reform: The Progressives' Achievement in American Civilization.* Champaign: University of Illinois Press, 1985.

McDonald, Lynn. "The Nightingale System of Training." Lecture given at American Association for the History of Nursing and European Nursing History Group Conference, London (September 14, 2010). http://www.uoguelph.ca/~cwfn/nursing/nightingale-system-of-training.html.

McKibbin-Harper, Mary "In Memoriam: Lena Kellogg Sadler, M.D." *Women in Medicine* (October 1939): 27.

McNeese, Tim. *The Progressive Movement: Advocating Social Change.* New York: Chelsea House Books, 2008.

Mehler, Barry. "The History of the American Eugenics Society, 1921–1940." PhD diss., University of Illinois at Urbana-Champaign, 1988.

Menand, Louis. *The Metaphysical Club: A Story of Ideas in America.* New York: Farrar, Straus & Giroux, 2001.

"The Message of Health for the Masses." *The Lyceumite and Talent,* vol. III, no. 10 (March 1910): 33.

Meussling, G. Vonne. "William S. Sadler: Chautauqua's Medic Orator." PhD diss., Bowling Green State University, December 1970.

Miller, Donald L. *City of the Century: The Epic of Chicago and the Making of America.* New York: Simon & Schuster, 2003.

Miller, Glenn T. *Piety and Profession: American Protestant Theological Education,* 1870–1970. Grand Rapids, MI: William B. Eerdmans, 2007.

Mills, Bill. *The League: The True Story of Average Americans on the Hunt for WWI Spies.* New York: Skyhorse Publishing, 2013.

Moyer, Ernest P. *The Birth of a Divine Revelation: The Origin of the Urantia Papers.* Hanover, PA: Moyer Publishing, 2000.

Mullins, Larry, and Meredith Justin Sprunger. *A History of the Urantia Papers.* Boulder, CO: Penumbra Press, 2000.

Nasht, Simon. *The Last Explorer: Hubert Wilkins Hero of the Great Age of Polar Exploration.* New York: Arcade Publishing, 2005.

Nobel, Nelle S. "Lena K. Sadler, M.D." *Journal of the American Medical Women's Association,* vol. 11, no. 6 (June 1956): 219.

Numbers, Ronald L., ed. *The Education of American Physicians: Historical Essays.* Berkeley: University of California Press, 1980.

————. *Galileo Goes to Jail: and Other Myths about Science and Religion.* Cambridge, MA: Harvard University Press, 2009.

————. *Prophetess of Health: A Study of Ellen G. White.* New York: Harper & Row, 1976.

O'Keefe, Katharine. *History of the American Eugenics Society,* 1922–1994. Stafford, VA: American Life League, 1993.

"An Opportunity to Help the Poor." *The Medical Missionary,* vol. XVI, no. 4 (January 23, 1907): 30.

Osborn, Henry Fairfield. *Man Rises to Parnassus: Critical Epochs in the Prehistory of Man.* Princeton, NJ: Princeton University Press, 1928.

O'Toole, Marie T., ed. *Miller-Keane Encyclopedia and Dictionary of Medicine, Nursing, and Allied Health,* 7th ed. Philadelphia, PA: Elsevier, 2003.

Owen County, Indiana. *Index to Marriage Records* 1850–1920. Inclusive vol. W.P.A. Original Record, book 30, page 402.

*Oxford English Dictionary,* online edition, Oxford University Press, 2010.

Ozick, Cynthia. "What Helen Keller Saw: The Making of a Writer." *The New Yorker,* June 16, 2003.

Pacyga, Dominic A. *Chicago: A Biography.* Chicago: University of Chicago Press, 2009.

Palmer, Harold D. *Review of Theory and Practice of Psychiatry. Mental Hygiene* (July 1937): XX.

Paul, Julius, "Three Generations of Imbeciles Are Enough: State Eugenic Sterilization Laws in American Thought and Practice." Paper 95. Washington, DC: Walter Reed Army Institute of Research, 1965.

Pearsall, Paul. *The Heart's Code: Tapping the Wisdom and Power of Our Heart Energy.* New York: Broadway Books, 1998.

Powell, Horace B. *The Original Has This Signature: W. K. Kellogg.* Battle Creek, MI: W. K. Kellogg Foundation, 1959.

Praamsma, Saskia, and Matthew Block. *The Sherman Diaries: with Letters, Notes, and Other Writings,* vol. 1: Dawning Revelations 1898–1942. Glendale, CA: Square Circles Publishing, 2002.

————. *The Sherman Diaries: with Letters, Notes, and Other Writings,* vol. 2: Revelation and Rebellion 1942. Glendale, CA: Square Circles Publishing, 2003.

————. *The Sherman Diaries: with Letters, Notes, and Other Writings,* vol. 3: Aftermath of Rebellion 1943. Glendale, CA: Square Circles Publishing, 2004.

————. *The Sherman Diaries: with Letters, Notes, and Other Writings*, vol. 4: The Turning Point 1944–1945. Glendale, CA: Square Circles Publishing, 2005.

————. *The Sherman Diaries: with Letters, Notes, and Other Writings*, vol. 5: Moving On 1946–1955. Glendale, CA: Square Circles Publishing, 2008.

Pratt, George K. *Review of The Mind at Mischief* (Tricks and Deceptions of the Subconscious and How to Cope with Them). *American Journal of Public Health*, vol. 19, no. 12 (December 1929): 1394.

Prince, Morton. *The Unconscious: The Fundamentals of Human Personality Normal and Abnormal*. New York: Macmillan, 1921.

Rauschenbusch, Walter. *Christianity and the Social Crisis in the 21st Century*. New York: HarperOne, 1907.

Robinson, David. *From Peep Show to Palace: The Birth of American Film*. New York: Columbia University Press, 1996.

Robinson, John A. T. *Honest to God*. 1963. 40th anniversary edition, with essays by Douglas John Hall and Rowan Williams. Philadelphia, PA: The Westminster Press, 2002.

Rydell, Robert W. *World of Fairs: The Century of Progress Expositions*. Chicago: University of Chicago Press, 1993.

Sadler letters. W. K. Kellogg Foundation Archives, Battle Creek, MI.

Sadler, Lena K. "Important: Here's Where We Must Give Our Service." *Bulletin Medical Women's Club of Chicago* (September 26, 1926): 6–8.

————. "Is the Abnormal to Become Normal?" in *A Decade of Progress in Eugenics, Scientific Papers of the Third International Congress of Eugenics*. Baltimore, MD: Williams and Wilkins,1934.

————. "Medical Women of Today." *Medical Women's Journal*, vol. 40, no. 5 (May 1933): 117.

————. "The Preliminary Survey of Emotional Analysis." *Medical Women's Journal*, vol. 39, no. 9 (September 1932): 221–23.

————. "The Relation of Women's Clubs to Organized Medicine and the Public Health Movement." *Illinois Medical Journal*, vol. 66 (July 1926): 52

————. "Report of the Chairman of Public Health" (June 1929): 1–4. AMWA Collection, Drexel University Archives, Philadelphia, PA.

Sadler, William S. *Bible Study, History Part One: A Survey of the Bible*. Chicago: Urantia Foundation, 1960.

————. *A History of the Urantia Movement*. Chicago: Urantia Foundation, 1960.

————. *Living a Sane Sex Life*. Chicago: Wilcox & Follett, 1946.

————. *The Medical Missionary*, various volumes.

————. "Psychiatric Educational Work." Paper presented at the Ninety-Second Annual Meeting of the American Psychiatric Association, St. Louis, MO, May 4–8, 1936.

————. *Race Decadence: An Examination of the Causes of Racial Degeneracy in the United States*. Chicago: A. C. McClurg,1922.

————. "The San Francisco Church Dispensary." *Pacific Union Recorder*, vol.3, no. 10 (December 17, 1903): 12.

————. *Soul-Winning Texts or Bible Helps for Personal Work*. Glendale, CA: Square Circles Publishing, 1999.

————. *The Mind at Mischief: Tricks and Deceptions of the Subconscious and How to Cope with Them*. New York: Funk & Wagnalls, 1929.

————. *The Physiology of Faith and Fear: Or, the Mind in Health and Disease*. Chicago: A. C. McClurg, 1912.

————. "The Story of the Life Boat." *The Life Boat*, vol. VI, no.12 (December 1903): 335.

————. *Theory and Practice of Psychiatry*. St. Louis, MO: C. V. Mosby, 1936.

Schwartz, Richard W. *John Harvey Kellogg*. Nashville, TN: Southern Publishing, 1970.

————. "John Harvey Kellogg as a Social Gospel Practitioner." *Journal of Illinois State Historical Society* 1908–1984, vol. 57, no. 1 (Spring 1964): 5–22.

*Seventh-day Adventist Year Book for 1890*. Battle Creek, MI: Review and Herald Publishing, 1890.

Sheldrake, Rupert. *The Presence of the Past: Morphic Resonance and the Habits of Nature*. Rochester , VT: Park Street Press, 1988.

Sheldrake, Rupert, Terrance McKenna, and Ralph Abraham. *Chaos, Creativity, and Cosmic Consciousness*. Rochester, VT: Park Street Press, 1992.

Sherman, Harold. *How to Know What to Believe*. Greenwich, CT: Fawcett Publications,1976.

Shermer, Michael. *The Believing Brain: From Ghosts, and Gods to Politics and Conspiracies—How We Construct Beliefs and Reinforce Them as Truths*. New York: Henry Holt, 2011.

Shurtleff, William, and Akiko Aoyagi. "Dr. John Harvey Kellogg and Battle Creek Foods: Work With Soy." Unpublished manuscript, 2004. http://www.soyinfocenter. com/HSS/john_kellogg_and_battle_creek_foods.php.

Shyrock, Alfred. "Summary of AMMC (medical school at Battle Creek)." Handwritten history, January 1929. E. G. White Estate Collection, WDF 1694, Loma Linda, California.

Simonton, Dean Keith. *Origins of Genius: Darwinian Perspectives on Creativity.* New York: Oxford University Press, 1999.

Sinclair, Upton. *The Jungle.* 1906. New York: Dover Publications, 2001.

"The Social Gospel." *The Biblical World,* vol. 40, no. 3, September 1912.

Smith, Christopher. "The Urantia Book as a Test Case for Statistical Authorship Attribution in Genre-Distinctive Texts." Unpublished paper, Claremont Graduate University, California, 2010.

Spinney, Robert G. *City of Big Shoulders: A History of Chicago.* DeKalb: Northern Illinois University Press, 2000.

Starr, Paul. *The Social Transformation of American Medicine: The Rise of a Sovereign Profession and the Making of a Vast Industry.* New York: Basic Books, 1984.

Stern, Alexandra Minna. *Eugenic America: Faults and Frontiers of Better Breeding in Modern America.* Berkeley: University of California Press, 2005.

Stewart, James, Jr. *The Union Army, A History of Military Affairs in the Loyal States 1861–1865—Records of the Regiments in the Union Army—Cyclopedia of Battles—Memoirs of Commanders and Soldiers,* vol. 3: *New Jersey, Indiana, Illinois, and Michigan.* Madison, WI: Federal Publishing, 1908.

Stilson, Gladys M. *Review of Psychiatric Nursing. American Journal of Nursing,* vol. 38, no. 5 (May 1938): 622–23.

Stott, Kelly McMichael. *Waxahachie: When Cotton Was King.* Mount Pleasant, SC: Arcadia Publishing, 2002.

Tarnas, Richard. *The Passion of the Western Mind: Understanding the Ideas That Have Shaped Our World View.* New York: Harmony Books, 1991.

Taubenberger, Jeffrey K., and David M. Morens. "1918 Influenza: the Mother of All Pandemics." *Emerging Infectious Diseases,* vol. 12, no. 1 (January 2006): 15–22.

Vaidhyanathan, Siva. *Copyrights and Copywrongs: The Rise of Intellectual Property and How it Threatens Creativity.* New York: New York University Press, 2001.

Vogel, Dan, and Brent Lee Metcalf. *American Apocrypha: Essays on the Book of Mormon.* Salt Lake City: Signature Books, 2002.

W. K. Kellogg Foundation Archives, Battle Creek, MI.

Walker, Aaron. "Did Sadler Write Papers 88 and 160? A Preliminary-Findings Report of a Stylometric Analysis." Unpublished article, April 2010.

————. "Findings Report: Stylometric Analysis of UB160 vs. *Issues of Life* (Wieman) andUB160 vs. Sadler to Determine Probable Authorship." Unpublished article, Summer 2010.

————. "Findings Report: UB130, 132, and 133 vs. Sadler and Flewelling." Unpublished article, Summer 2010.

————. "William S. Sadler and Papers 39, 88, 160, the Forward and Acknowledgments of *The Urantia Book*: A Stylomertic Analysis—Report #2." Unpublished article, June 2010.

Westcott-Wieman, Regina. *Review of Theory and Practice of Psychiatry. The Christian Century*, September 23, 1936.

Weinberg, Arthur and Lila. *The Muckrakers*. Champaign: University of Illinois, 2001.

Weisenberger, Carol A. "Women of the FCC: Activists or Tokens?" *Business and Economic History*, 2nd series, vol. 21 (1992): 192–98. http://www.thebhc.org/publications/BEHprint/v021/p0192-p0198.pdf

White, Arthur L. Ellen G. White, vol. 1: *The Early Years 1827–1862*. Hagerstown, MD: Review & Herald Publishing Assocation, 1985.

White, Ellen Gould. *Manuscript Releases*, vol. 13, no. 26: "The Purposes of Our Sanitariums." http://www.gilead.net/egw/books/manuscript-releases.

White, W. B. "Medical Work in Seattle." *North Pacific Union Gleaner* [Spokane, WA], vol. 1, no. 27, November 1, 1906.

White, William, Jr., and C. Howard Hopkins. *The Social Gospel: Religion and Reform in Changing America*. Philadelphia: Temple University Press, 1976.

Wiebe, Robert. *The Search for Order, 1877–1920*. New York: HarperCollins, 1967.

Wiggam, Albert Edward. *The New Decalogue of Science*. Indianapolis, IN: Bobbs-Merrill, 1923.

Wilford, John Noble. "Camels Had No Business in Genesis." *New York Times*, February 10, 2014.

Wright, Willard H. *40 Years of Tropical Medicine Research*. Baltimore, MD: Reese Press, 1971.

Zinn, Howard. *A People's History of The United States, 1492–Present*. New York: Harper Collins, 1999.

# SOURCE BOOKS CITED

Cooper, James F. *Technique of Contraception: The Principles and Practice of Anti-Conceptional Methods*. New York: Day-Nichols, 1928.

Dickinson, Robert Latou, and Lura Beam. *A Thousand Marriages: A Medical Study of Sex Adjustment*. Baltimore, MD: Williams & Wilkins, 1931.

Eddy, George Sherwood. "The Problems of Marriage." In *Twenty-Four Views of Marriage: From the Presbyterian General Assembly's Commission on Marriage, Divorce and Remarriage*, ed. Clarence A. Spaulding. New York: Macmillan, 1930.

Ellis, Havelock. *Psychology of Sex: A Manual for Student*. New York: Emerson Books, 1938.

Everett, Millard S. *The Hygiene of Marriage: A Detailed Consideration of Sex and Marriage*. New York: The Vanguard Press, 1932.

Exner, M. J. *The Sexual Side of Marriage*. New York: W. W. Norton, 1932.

Fielding, William J. *Sex and the Love-Life*. New York: Blue Ribbon Books, 1927.

Hamilton, G. V. *A Research in Marriage*. New York: Albert & Charles Boni, 1929.,

Hamilton, V., and Kenneth MacGowan. *What Is Wrong with Marriage*. New York: Albert & Charles Boni, 1929.

Keyserling, Count Hermann. "The Proper Choice of Partners." In *Twenty-Four Views of Marriage: From the Presbyterian General Assembly's Commission on Marriage, Divorce and Remarriage*, ed. Clarence A. Spaulding. New York: Macmillan, 1930.

Lindsey, Benjamin B. "An Answer to the Critics of Companionate Marriage." In *Twenty- Four Views of Marriage: From the Presbyterian General Assembly's Commission on Marriage, Divorce and Remarriage*, ed. Clarence A. Spaulding. New York: Macmillan, 1930.

Popenoe, Paul. "Broken Homes." In *Twenty-Four Views of Marriage: From the Presbyterian General Assembly's Commission on Marriage, Divorce and Remarriage*, ed. Clarence A. Spaulding. New York: Macmillan, 1930.

Popenoe, Paul. *Preparing for Marriage*. Los Angeles, CA: American Institute of Family Relations, 1938.

Van de Velde, Th. H. *Ideal Marriage: Its Physiology and Technique*, trans. Stella Browne. New York: Random House, 1926.

Wiggam, Albert Edward. *The Fruit of the Family Tree*. Indianapolis, IN: Bobbs-Merrill, 1924.

Wright, Helena. *The Sex Factor in Marriage: A Book for Who Are About to Be Married*. New York: Vanguard Press, 1937.

# ACKNOWLEDGMENTS

There are many people whose support and assistance made this book possible. First, and most importantly, is the man behind the writer. He has my deepest gratitude. That man is my husband, George Oliva III. He patiently supported me through this process for five years as I wrote the manuscript; he edited the copy and offered invaluable advice on improving the book.

Thank you to the artist Tonia Baney for the wonderful drawing of Dr. Sadler. The illustration alone may be the reason you bought the book.

Much obliged to photographer John Konkal for taking the back cover picture of me.

I am indebted to Saskia Praamsma and Matthew Block for reading the manuscript and offering many editorial suggestions that were extremely helpful in both substance and fact.

Several professors offered their knowledge to my queries as I moved through the research. The assisted me in gaining greater understanding and context of the topics presented. Dr. Richard Bushman at Cornell, Dr. Anthony Grafton at Princeton, Dr. John Klimo at The American Schools of Professional Psychology, Argosy University, and Dr. Ronald Numbers at the University of Wisconsin, Madison, all gave me feedback that elevated my thinking. Thank you.

Many Urantia Book readers offered research tips, listened to my latest research updates, asked questions, and gave me feedback that served me well. Lyn Lear, Steve Dreier, Carolyn Kendall, Marilynn Kulieke, David Kulieke, Mark Kulieke, Gard Jameson, Richard Keeler, John Hales, Vern Grimsley, Meredith Sprunger, Jay Peregrine, Barbara Newsom, Judy Sadler, John Ploetz, Byron Belitsos, Scott Forsythe, Patrick McNelly, and Carol Schindler, all have my appreciation for their input and asking me challenging questions about the manuscript.

My gratitude also goes to Urantia Foundation for admittance to their records on the printing of *The Urantia Book*. Learning when the book was typeset was important. I thank Jay Peregrine for his assistance in accessing this information.

My thanks to Leigh Hyndman who read the manuscript and asked many questions that assisted me in elucidating concepts that would be unfamiliar to person unfamiliar with *The Urantia Book*.

The archives I visited all gave me excellent service in locating documents that would help me tell the story of William Sadler's life. Alicia Shaver at the W.K. Kellogg Archives sat by my side while I transcribed 400 letters. I am indebted to Lori Curtis at the Loma Linda Archives, Juliette Johnson and Carol William at the Center for Adventist Research, Alice Williams at Andrews University, Carolyn Marr at the Museum of Science and Industry in Seattle, Diana Wallace at the American Medical Association Archives in Chicago, Harold Blum at the Sigmund Freud Archives, Matt Herbison at the Legacy Center and Special Collections at Drexel University, Teresa Johnson at UCLA History and Special Collections, Jon Schmitz at Chautauqua Institution Archives, Edward Kelly IV at the University of Iowa Special Collections, Louise King at the Royal College of Surgeons, Laura Kissel at the Byrd Polar Research Center Archival Program, Ellen Keith at the Chicago History Museum Research Center, and Tim Poirier at the Ellen G. White Estate, for guiding me to new treasures stored in their archive's holdings.

# SIOUX OLIVA

Sioux Oliva is an American historian and lecturer. Born in in Buffalo, New York and raised in San Diego, California, Sioux earned her Ph.D. in History from the University of Southern California in 1999. Her first project was managing a non-profit website to introduce the teachings of *The Urantia Book* to a wider audience sponsored by Lyn and Norman Lear. Some of her other notable projects and clients include assisting Mrs. Robert F. Kennedy organize her personal papers at her home, Hickory Hill, in McLean, VA; designing a research scheme for the Estate of Marilyn Monroe; doing four family history projects and cataloging thousands of documents found in Grey Gardens for Sally Quinn and Ben Bradlee; and research projects for The Getty and The City of Los Angeles, and The Autry Museum of the American West. Sioux lives outside of Asheville, North Carolina, with her husband and their two Field Setters. More information is available on her website: www.SiouxOliva.com

# TONIA BANEY

Cover artist Tonia Baney served for seven years as the Executive Director of Urantia Foundation and has been a student of *The Urantia Book* since 1968. She is also an accomplished portrait artist. Her portraits reveal a particular life, light and character signifying the individual subjects true and inner beauty. Tonia deemed it an honor to present and prepare the cover art for this book. She said, "Dr. Sadler is a person whom I had thought and wondered about most of my life, a man whose existence influenced my religious faith, as well as those who hold this book in their hands." Prints of the portrait of the young Dr. Sadler are available on her web site. www..toniamarksbaney.com or email: artbaney@aol.com